THROUGH NEW YORK'S
GOLDEN DOOR

www.mascotbooks.com

Through New York's Golden Door: An American Journey

For more information, please contact:
Mascot Books, an imprint of Amplify Publishing Group
620 Herndon Parkway, Suite 320
Herndon, VA 20170
info@mascotbooks.com

Library of Congress Control Number: 2021923515

CPSIA Code: PRV0422A
ISBN-13: 978-1-63755-167-7

Printed in the United States

THROUGH NEW YORK'S
GOLDEN DOOR

An American Journey

H. CLAUDE SHOSTAL

To the countless public employees who serve in myriad capacities with integrity, dedication, and professionalism.

CONTENTS

From "The New Colossus"
Emma Lazarus, 1883

Keep, ancient lands, your storied pomp!" cries she
With silent lips. "Give me your tired, your poor,
Your huddled masses yearning to breathe free,
The wretched refuse of your teeming shore,
Send these, the homeless, tempest-tost to me,
I lift my lamp beside the golden door!

From the First Inaugural Address
Abraham Lincoln, 1861

We are not enemies, but friends. We must not be enemies. Though passion may have strained it must not break our bonds of affection. The mystic chords of memory, stretching from every battlefield and patriot grave to every living heart and hearthstone all over this broad land, will yet swell the chorus of the Union, when again touched, as surely they will be, by the better angels of our nature.

From the Gettysburg Address
Abraham Lincoln, 1863

It is for us the living, rather, to be dedicated here to the unfinished work which they who fought here have thus far so nobly advanced. It is rather for us to be here dedicated to the great task remaining before us—that from these honored dead we take increased devotion to that cause for which they here gave the last full measure of devotion—that we here highly resolve that these dead shall not have died in vain—that this nation, under God, shall have a new birth of freedom—and that government of the people, by the people, for the people, shall not perish from the earth.

PREFACE

With the twenty-first century having come of age, it seems a good time to sit down and take stock. Research scientists have developed safe and effective vaccines and new treatment medicines for COVID-19 in record time. This stunning success gives us some basis for thinking that the pandemic might soon be in the rearview mirror, mostly behind us but still visible. Ahead, our social and economic "new normals" will be different—though no one is yet quite certain what those new paradigms will look like. Politically, after the horrific years of the Trump presidency, there is some reason to hope that we have at least begun a conversation with the better angels of our nature.

This interstitial time strikes me as a special opportunity to look back—hopefully with more clarity of vision—on the time and experiences that have made up my life, and to try to write it all down. Early in the first year of the pandemic, I marked my eightieth birthday. Turning eighty is different. One's future just doesn't stretch out endlessly anymore. I know that there will not be very many more soft spring days, exquisite songs of the hermit thrush, or thrilling outdoor adventures before significant debilitation starts to set in and living becomes a mostly dead-end job rather than an ongoing source of joy and wonder.

Mine has been a rich life marked with more excitement and fulfillment than despair and disappointment. The journey has also included enough adversity to allow me to appreciate how fortunate, for the most part, I have been. Conventional wisdom suggests that a dearth of angst and melancholia might make for a boring narrative. The reader will have to be the judge, but I do not believe that to be the case.

When I was born in France in 1940, I was given my exquisitely Gallic name, Henri Claude, but grew up speaking only English. My earliest years were filled with hair-raising adventures that I was lucky to survive. We were among the few fortunate families who, in 1941, succeeded in making a hazardous escape from wartime Europe. We arrived in America penniless and in debt, but my parents were able to carve out a good life here. Because of their heroic efforts, as well as the opportunities that our adopted country provided in those years—and boosted in no small measure by the privilege of my white ethnicity—I have had the good fortune to be able to live out much of the American Dream.

My professional career began in 1967 on the staff of Governor Nelson Rockefeller, where I would meet larger-than-life personalities like Jackie Robinson and Henry Kissinger, as well as a host of dedicated and talented public servants. From that special perspective, I witnessed the drama of the urban and campus unrest of the 1960s, the dire events of 1968, the Woodstock Music Festival, and the Attica uprising. I then moved to New York City government during the fiscal crisis of the 1970s, becoming the first commissioner of New York City's Department of Cultural Affairs, appointed by Mayor Abraham Beame in 1976. I dealt with Isaac Stern, Harvey Lichtenstein, Thomas Hoving, and many other luminaries from the cultural world. Later, after a decade in commercial real estate working on large-scale development projects, I had the honor of leading Regional Plan Association, perhaps the country's premier nonprofit metropolitan planning organization. During breaks from these wonderful assignments, I made time to climb to the summits of Kilimanjaro and two 20,000-foot peaks in the Himalayas.

How did a sickly infant smuggled through France in 1941 become a "Rockefeller guy," grow into something approaching an elder statesman in New York's civic community, and along the way amass a respectable portfolio of adventure travel? My odyssey took shape in what looks more and more like a golden age—the 1950s and '60s—compared with the darker colorations of the present time. My passage was aided by many remarkable people—my parents, mentors, colleagues, and friends.

Of one thing I am quite certain: my story could not have happened anywhere else. While my heritage and culture growing up were purely European, my life has been a quintessentially American story. And this memoir is a series of stories based upon my recollections. Mindful of how flawed memory can be, I have done my best to be as factually accurate as possible. With the help of the internet and access to a few seminal documents, I believe I have largely succeeded. But I am sure I have inadvertently missed, misconstrued, or rearranged certain details, for which I apologize. Nevertheless, I know that the arc of what follows is essentially true. These are my stories as I have come to understand them and as they have formed me. I invite the reader to join me and share this travel in time. Let us lift off, escape the gravity of the present, and share the journey that this imperfect and still unfinished nation allowed me to make.

ONE

VIENNA TO FRANCE

My parents met at the University of Vienna in the late 1920s. My father, Walter Leo Schostal, born in 1908, was a Viennese Jew of an urban but very secular bent. He did not wish to be identified as a Jew. As he would prove again in France, he insisted on being identified by his allegiance to his country, not by his religion or ethnicity. As Edmund de Waal described in *The Hare with Amber Eyes*, many Jews coming out of the diaspora from Russia in the latter part of the nineteenth century desperately wanted assimilation rather than a separate Jewish identity. My father's family, though of much more modest means than de Waal's, shared that desire.

Like de Waal, my father joined a saber fencing fraternity at the University of Vienna to establish his *bona fides* as a regular young Austrian man. He was proud of his scars—badges of honor testifying to his un-Jewish youth. He happily explained to me that since fencing was technically illegal, medical students patched their friends' wounds, taking care not to stitch the cuts too neatly so that the manly but minor disfigurements would be clearly visible.

As with many Jewish families, education was fundamental to my father's *Weltanschauung*—his view of the world and our place in it. He pursued a classical education at the university and became proficient in Latin and Greek. He probably should have become an academic, which would have suited him very well, but the real world interfered. First, he had a very slight stutter, a major barrier to a profession that, at the time, prized verbal presentation and oral dexterity. Second, in the early 1930s, the worldwide depression made jobs of any kind very hard to find. Finally, of course, being Jewish would have made it virtually impossible for him to gain a foothold among the *intelligentsia* of Vienna at a time when the *Anschluss*—the Nazi takeover—was just around the corner.

My mother, Theresa Magdika, born in 1906, had a very different heritage. She came from a small rural Hungarian community named Tolna. My parents' personalities were also in stark contrast. She was a Magyar; intense, emotional, and passionate. He was reserved, guarded, even remote. We know almost nothing of my mother's family except that they were quite poor. Her mother abandoned the family when "Risa" was only several months old, and she was sent to grow up with her aunt and uncle Wesely—Maria and Anton—in Vienna. I never met either of them, but my older brother, Pierre, did meet Aunt Wesely. They were kind and loving people. Although uneducated herself, Aunt Wesely recognized that my mother was an extraordinarily gifted little girl and encouraged her intellectual growth. As my father wrote in a personal memoir:

Uncle and Aunt Wesely were simple but marvelous people. Aunt Wesely could sign her name but she could neither read nor write. Her husband had been in the military for some fifteen years. For such faithful service, the K & K ("Imperial and Royal")* government rewarded him with a minor job in one of the governmental offices in Vienna. There, Magda [as my father called her] grew up, cared for by Uncle and Aunt as if she were their real daughter. They had no children of their own.

My mother was raised in a strict Catholic environment and was sent to a Jesuit convent school. The head of the school, Father Novotny, was so impressed by her that he talked about founding a new female Jesuit order around her.

To do so, she would have to get a solid education and attend university. The first step would be to pass the so-called Matura, the final exam of the academic

---

* Imperial and Royal (translates to *Kaiserlich und Königlich* in German) stood at that time for the Emperor of Austria and the King of Hungary, the "Dual Monarchy" of Austria-Hungary.

high school that was required for admission to the university… Father Novotny was laying the foundation, tutoring her in all subjects, including Latin, which was required for this dreaded exam.

However, this path was not to be hers. After having been discovered secretly attending a dance as a teenager, she was forced to kneel in penance all night on a cold marble floor. My mother deeply resented this stark punishment, and it began to turn her against Catholicism. The rupture was completed some years later when her name was posted on the church door announcing her excommunication for the sin of marrying my father.

The spark lit by the father, however, did not die. Risa got herself books and continued studying on her own. When she got her first boyfriend, sure enough it was one who could help her with her endeavor. (Yes, she could even be ruthless, if she wanted something badly enough.) He was a young Jewish physician doing his internship at the hospital. He tutored her in Latin and math; the other subjects she could study on her own.

Her tutor was, in fact, the first and true love of her life, a doctor who would later play a tragic role in her life. My father's memoir goes on to describe his own lifestyle at the time:

My schedule was a little different. I spent about half of my day in my brother's business, the other half attending classes or at the university library; the evening hours, however, I spent at my fraternity. There was no drinking, but never-ending talks—I have no recollection about what—a little card playing, and above all, almost continuous training in the art of fencing, the goal of which was preparation to fight duels with sharp weapons. The tradition of dueling goes back centuries at German universities … With a great deal of patience, Magda tried to wean me from this waste of time. Since she finally succeeded, I can now and for the remaining days of my life have the title of "Doctor" precede my name when in Austria and Germany.

My father's somewhat elliptical prose tells us that he indeed received his PhD, but only with a good deal of help from my mother. Much more impressively, she, too, received her doctorate in what we might today call philology—an extraordinary accomplishment for a woman at that time, particularly a woman of humble origins. I grew up appreciating my mother's brilliance and determination, and I am sure that she is the reason I have always been drawn to strong and intelligent women.

My parents decided to marry after completing their degrees. They wanted a church wedding, mostly to please the Weselys, but the powerful Catholic Church forbade divorces, and its stance was recognized at the time by the civil authorities. So, although they did not anticipate divorcing, they decided to become Protestants. After an anti-Semitic encounter with a Lutheran pastor, they found a welcome with the head of a small Calvinist congregation.

Magda remembered in time that her father actually was a Protestant of the Calvinist persuasion. It was no lie that she told the holy man, who was delighted.

Clearly, where religion was concerned, my parents were flexible. While my parents never talked much about their religious beliefs, they made little secret of the fact that neither of them could believe in a god or an afterlife as depicted in most religious practices. They were supremely rational people, and those ideas just did not make sense to them nor, therefore, to me. My father never set foot in a synagogue and my mother no longer wanted anything to do with Catholicism, but they valued religious traditions as important parts of our culture. We celebrated Christmas like Christians, with a tree and presents. Ours was a very European household, so Christmas gifts were opened on Christmas Eve and Santa Claus had a very short life span. My brother and I were sent to Dutch Reform Sunday school. Later, I would become an Anglican altar boy when my mother taught at an Episcopal prep school in exchange for my tuition. But despite going to services nine times a week in my senior year, religion never could establish a beachhead in my psyche. For her part, my mother told us—after agreeing to be confirmed in the Episcopal Church as a favor to the beloved head-master of Saint Peter's School, Rev. Frank Leeming—that if she were ever to return to religion, it could only be as a Catholic, so deep was her early connection. It did not happen.

Picking up my father's story:

I graduated from the University of Vienna in 1933. It took me more than seven years to do so, instead of the usual minimum of five. One reason for this slow progress was that I was working part-time in a business that my brother, Robert, had started. Incidentally, Robert was a handicapped person. He had a spastic condition that goes by the scientific name of "Morbus Little" (infantile cerebral palsy). He could hardly write, he had only limited control of his arms and legs, and even his speech was affected.

Despite all of these limitations, he was able, by sheer willpower, to lead a successful and mostly happy life; a lesser person would have sat in a corner and let other people take care of him. He started this business as a student in an attempt to earn a little pocket money. It was an agency, a link between photographers and their customers, such as magazines, newspapers, or whoever else needed to reproduce photographs. While Robert's enterprise changed from a student's plaything into a real business, my father's commercial attempts dwindled into insignificance; in the end, he became a bookkeeper in his son's business.

I only recently became aware that the business that Robert had launched in Vienna had grown to become a substantial enterprise before being "Aryanized," a euphemism for its expropriation by the Nazis. Somehow, a portion of the files of the Schostal Press Agency ended up in Toronto, in the Art Gallery of Ontario, a major museum. An academic thesis written in 2014 about that collection stated:

> It was at this time, in the late 1920s, that the Schostal Press Agency became the exclusive Austrian distributor of photographs for the Keystone Press Agency (based in New York). They were given a fixed monthly fee to distribute Keystone photos in Paris, London, and Berlin. It was this fixed income that allowed the brothers to keep their business afloat, and by 1933 they were able to expand their base. Walter and his wife moved to Paris and set up a branch office there . . . The Schostal Agency thrived from 1934 to 1938, employing up to ten people in its Vienna headquarters, and boasting

an inventory of over one million photographs depicting events and daily life both locally and globally.[*]

My father's memoir presents a more modest picture, making it likely that the Nazis incorporated other photographic collections into the files that bore our family name:

When I graduated from university, I could see no hope to find a job that offered any future, or for that matter, to find any job at all. I had hoped to become a writer—maybe a journalist—but first one had to make a living—somewhere, somehow. Robert's business—while growing—seemed too weak to support two families; we got the idea that I should move to Paris and start a branch of the business there.

My father's family had been successful merchants. The family business was a fashionable women's clothing store on Vienna's main square, the Stephansplatz, next to the famous Stephansdom, Vienna's great Catholic cathedral. The Schostal store was well known in Vienna, and in 1870 or thereabouts, a branch of the family moved to Rome where the Schostal store still exists at Via della Fontanella di Borghese, 29, albeit under different ownership. The family talent for business was not inherited by my grandfather, who died of a heart attack shortly before the Anschluss of April 1938.

My father's memoir continues:

At that time (the late 1930s), many Jews had left Vienna—most of them not for places of their choosing, but to wherever they had been able to get (or often buy) visas: Cuba, Shanghai, Istanbul, New Zealand, etc. Never mind where to, but to GET OUT. For most, the United States was the goal, but many more Jews remained in Vienna—among them Aunt Jenny, my mother's only sister. A tiny, slightly humpbacked, sweet, and very intelligent woman, she was quite hard of hearing, too. Her husband was dead. Her two sons in Paris were (sorry to report) not too eager to have their mother join them; their own lives in

---

[*] Rebecca Madamba, "Honours Bachelors of Arts, Studies in Arts and Culture, Concentration in Curatorial Studies, Brock University, 2008. A thesis project presented to Ryerson University/Art Gallery of Toronto."

emigration were difficult enough, and I could do nothing for her. What little connection I had with French authorities I had used to secure temporary visas for my mother and brother.

Aunt Jenny had been chased out of her comfortable apartment, where she had lived all her life. She found a miserable hole somewhere in the historic ghetto of the city. I still have her last letters—heartbreaking, begging for help; she was all alone. The only people left who would befriend her were Uncle and Aunt Wesely, although they had not even known her before the calamity. Uncle and Aunt thought it was the right thing to do. They could not really help, as they had little money, but they met with her and talked to her up to the day when a transport took her to an unknown destination. Was it Treblinka, or Auschwitz, or some other such terrible place? We never knew. If anybody up there is keeping book of the poor souls who lived their faith, the names of Anton and Maria Wesely must be written there in golden letters. "Requiescat in Pace."

My parents did move to Paris in 1933 or 1934, and they fell in love with the city and all things French. They quickly became fluent in the language and eked out a living with the stock photo business, no small feat during those hard economic times. My older brother was born in Paris in February 1937 and was named Pierre Philip Oscar (the latter after his grandfather, a name he disliked and never used) with the expectation that he would grow up to be a Frenchman.

But the storm clouds of war were approaching and everyone was struggling with how to deal with the imminent crisis.

I did not want to go to America. I told her so. It was late summer or early fall of 1938 in Paris ... I was facing an elderly, somewhat stout, rather stern yet friendly-looking woman. She was a relative from America whom I had never met before. I was facing her at the sitting room of her suite at the Hotel George V. Its quiet elegance impressed me greatly. She had come to Europe with her husband [Paul Sachs] to find out how their respective families were faring in all that turbulence, since Hitler had marched his troops into the Rhineland in violation of the terms of the Versailles peace treaty; he had also gobbled up Austria and then Czechoslovakia, and threatened to eliminate Jewish life from German lands as well as all of Europe, and he made all sorts of noises threatening his neighbors.

I don't remember what language we used. Hardly English, I think. My knowledge of that language was quite poor at the time. I had been given private lessons for a few years, but had disliked both the lady teacher and the language itself. As a consequence, I was making very little progress. We must have talked either in French or in German. Aunt Meta asked whether I would not like—with my family—to come to the United States. It was a much better and safer place to live than Europe. She would gladly give me the needed affidavit and help me to obtain immigration visas. I agreed with her that things did indeed look bad in Europe, that war was a distinct possibility. I felt, however, not personally threatened. Yes, I had lost my nationality: a pusillanimous French government did not recognize any longer my Austrian passport, so as not to displease the German dictator; I could have obtained instead a German passport with a big "J" stamped in, which would have identified me as a Jew, second-class citizen, but I did not like that.

I accepted instead a French piece of paper which specified my nationality as Exautrichienne ("former Austrian"). In other words, I had become stateless. This did not disturb me greatly, as I could travel nevertheless. And, I hoped the troubles would not last. Before too long, I had expected to become a French citizen. My two-year-old son born on French soil was already one, as we had registered him as such at the mairie of our arrondissement. I had been given the right of permanent residency in France, even the Carte de Commercant which carried the right to exercise my profession and which was so difficult to obtain. Most important, I loved France, the French language and French literature; I felt at home there. And, if the war came, I would take my chance with the French people, as I had confidence in the French army. They had held back Le Boche (a hateful French term for "the Germans") once before.

Aunt Meta made a slight attempt to move me, but could not. I begged her to get affidavit visas for my mother and brother instead. They were still in Vienna, but I hoped for their arrival in Paris within a few weeks. I had gotten for them temporary visas, but knew there was little chance that they could get permission to stay. France was already overrun by refugees. I begged Aunt Meta to get affidavits and visas for them; she was reluctant. She knew that my brother was a handicapped person, and she thought that America—with its ruthless competition—was not a good place for such. I insisted and she relented.

War did come—and it changed our lives completely. First there was la drôle de guerre ("the phony war") in autumn 1939; France did nothing while the Germans annihilated Poland and divided it up with their newfound Russian ally. In the Paris region, all Germans—including Jewish refugees and all Austrians—had to report to the large football stadium for internment. The French were just as distrustful and jittery with regard to these people as a little later after Pearl Harbor the Americans were of the people of Japanese ancestry, and they treated them just as badly. They feared a "fifth column"* as they called it—a term taken from the recent Franco war.

Conditions at the stadium were bad. The French had nothing prepared and were not good at improvising. As food there was nothing but pâté de foie, (liver paté) and bread—very good pâté de foie, but if you eat nothing but that for weeks, you get nauseous even at its looks. Hygienic conditions were deplorable, with four or five big drums for perhaps 10,000 men. The regular toilets were outside of the stands and not accessible. I could not bear to get near these drums and simply did without. How I could survive this without permanent damage to my health is a piece of good fortune.

After about two weeks, the stadium was emptied and we Austrians were sent to a place in Normandy, a night's train ride away; I do not remember where the Germans went. The new place was a slightly sloping meadow surrounded by barbed wire. Nothing else. The first night was miserable. There was a slight rain. After a few days, the situation improved. Cesspools were dug, a kitchen built, a barracks with cots inside erected and camp life began to get organized. We had lectures and bridge games, played soccer, and waited. After a few weeks, we were told that those of us who could prove des attachés Francaises (French family relations) could be released. I had such an attaché—my two-year-old son, Pierre; he was a French citizen. After this was duly proven with several official stamps, I could get out and went home.

I will keep quoting directly from my father's memoir rather than trying to paraphrase because it captures so much about him. Although he was far

---

* The term refers to the Spanish Civil War and General Francisco Franco's boast that he would march into Madrid with four columns of soldiers, reinforced by a fifth column of Madrileños who would rise up in support of his fascist rebellion.

from a perfect man, I admired my father, and I find myself becoming more and more like him as I age. His greatest shortcoming was an inability to show and share emotion, which was devastating for my mother. He was reserved to a fault—and I have struggled, not always successfully, to be more open. It does not come naturally. Near the premature end of her life, my mother asked me, "What makes your father tick? I never could figure that out. You are so much like him. Can you tell me?" I could not, so I will continue to let him speak for himself:

Paris had changed. The lights had gone out for fear of aerial attacks which had not yet come. All able-bodied men were gone—all in the army were manning the Maginot Line (the "impregnable" defense structure between Paris and the German border), or standing guard elsewhere. My business had shrunk considerably, so we had to live on our small savings. Things were difficult, both practically and morally: could I sit home and let the French fight their war as if it did not concern me? When all was over and victory won, whom could I look in the eye and say, "I want to be a 'Frenchman'"? There was only one answer: I had to enlist and be one of them.

I went to the right place, signed a certain paper, got a receipt for that noble act, and was sent home. I would be called up in "due time." After a while, I received a notice that there was a certain change in my enlistment. It was not any longer simply for the armed forces. It was à titre de la legion etrangère. What did that mean? I went back to the place of enlistment: a friendly captain explained this measure was taken in the interest of people like me. If I were to be taken prisoner by the Germans, in all likelihood they would shoot me immediately as a traitor to the Vaterland. If I was sent to Africa, I was more likely to face Italians, who in a similar case might be less ferocious. It sounded reasonable enough. And anyway, I had no choice if I wanted to serve. Furthermore, the officer explained, it was not really the Foreign Legion. It was only à titre de la legion, the Legion in name only. There would be special units for those enlisted for the duration of the war. There would be no mix with the real Legionnaires who had to enlist for five years. The truth of the matter was—as we learned later—the government did not fully trust us. They feared spies, saboteurs, and the "fifth column." They preferred to have us out of the way; we were less dangerous in Africa than on French soil. I received my call-up notice and left Paris on Christmas Day 1939. Magda was pregnant.

Our group traveled south in several slow stages, from encampment to encampment, which were most uncomfortable. I remember particularly one, where we spent several days. It was an airplane hangar: no heat; no blankets . . . a thin layer of straw on the floor was all; no water, either. Two waterspouts were frozen solid. I was still in good shape, as I had my warm civilian coat; others in our group had nothing.

Our last stop in Europe was the Fort St. Jean, overlooking Marseille. It was a magnificent spot on a promontory high above the city. There we had a little foretaste of our future. We

My father as a Legionnaire, 1939.

were treated to a welcoming speech by the commander of the fort, a gray-haired captain with only one leg. There was much in his speech about glory and valor, and all about the Legion and what an honor it was to serve in its sacred ranks. We felt sure he lost his leg on some champ d'honeur (field of honor)... He ended with the somewhat chilling words: la-bas vous servirez la Legion d'abord, la France ensuite ("Over there you will first serve the Legion and then also France"). It was not exactly what we had in mind when we enlisted. We ended up staying at Fort St. Jean for four or five days; never did I meet with bedbugs as ferocious as they were at St. Jean!

It was still daylight when we embarked. The ship left after dark; we sailed with all lights out, with even no smoking on deck as there might have been enemy U-boats lurking in the dark. I lay on my back looking up as the top of the mast drew circles against the incredibly starry sky. It was almost romantic. "Adieu, Europe; adieu, family"—but toward what fate?

It was morning when we arrived at Oran and were put on a slow train, which got us to Sidi Bel Abbès, headquarters of the French Foreign Legion. It did not take us long to discover that it was the Foreign Legion, alright. "Special units, special treatment?" What was that nonsense? We were in the Foreign Legion, weren't we? Those gentlemen in Paris could say and write whatever they wished: the Legion made its own laws.

I received a wire announcing that I had become the father of a second healthy boy. I knew that gave any French soldier the right to a one-week furlough. I went to the company office, proudly showing my telegram. I did not even get to see the lieutenant: I was laughed off the premises. "Furlough? Who ever heard of such a stupid thing?" If I knew what was good for me, I would disappear, "and on the double."

It was a hard but healthy life. I doubt that we became Legionnaires worthy of that name, but they were beginning to make soldiers out of that bunch of civilians. We did not see any fighting, and that was good, as our equipment was miserable. Our rifles dated from the First World War, our ammunition (which had to be used most sparingly) came in boxes which were stamped "1917"; every fourth shot was a dud. We did not even see any enemy.

We also knew little of what was happening in the outside world. Nobody had a radio. The little newspaper which came from Oran reported little, heavily censored as it was. But we understood the "phony war" was not so phony any longer. The real thing had started and did not seem to go so well. There were words like "strategic retreat," "regroupments," as well as "shortening the front" and the "establishment of a new line." Finally the blow came; the truth could not be hid any longer: the Germans were in Paris.

Never had I felt similar despair and utter hopelessness. Our life had come to an end; the Germans parading on the Champs-Élysées! The day the news reached us happened to be payday at the Legion. As night fell, les anciens, the true Legionnaires, sat around at the canteen, more or less drunk, bawling to the "Horst Wessel Lied"—the Nazi hymn. It was the saddest day of my life.

What was to become of us who had enlisted for the duration of the war? The French government of Marshal Pétain had signed the armistice; was the war over? The Germans made the decision for us. According to the armistice terms, the French had to reduce its military establishment in North Africa; the Legion had to let us go. Where to? The country was in chaos; millions who had fled the German invasion were on the roads; a quarter of its population was uprooted. Let these soldiers go to Morocco and Algeria with no place to go and no money to live on? That seemed a sure road to brigandry and civilian disorder. There was but one way out. One could form these men into so-called civilian units—"companies de travailleurs," they were called. They could work the coal mines and build the long-planned railroad across the Sahara; maybe the Germans might allow that.

In this thoroughly confused situation, only a few of us succeeded in being sent back to France. It took a good deal of persistence, luck, and finally cheating to be among them. It really seemed stupid to go there, so why was I so eager to return to Nazi-dominated Europe? I wanted to be with my family. It did not turn out to be such a stupid decision, as most of the ones who stayed were indeed to become soldiers again; after the Allied landing in North Africa, they became part of the Eighth Army, which fought its way against stubborn German resistance up the Italian Peninsula. I was told that after the Sicilian landing, Anzio, and Monte Cassino, not many of my friends were to reach France.

Oddly, my father did not include in this written memoir a story which I found particularly moving. Whether he or my mother told us, I do not remember, but it was an important element of the family lore. In order to be sent back to Vichy, France, a Legionnaire had to prove he would not be "a burden on society." That meant proving that one had 5,000 francs to one's name. By my admittedly very rough calculation, that might have been six months' pay for a Legionnaire, possibly more; few could have saved that much.

Fortunately, one of my father's fellow soldiers, a Sergeant Cohen (I believe), did have that kind of money. He bought his way out and then deposited the necessary funds in a bank in Marseille in the name of the next one of his comrades who wanted to follow suit. Each one thereafter did the same—paying it forward, as we might say today—and, as a result, all of the Legionnaires in my father's small unit who wanted to risk going to France were able to get out. Any one of them could have absconded with the money; none did.

It was the winter of 1940 and freezing cold when I debarked in Marseille. An icy mistral (a violent cold and dry wind) blew. I came from Colomb-Béchar, an oasis on the edge of the Sahara, so I had nothing but my tropical summer uniform. All I had was my discharge paper, a small yellowish sheet that said I had served with honeur et fidelité *in the most splendid regiment of them all.*

France was divided into two separate parts. The north including Paris, the so-called "occupied zone," was under direct German rule; the so-called "free zone," which was not really free, was administered by the puppet government of Marshal Pétain at Vichy. There was no communication whatsoever between the two zones; no travel, no mail, no telephone. The only messages which could reach across the dividing line were pre-printed Red Cross cards, one-liners where you could check off one of five messages. And then there were messages smuggled through the underground; this way I learned that my family was still in Paris but hoped to leave soon and join me in Marseille. Clearly, I had to find a place for them to stay. That seemed almost impossible, as Marseille's population had almost doubled, swollen by the number of refugees from the north.

In my desperate search for that elusive apartment, I had a strange encounter with an American Quaker woman. Somebody had told me that the Quakers were nice and helpful people. I went to their office and was received by a friendly, middle-aged lady. I told her my story and she asked a number of questions, which I answered at my best. "No," she said, she would like to help, but knew of no place. When I left, it was a strange leave-taking. She held my hand for a long time, maybe a full minute, and looked me straight in the eyes. It seemed like she wanted to say something and then did not. This unusual scene stuck in my mind, its memory haunting me for a long time.

Many, many years later, I learned the explanation of this unusual scene. I saw a movie on television, a documentary, naturally on PBS; its title was, A Village in the Cévennes. *It told the wartime story of a Protestant community* up in the wilderness of the Plateau Central, far away from city life and centers of civilization … These people, peasants and other simple folk, felt called upon; when this war came and Jews were persecuted on French soil, they thought: "We are people of the Book and they are, too, so we are one and the same." So they offered refuge to hundreds of them in the woods when search parties of the German police came hunting Jews, hid them also (with shame it must be told) from the French police, who were equally searching.

Today there is a stone monument at the village, paid for by American Jews. It has the shape of an open book, its lettering in both French and Hebrew. A French filmmaker, the son of German Jews, had himself spent part of his childhood there. The film was his testimonial. It reported that a small group of American Quakers in Marseille acted as a link of an underground railroad which funneled people up to that mountain hideout. Now I had the answer to what the woman had been thinking about. She must have concluded that other people were more severely threatened than I. Had she spoken up, how different our lives would have been!

I found a place for my family, a small summer home on the outskirts of the city—Villa Santuzza was its name—at Château-Gombert; Route des Grottes Loubière was the address. The tram #5 got us there. The rent was exorbitant; it took most of the money I had. There was no heat, no gas, but there was water and electricity, if it worked. There was a small garden where we might be able to grow things … it seemed like heaven.

In the meantime, I was waiting for my family to arrive. I hoped they had received my message with the address, but could not be sure. I spent endless hours observing the train station where I expected them to arrive, but did not dare to get too close, as there were too many police around, checking people and asking for papers. Anybody who was not French or who spoke with an accent was likely to be taken along. And once "inside," only heaven knew when you would see daylight again.

We met in the streetcar as I headed home on #5, the last tram to run that evening. It happened on my birthday, February 25, 1941; Pierre did not recognize me. The family was at last reunited—but we were not complete.

My brother, Pierre, and my father in Marseille, 1941.
The attaché case contained batteries he was peddling to earn
a little money.

TWO

ESCAPE FROM NAZI EUROPE

I have always been perplexed by that last paragraph. Behind it lies an astonishing story of how my indomitable mother managed to get herself and my brother to that streetcar, with me joining them several months later. It is a story of danger, heroism, narrow escapes, altruism, and even something of a "Sophie's Choice" that my mother was forced to make. Perhaps my father did not include those details because he knew that my mother had written them down and they did not need to be repeated. But it would have been equally in character that he could not face recounting a story that likely caused him considerable guilt at having exposed his family to such hardship and danger.

Even more compelling is my mother's telling of the story. She composed it in English, barely a few months after coming to this country and learning the language. Its unadorned direct narrative style makes it completely alive and immediate for me—and it has deeply moved everyone with whom I have shared it.

Through the Occupation of France, 1940
by Theresa Magdika Schostal

*More than two years have passed since the fall of Paris, a relatively long time
for memory, but I remember those days in all their terrible details and I will
remember them even twenty years from now. I have read books and stories, and I
have seen motion pictures which dealt with these events, but none of them could
give a real picture of the atmosphere of terror and misery. I can't hope to be able
to describe it myself but I will try to tell simply my own story of these days, and it
will be at least absolutely true. I am well aware that all that happened to me was
not the worst because there was a happy end: we are all together and safe in this
country. But a great deal of our life and energy, even of our health, remains there
and we can't be as happy as we have reason to be, thinking of our friends who
live there under terrible conditions. Sometimes I feel ashamed that we escaped.*

*The first months of war didn't bring a great change in our life. Walter, as an
"enemy alien," had to go to a camp but he came back after a few weeks because
he was the father of a French-born child. He enlisted in the French army but he
was called only at Christmas '39. He left us on Christmas Day and it was a very
sad Christmas, the first and only one in my life without a Christmas tree. I had
hoped that he would stay with us until Claudie was born, but Claudie arrived
four weeks later. I continued our business after his leaving. I was able to do it
because I had always worked with him in the office. I didn't even feel very lonely
because my mother-in-law, who already had her American visa, waited until after
Claudie's birth and left me only in March 1940 for the United States. All our
male employees joined the army but it didn't matter, business was very slow and
I worked with a secretary and a young apprentice. I had all the advantages the
Frenchwomen had whose husbands were mobilized—that means I hadn't any
rent to pay, and I received seven hundred francs monthly from the government.
It wasn't enough to live on but it helped a great deal toward supporting us. In
all these months, we sometimes had air-raid alarms and we heard the shots of
the anti-aircraft guns. This was a sign that enemy airplanes were over Paris, but
they never dropped any bombs. In the beginning, we always went downstairs*

into the cellar, as we had orders to do. It was very hard for the children, in the night, especially for Claudie who was only a few weeks old. I knit many pairs of woolen socks for Walter during those nights in the cellar, and we joked often saying if only there would be more alarms. I was so busy during the day that I never had time to knit, and Walter needed so badly woolen things for the night. The climate in Algeria was so bad—a terrible heat during the day and very cold nights.

Later on, we remained in our apartment during the air raids since, indeed, nothing happened. We even became a little accustomed to the sirens, which we never could hear without shuddering. I heard the sirens again in New York, but it wasn't the same. They didn't get through your nerves and were not half as loud as in Paris. Pierre always screamed when he heard them, even Claudie showed signs of excitement and he was only a newborn baby.

In May, the alarms became more frequent with the German advance in Holland and Belgium. We began to feel uneasy but never thought that the Germans would reach Paris. We saw the refugees come through Paris, first the Belgians and later the refugees from northern France. It was heartrending to see these tired children in the halls of the stations where the refugees assembled. Most had walked on foot, their clothes were torn and they had nothing with them. They had had no time to save anything, and if they had a few things, they had thrown them away on the roads, they were too tired to carry them. We gave them whatever we could spare. We heard them tell stories of how they had been machine-gunned and bombed during their escape, and that many had died on the roads either by guns or from exhaustion. We were shocked and frightened, but you know how it is—down in your heart you can't believe it, you simply have not the imagination to feel it. We felt so secure in Paris; we always thought it would be as it was in the other wars. The Germans would be stopped before reaching the city. We read in the papers that French cities in northern France had been bombed and we knew it would be Paris' turn soon. Thousands left the city, but most of the people chose little places not too far from Paris, only in order to escape the bombings. So did I. I rented a little apartment in a small village which could be reached in about half an hour on the train. But we remained in

Paris, even the children. I could not decide to send them away with Catherine, our old alsacienne, who was the maid for the children, as I worked in the office and nursed Claudie. She had already brought up Pierre and belonged to the family, and I knew I could leave the children in her care, but I was afraid to stop Claudie's nursing.

Then came the collapse of the Belgian army and the tragic days of Dunkirk. Business was practically nonexistent and we sat all day before our radio hoping that finally the news would come that the Germans had been stopped. We had a powerful radio and I could easily hear stations in Germany. On the evening of Sunday, June 2, I heard a German broadcast which was intended for the Parisian population. The speaker said, "Parisians, this was your last quiet Sunday." When on Monday at noon the sirens began to scream, we knew this time it was serious and we went down in our cellar. It was horrible. We heard as usual the anti-aircraft guns and besides there was the thunder of explosions. The walls trembled. We tried not to show our fear because of the children. I spoke to Pierre and told him a story to divert his attention from the terrible noise, but my lips trembled. When I looked around, I saw white faces and eyes full of fear. In an hour all was over. In the next broadcast we heard of the disaster. They didn't tell where the bombs had fallen, but we soon found out that the Citroën factories were destroyed, and that especially the Porte de Versailles and some suburbs had suffered most. (I saw the Citroën factories months later and it was a terrible sight.) We heard soon that there were nine hundred victims of this bombardment.

Late in the evening, a friend of mine, the wife of our salesman who served now as a lieutenant in the army, came in with her children to see me. She lived in Issy-les-Moulineaux, a suburb near the Porte de Versailles. She was frightened and excited, and told us that Issy-les-Moulineaux had suffered terribly. Bombs were dropped on the railroad a few yards from her house. At the time of the bombardment she was in Paris for some shopping. She had a daughter of eleven and a baby of about the same age as Claudie. She had kept her daughter home from school to watch the baby and she knew the children were alone in the apartment. When all was over, she could not go home, her subway line was not operating, and she heard that Issy was heavily bombed. Poor woman, she was nearly crazy from fear. After several hours, the line was repaired and she went home to find her children crying but safe in the apartment. She learned that the fact that her daughter was home and not at school had probably saved her life. In this school there was no cellar for shelter but only a covered trench in the garden, and a bomb fell on top of this improvised shelter and killed a great number of little girls.

My friend was afraid to stay home and asked me to keep her and the children for the night. We decided to move the next day to our little summer apartment, thinking that from now on Paris would be bombed every day. She was invited by friends not far from the village where I had rented the apartment. She left me in the morning, crying and unhappy. In addition to the troubles we all had, she had no news from her husband and she knew he was in Belgium. It was not until months later that she heard that he was a prisoner in Germany, where he probably is yet. She was the best friend I ever had. She kept Claudie when I went with Pierre to Marseille and took over a responsibility which not many would take.

At that time I could be considered happy in comparison with her situation. I knew Walter was safe in Africa. There was no war there.

The next day, I prepared for our departure from the city. I myself intended to stay in Paris and go to see the children twice a week. Claudie's nursing was no longer a problem; all the troubles and especially the bombing had affected my ability to nurse him. Poor Claudie had to change his diet suddenly, but fortunately he was a healthy baby and it didn't do him any harm. I hired a taxicab and accompanied Catherine and the children to their new home. On our way there, we saw the effects of the bombing. Not far from our house a bomb had fallen in the street, leaving a big crater. All the windows in the street were broken, but there were not victims in our neighborhood.

The well-known roads out of Paris, which we took so often in peacetime for trips to the nice environs of the city, had a strange aspect. Hundreds of soldiers occupied the crossings and bridges. Our car was searched and our papers inspected many times before we arrived. The apartment I had rented was on the estate of friends of ours, who once had money and had lost it. All looked a little neglected but there was a large garden once cultivated but now a wilderness. Pierre liked it very much and was happy. It was so peaceful and quiet. Then came the first night, and it was hell. The sirens screamed, the anti-aircraft guns were fired all night, and bombs fell not very far from the village so that we could see the fires from our windows. It was worse than in Paris. I regretted having left Paris, but it was too late. The next day I returned to Paris, but I was anxious, and for the following week I took the train nearly every evening and spent the nights with the children. It was the same hell every night, and often even during the daytime. I remember the Sunday before the occupation. We were in the garden and Pierre was picking strawberries which grew wild everywhere. Suddenly we saw several airplanes above our heads, which we recognized as German. The anti-aircraft guns began to shoot and we saw the explosions in the sky. I called Pierre, who was angry at the interruption of his picking, and we ran and sought shelter under a tree. It was too late to go into the house. Suddenly the guns stopped and a group of French planes arrived. For half an hour we could observe a battle in the air, which excited us like a sport game. We felt more secure than under the anti-aircraft guns, which often injured persons who were outside during their shots. Finally, the planes disappeared in different directions and Pierre went back to his strawberries. There wasn't even an alarm during this battle. They had no time to give it.

The following days the situation became more and more confused. We began to be afraid of an occupation. Thousands and thousands left Paris with cars and trains and tried to go to southern France. Most of them didn't go very far. There were fewer and fewer trains and no more gas for the cars. The French began to blow up the bridges over the Seine River and it became nearly impossible to travel between Paris and the little village where we were. An atmosphere of fear and panic came over us. There was no order anymore. The mayor of Paris made a speech over the radio saying that Paris would be defended house by house and stone by stone. This was one of the most horrible crimes of this war because everybody became sick with fear, and millions began to leave the city on foot. It was an indescribable chaos. The last chance to stop the Germans was taken away by this exodus. The roads were crowded by refugees and soldiers who moved without order.

I made desperate efforts to find a possibility to go south. Nobody would take me with the two children. One person could find a place in a car or even try to escape on foot, but we were four. People paid astronomic prices for a place in a car. For us, it was hopeless. When on June 10, Italy declared war on France, I had one thing more to worry about. I knew now war would begin in Africa and Walter would no longer be in security.

Our little village became completely deserted. All civilians were gone and the shops closed. We couldn't even buy milk. The milkman was gone too. It was no longer possible to stay, and since we couldn't go south, the only possibility was to go back to Paris. I thought, if there is a way to escape, we would find it more easily in Paris than here, and if not, the cellars of the old Parisian houses were safer. So we packed up and hurried to the station. But there we had a terrible surprise. There were no more trains. We waited for hours and hours and did not know what to do. There was a strange atmosphere around us, a kind of smoke or fog was in the air, which made us cough and our eyes water, and nobody knew what it was. There were rumors that it was an artificial fog in order to hide the retreat of the French army. Others said it was the smoke from the big gas reservoirs which the French blew up to destroy their stocks for fear they would fall into the hands of the enemy. We never knew what it really was, but the last explanation seemed to me to be the most probable because we heard explosions far away. During all this time, the anti-aircraft guns were firing and German planes were above us. Small groups of French soldiers came along. To see their hopeless faces made us cry. Most of them were drunk, and they had no officers with them. It was a retreat without order. Nobody knew where to go.

Finally, the station master advised us to go to the next town from where, as he had heard, a train would leave for Paris. It was only a few miles away. We immediately set out. I was well aware that it was dangerous because the retreating French army took the same road to Paris. But we had no choice. We walked and walked. Catherine pushed Claudie's carriage. Pierre could not walk fast enough, and so we put him into the carriage with Claudie. I carried a suitcase, but we had left most of our things at the station. It didn't matter. If we could reach Paris and our apartment, we would find there what we needed. Claudie cried. He was hungry, but we could not stop to make a bottle ready for him. We were so afraid of the planes which were constantly above us. The road was crowded with soldiers moving in the direction of Paris, and cars and people on foot who were coming from Paris and going I did not know where. Probably nobody knew where they were going. After one hour, we stopped for a few minutes at an inn and Claudie had his milk warmed up. We had just left the inn when I heard a strange noise. I did not realize what it was until I heard some soldiers calling and I saw them running to bushes. Now I understood that we were machine-gunned, and at the same moment, the plane was only a few yards above our heads. I could clearly see the faces of the pilot and the gunner. All the time, this noise did not stop. It continued in a terrible regularity. I screamed and was heedless for a second, but Catherine was already in the bushes with the children. I fell in the ditch beside the road and somebody pulled me into the bushes. I remember they were currant bushes, and the berries were red and ripe. Pierre was hungry and began to eat the berries. We remained there for a long time. We heard many planes above us but saw only a few which dived low because of the strange fog. Nobody was hit, but when we finally continued to walk, we saw several dead soldiers in the ditches. After another hour we arrived at the station of the town and a train was waiting there. Hundreds tried to go in, but it was hopeless. When the station master saw us with the children, he pushed us in. But we couldn't take Claudie's carriage with us. It remained there. The train left and many remained behind who couldn't go in. A few minutes later we arrived.

In Paris, the fog was worse than out in the country. It was hard to breathe. There was soot in the air and our clothes became greasy. The streets had a strange aspect. All the shops were closed. Small groups of tired-looking people moved in the direction of the different portes pushing all kinds of vehicles loaded with their personal belongings. There were no cars at all. Fortunately, the subway was operating, and we hurried to our apartment and went to bed. I had a strange feeling and everything seemed to me like a dream. A few hours ago we were hiding in bushes from the firing planes, and now I lay in my bed at home. It was Tuesday, June 11, 1940.

The next day, I ran around looking for a chance to leave Paris by car. There was none and I gave it up. It was nearly impossible to find anything to eat. The only open shop in our neighborhood was a pharmacy where I could buy evaporated milk. We had some fruit preserves and cookies at home and we lived on them. In the afternoon the druggist told me he had heard good news. Paris had been declared "ville ouverte" (open city). That meant the city would not be defended. There would be no battles in the streets, no bombing. In one sense, it was good news, but in the other, there was no hope anymore. It was perhaps a question of hours and the Germans would be here. Indeed, a few hours later we heard it over the radio, but it was too late. If this decision had been taken two or three days earlier, most of the people would have stayed at home and many lives—especially those of children—would have been spared and a great deal of misery avoided. I learned later that the fact that we couldn't find any possibility of leaving Paris was good luck and probably saved our lives, at least the lives of the children. Besides the soldiers, thousands of women and children died on the roads. Our adventure was short but I can imagine the hardships of those who were out for days and even weeks.

In the end, when I had given up hope of leaving Paris, my neighbor, a very good friend of ours, spoke to me about a possibility. It was Thursday evening, and early the next morning a truck would leave Paris for Orleans. The driver had agreed to take us with him and we should wait for him at Place Pigalle at seven o'clock in the morning. I was afraid to go. I had already settled my mind to stay in Paris. I began to understand that it was foolhardy to leave without knowing where to go, as millions did. But the thought that, if we could escape from the Germans, I would have the chance to write and receive news from Walter made me change my mind. We packed up once more—only a few things, and evaporated milk for Claudie. I did not go to bed at all that night. I was too excited. I sat down at our window and waited. The last two days had been relatively quiet. We had no more air-raid alarms. But that night was a hell. Heavy guns—not the anti-aircraft guns to which we were already accustomed—fired all night and they were not very far away. The walls trembled. The sky was red, and from time to time huge flames rose. My eyes watered because of smoke and fog. At dawn, the guns suddenly stopped firing. The quietness was strange. I woke the children and we got ready to leave. Catherine carried Claudie and I had a heavy rucksack. Pierre staggered. He was so sleepy and frightened. At seven, we arrived at the Place Pigalle and waited for the truck. The Place Pigalle is Paris' amusement center at Montmartre, a nice and gay place in the happy days, but now it had a desolate aspect. Groups of French soldiers came along, some on foot, some on bicycles; their uniforms were torn, and they looked exhausted. One of them collapsed and lay on his knees, crying like a child. His comrades boxed at his ears to make him rise and walk. They told him not to lose his nerves, one porte was still free, the Porte d'Orléans, and they would escape if he could run. He rose and staggered away. Through their conversation we learned that Paris was already encircled. Suddenly we heard a woman's voice screaming. We saw her under the gate of a house crying for help. She was in labor pains and there was no vehicle to take her to a hospital. Finally, two policemen helped her to walk to the next subway station. After a few steps she collapsed and refused to walk. They took her to the next stop, and a few minutes later the child was born with the help of the policemen. We waited outside in great tension and forgot all the war and were even happy when we heard that everything was all right with her.

One hour had passed and the truck had not arrived. There was no sense to wait any longer. We decided to go home. As we were starting, I saw a group of soldiers in a strange uniform. One of them made signs for us to go out of the way. It took me several seconds until I realized that these were not French soldiers. I stared at them and then I understood. All was finished. The Germans were here.

To a certain degree I was relieved. There was nothing to do except to go home and sleep. For the first time in weeks we could sleep without fear. There would be problems and misery later I knew, but for the moment, for us, the war was over.

It was in December 1940 that I received the first news from my husband who had been in Algeria since June. It was a printed postcard with his signature, the only kind of mail the Germans permitted between the zone libre and the zone occupée. He informed me that he would soon come to Marseille to be demobilized. I knew that he never would dare to come back to Paris, and so I tried to find a way to go and meet him in Marseille. It was impossible to get a permit from the Germans and the only way was to be smuggled across the line.

A few weeks later, I was introduced to a woman who was a smuggler and who agreed to take me and Pierre with her, but she refused to take Claudie, who was only a baby of twelve months at that time. It would be too dangerous and difficult because we had to walk miles and miles in the night through forests. It was the hardest decision I ever had to make in all my life; to leave Claudie behind me and not to know if and when I could see him again. A friend of mine agreed to keep him, and I knew he would be well treated, and I hoped the Red Cross would bring him to Marseille a few weeks later.

One Sunday evening, we had a date with the woman at the station. I had already sent our things to Marseille. It was allowed to send clothes and personal belongings from one zone to the other. We left behind all our money, jewelry, furniture, etc. We waited and waited until the train was gone, and the woman didn't come. I was crying and so was Pierre. It was late and we had only half an hour until the curfew. Nobody was allowed to be in the streets after eleven o'clock. We took the subway to the woman's apartment. I had to know what happened to her. From her superintendent I heard that she had been arrested two hours before by the Gestapo. I knew she had my address in her pocketbook, and so I couldn't go back to my apartment where the Gestapo, who knew me very well, would find me. And it was eleven o'clock. So we took a little room in the next hotel, an awful dirty place with a "patron" who looked like a criminal. I could not sleep, and I cried. It was a terrible disappointment. I did not know where to go the next day, and I had only a handbag with me.

The next morning, I went to a friend of mine and asked her if I could stay with her for a few days until I had found another way to go to Marseille. She received me very nicely and I spent a week in her apartment. I tried to buy a permit, but it was impossible to get one at the moment. I was desperate and I knew my husband was anxious because he was expecting us. I had to get away from Paris, and so I tried to do it alone without any help. Somebody told me about a little town on the frontier where the bus drivers helped people to go on the other side. But it was all very vague.

One evening, we took the train to Bordeaux. I remember there was a terrible snowstorm in the streets when we went to the station. We had to change twice. I always will remember some of the details of the trip. We arrived in Bordeaux early in the morning and went to the station cafeteria to get some coffee, or what they called coffee. There was a drunken German soldier drinking champagne at seven o'clock in the morning. He offered everybody a glass and I didn't dare to refuse because he was drunk and I was afraid of having trouble with him. I was so glad that Pierre didn't understand German. He would certainly have answered in German, and that would have been bad.

Then I remember a group of young Frenchmen in the train who told me they would try to go over the frontier to Spain that night and go to England to fight with the Free French. I wished them good luck and they wished the same to me. A few minutes before we arrived in Mont-de-Marsan, I began a conversation with a man who asked me what I was doing in this little town where he lived. I told him the truth, knowing I could trust a Frenchman in things like that. "My poor lady," he told me. "What are you doing! It is impossible to go through here. It was possible a few weeks ago, but since then so many people have been arrested by the Germans, and in the night they make patrols with dogs along the frontier and everybody is shot on sight." When he saw my tears and my hopeless face, he tried to console me. "I will try to help you, don't despair," he said.

When we left the train I had a terrible surprise. There were German soldiers on the passageway inspecting the papers of every traveler. I knew I could not show my papers. It would have shown them that I was an Austrian and inhabitant of Paris. It would have been easy to find out what I was doing in this little frontier village where I knew nobody and the Germans knew each one of the few inhabitants. At the last moment, my new friend gave me his name and address so that I could give a name to the inspector. But I had a bright idea. Now I can understand how it is possible in moments of great danger to find a solution which you never would be able to find in normal life. Pierre was always afraid of German soldiers, and so I told him, "Pierre, run away. You see the German soldier. He will put us in prison if he can seize us." And Pierre ran and ran, and I after him, calling his name. The German believed that I was a poor mother running after her naughty boy, and he let me run through the passageway with a smile, perhaps remembering his own naughty boys. He didn't even look at my papers. I was through the passageway and the first round was won. But the most difficult was still before us.

Outside of the station, Monsieur B., my new friend, was waiting for me. He gave me his arm, and so we went down to the town (the station was situated on a hill). In Paris the streets were always crowded with German soldiers but I never before saw so many in one place as here. I was afraid, and I understood that it would not have been possible to ask the bus drivers to help me. Every step was observed by the Germans, and especially people who approached the bus going to the unoccupied zone had to pass a lane of inspecting soldiers. But talking to Monsieur B. like a just-arrived friend, we moved safely in the streets without troubles. "The first question," he told me, "is to find a room for you. It will not be easy. Every hotel room is taken by the Germans."

There were only a few hotels in the town, and it was true. I could not find a room. Finally, he went with me to a friend of his, a nice elderly woman who had a hotel with a few rooms and she gave me her own room for one night. It was a very cold and foggy day in February. "You can't stay in the streets with your poor little boy," she said, and I knew she understood my situation and was willing to help me. At noon we had dinner with her and a lot of German soldiers. She introduced me as her cousin, and so nobody asked me a question. It was a funny situation. The Germans had not the slightest notion that I understood every word of their conversation. They tried even to speak to me in French and it was hard for me not to laugh. Their conversation was not very interesting. I noticed it very often when I heard German soldiers talk together. They never said anything personal. I think they don't trust each other. After lunch, Monsieur B. came for a visit in my room. "I have thought it over," he said. "There is only one man here who can help you. Go to Monsieur Dasse, the electrician. He hates the Germans. He is a Gaullist (as are called the followers of General de Gaulle in France). I am sure he will do something for you."

We went to Monsieur Dasse and I told him my story. He was a very nice man, but first he hesitated. "You know very well," he said, "that I risk my position and even prison, and I promised my wife never to do it again." But his wife, who was the midwife of the village, when she saw Pierre, said to him, "Do it for the little boy, so he can see his father again." He told me to go back to my room and stay there for the rest of the day. It was a Sunday and he couldn't do anything *before Monday morning. He told me nothing about how he would help me, and so I was in a state of uncertainty and the day seemed to me very long. In the evening, before we went to bed, the landlady told me I had better leave the hotel early in the morning because at seven o'clock the Germans always come in the hotels to inspect the papers of every stranger. I could not sleep that night, and at six o'clock we were in the streets. It was dark and cold, and in reality, it was only four o'clock because we had in France at this time German wartime, that means two hours earlier than the real western sun time. I did not dare to go to Monsieur Dasse so early, and so I found an open gate where we stayed for two hours in a terrible cold, always in fear of the German patrols which we could hear in the streets. Pierre cried, he felt so cold, and I tried to keep him quiet. Those two hours seemed to me longer than two years. Finally, it was eight and we went to Monsieur Dasse. His wife gave us tea and milk, and so we came back to life. And only now Monsieur Dasse explained to me how he would manage it, to get us on the other side. Most of the inhabitants of a frontier village had regular permits to go on the other side of the frontier. Often they had ground and property there. The frontier line was artificial and arbitrary, and in many cases, the house was in one zone and fields in the other. I heard, for instance, about a church in the occupied zone whose cemetery was in the unoccupied zone. (In Europe the cemeteries in the country are always around or behind the churches.) When there was a funeral, hundreds of "friends" followed the coffin and only a few of them came back. But soon the Germans found out the trick, and the minister is now in a concentration camp and you need a special permission for a burial.*

Monsieur Dasse borrowed a permission from a friend of his, a dressmaker. She was forty-eight and her picture was not at all like me, but with a little retouching we tried to make me look old enough to look like it. It was easy. I was so tired and looked so grieved. I put on my glasses and a shawl instead of my hat. Then I had to learn the woman's birthdate and birthplace and all the data about her husband and children. And so I was Madame Guerin. I never saw her in my life but I never will forget her kindness. I tried to leave a present for her but Monsieur Dasse didn't accept it neither for her nor for himself or his wife. It was all pure goodness. When the war is over I will write to those people who did more for me than the best friends can ever do. I feel so sorry for them knowing how much they suffer.

When we all found my disguise very satisfactory, Monsieur Dasse asked for all my papers and money, and all the little things in my handbag like a compact and a lipstick, things which a country dressmaker certainly never carries with her, and he hid everything in the rim of his wheel. People going on the other side were only allowed to have ten francs which is about a quarter in American money. Then he instructed me to tell the German officer inspector that I was going to a fitting for a dress for a customer. Now we were ready and got into the car. He told me that all depends on the German officer. Some are nice but all is a question of luck. When we left the last houses of the village behind us, we could already see the barrier of the frontier and a hundred yards behind it was the French barrier. I could feel the palpitations of my heart as we approached it. "I think we are lucky," said Monsieur Dasse. "The only Austrian officer we have here is on duty. He is nice and easy. He is not all like the Germans." And at this moment we stopped before him. On the right there was the officer and on the left of the car several soldiers who asked for our permits. And once more Pierre helped a great deal. The officer began to speak to him and to caress his hair because Pierre looked at him anxiously. I tried to intervene and told Pierre not to be afraid because the officer was a nice man. So I looked always in the other direction and the inspecting soldiers could not see my face. They looked in the car and in my handbag, and at this moment several other cars arrived which diverted their attention from us. The officer gave the signal, the barrier was lifted, and we went through. When I heard the barrier fall down behind us, I began to cry and to sob. Monsieur Dasse smiled, "Cry as much as you can, it will do you a lot of good. You are not the first one I saw crying in this situation."

I was still crying when the French barrier rose for our car and I saw for the first time in eight months French uniforms and the Tricolor. They opened the door and helped me out. They understood everything after looking at me. "Don't cry any more Madame, now you are in France, safe. Forget the Boches."

Monsieur Dasse, well known by the French soldiers, introduced me, saying, "This is the thirtieth I have helped to come through."

They congratulated us and invited us to have a drink with them. I looked back toward the German barrier. The other cars were still there. The Germans were still inspecting them and searching their occupants. I realized the lot of luck we had had, thanks to Pierre.

Monsieur Dasse hid his car behind the French customs house and took my things out of the tires. One could see perfectly well from the German side what one was doing here, and since he had to go back, he had to be cautious. Then he said goodbye to us and went back, leaving us with our new friends, the French customs officers and French soldiers. When I think it over, I am sure that never before in my life I was so happy as in this moment.

What followed then was so easy compared to what we had gone through. We had to wait two hours for the bus going to Pau, a watering place at the base of the Pyrenees mountains. We had dinner with the customs officers and gendarmes, and the sergeant sold me a dozen eggs, which made me very happy because we had not seen eggs for a long time. I carried them with me in my handbag very carefully.

When the bus arrived, the sergeant inspected the papers. Even in the unoccupied zone the inspection was very severe in the frontier zone, and it was not allowed for aliens to travel without permission. But the sergeant did not even think to ask for my papers. He was a polite Frenchman and we had had a drink together, so he could not distrust me. In Pau, I sent a postcard to my husband, hoping that it would arrive before us. We had no time to send a telegram because every telegram had to be censored by the police and our train for Toulouse was leaving in a few minutes. We arrived in Toulouse late in the evening and had to stay there for the night. You can go from Paris to Marseille in twelve hours, but as we did the trip, it took two days. We made a tour through France. The next day at noon, we took the train to Marseille where we arrived in the evening. We had left Paris in a snowstorm, but here in southern France, it was spring with blossoms on the trees.

In Marseille, it was rainy and dark, and there was no Daddy at the station. Walter had written to me that he had rented a little cottage in Château-Gombert near Marseille and that it took to go there half an hour by streetcar. It was nearly impossible to find a room or an apartment in Marseille. There were so many refugees from the occupied zone. The population had increased from 800,000 to 1.5 million since the fall of Paris. I couldn't even find a room for the night and I tried to go to Château-Gombert immediately, without hope of finding Walter there because it was February 25, his birthday, and I thought he would stay in town for a little party with friends. It seems ridiculous all the trouble it took to go from a town to a suburb, but all these things are very difficult now in Europe. There are no taxis at all, very few trains and streetcars, and in most of the big cities a blackout, so you can't find a street when you are a stranger in the place. But we found the place from which the streetcar went to Château-Gombert. We had to run to catch the last car leaving at nine o'clock and we just got in as it was leaving. And there I saw a very well-known silhouette a few seats before us. It was Walter, who also took the last car to go home. It was very funny for me to meet my husband in a streetcar after a separation of more than a year. I crawled forward and, covering his eyes with my hands, I asked, "Who is it?" You can imagine his surprise. I asked Pierre if he could recognize the gentleman. But even knowing that we took the trip to join Daddy, he did not recognize him. Walter told us that he had been at the station every day until the day before. Then he had lost hope of seeing us now, thinking we had been arrested by the Germans. Our postcard arrived two days after we did.

There began a very happy time for us three, spoiled only by Claudie's absence. The little cottage was nice, and we had a garden where the cherry and apple trees were already flowering and the lawns were blue with violets. We had no comfort at all. I had to cook on a stove but there was no coal and we took the wood out of our garden. Often it was wet and did not burn, and we were on our knees before the fire like bellows blowing and puffing to make it burn. Our menu was very poor. The nutrition situation in Marseille was even worse than in occupied France, especially the first weeks. Later on we had vegetables and fruit from the country and from our garden. Walter had tried to plant radishes and lettuce but they never came up. By chance we made the acquaintance of a good policeman from Marseille, Monsieur Paul we called him, who came several times a week to work in our garden. We did not pay him but he had the right to take half of all that grew. We always had lived in big cities, and for the first time in our life, we ate vegetables from our own garden. The country around Marseille is very lovely and there is always sun, the bright sun of southern France. We had a good time and we were very happy.

But week after week passed and Claudie did not arrive, and I had hoped that he would be with us two weeks after my arrival. I had two possibilities of bringing him over. The first was with a permit from the Germans. Before I left Paris, my friend who kept Claudie went to the commander to ask if she could have a permit to accompany a child whose parents were in Marseille. Cases in which parents were in one zone and the children in the other were frequent. So many parents had lost their children during the escape on the roads and didn't even know where they were. I knew, for instance, a case of friends of mine. They had left Paris on foot and they met a car with friendly people who proposed to take the children to the next town. The parents accepted because the children were so tired and could not walk anymore, and the roads were constantly machine-gunned by airplanes. The parents never reached the town and came back to Paris. Only months later they heard from the Red Cross that their children were safe in the unoccupied zone. So thousands and thousands of children were separated from their parents, and when I left Paris eight months after the fall, there was always a daily column in the newspapers with parents asking if somebody had found their children, or a hospital or a nursery advertising that they had young children who knew only their first name and had lost their parents.

My friend came back from the German commander with the answer that, naturally for a case like this, she would receive a permit if she could show a postcard from the other zone that really the parents asked for their child. When I arrived in Marseille, the first thing I did was to write such a postcard. But in spite of this promise, my friend never got the permit. After weeks of delay and vague promises, the final answer was a refusal.

Then we went to the Red Cross to ask for help. They promised us to bring Claudie over with their next transfer but they could not tell us when it would be: perhaps in two weeks, perhaps in three months. For several reasons we were anxious to have Claudie with us as soon as possible. My friend could not keep him any longer. Claudie had diphtheria and was for a few days in a great danger, and he had not yet recovered when her own little daughter (who was of about the same age as Claudie) fell ill of the same sickness. You can imagine my anxiety when I heard of it. Fortunately, I received her card announcing his sickness and that he was out of danger at the same time. That wasn't all. My friend lived in Issy-les-Moulineaux, a suburb of Paris which suffered the most of the great bombardment on June 3, 1940. Her house was on a hill, at the foot of which was a railroad. This railroad was hit by several bombs, and big craters remained in the neighborhood. Now several months later, a landslide resulted from these bombs and her house was in a great danger of falling in. She had to evacuate her apartment within a few hours and find accommodations with her family where she could not keep Claudie with her. She wrote desperate cards asking me to find a solution. And to make her troubles greater, the Gestapo made searches in her apartment considering my affairs.

I always had had troubles with the Gestapo who visited me several times with a search warrant. We had a news picture agency before the war and they were looking for anti-Nazi pictures and articles. As a matter of fact, we had none of this kind of feature, but one of these gentlemen was a personal enemy of Walter's (or to be more exact, a business rival before the war) who had lived for years and years in Paris and who, after the fall of France, came back in a German uniform—an excellent example of fifth column. He had an important situation as a news picture censor and misused his position to have the Gestapo investigate all his old correspondents and rival firms. This excellent gentleman, who had the tact to visit personally all his former acquaintances to bother them, had forbidden me to go away or to move anything from our office or apartment. He soon found out that I had decamped, but our superintendent, who knew that Claudie was with my friend, gave him her address and now he tried to revenge himself upon her. All this she could not write me. But we had arranged a code for our writing, and so I understood perfectly well what had happened, and later from a smuggled letter I learned the details. This man even tried to intimidate her, saying he would keep Claudie as a hostage. My friend fortunately was courageous and told him that the Red Cross knew about Claudie's case and would take care of him. So he did not dare to keep Claudie. The Germans always avoided open scandals, trying to seem human and to make believe they were not as bad as people always thought they were.

These were my friend's reasons for getting rid of Claudie, and we from our side needed him very desperately. Our American visa was ready, but the consul in Marseille refused to deliver it because the family was not complete. He wanted to see Claudie. We had an appointment for a certain date, and a week before Claudie had not yet arrived. It was very difficult to obtain an appointment, and when one could not keep it, one had to wait for months for another one. Our situation was so desperate from every point that we wanted to go away as soon as possible and Claudie had to come within a few days.

I asked everybody I knew about the possibilities of smuggling and finally I heard of a village near Chalons-sur-Saône where the inhabitants were willing to help, for money naturally. Chalons-sur-Saône was occupied, the Saône River was the frontier and the villages on the other side of the river were already unoccupied zones.

I decided to go there, but as an alien I needed a permission to travel, and after inquiry at the police, I heard that first of all it took a week to get a permission and then that I never would get one for a place so near the frontier. But I was not willing to abandon the plan for such trifles after all I had already overcome. We had a friend in Marseille whose cousin was a high functionary in the police. He procured an appointment for me with his cousin and I told him the truth. I never met a Frenchman who was not willing to help children, and so, one hour later, I had my permission.

I left Marseille the same evening, once more only knowing the name of a village. But I hoped to come back with Claudie. I arrived in Saint-Loup-de-Varennes, the frontier village, the next morning and found an entirely different situation than in Mont-de-Marsan. Here soldiers smiled at every stranger and wished them good luck, knowing very well that they came to this forgotten village only for some smuggling affair with the other zone.

The Germans did not allow departure from the occupied zone but they did not allow entrance either. It was likewise impossible to get a permission to go to Paris from the unoccupied zone as it was in the other direction. You had to ask for such a permission in Vichy at the German consul and you never got one.

When I left the station, looking around, a young man introduced himself and asked whether I wanted to go on the other side. I was so happy. What a difference between here and my previous experience! I explained my situation to him. I did not want to go myself, but I wanted my baby to be smuggled. He said this would be easy and only a matter of a few days. He was the son of the landlady of the "I des Platanes," an inn on the road to Chalons and, since the German occupation, an honorable smuggler.

He accompanied me to his mother's inn, where I found a nice comfortable room and friendly people. I had a good time there. I found out that everybody in this region was a smuggler and they smuggled whatever you wanted, persons and money and merchandise. They were proud of their new job and very respectable, asking only what one could pay and often helping poor people for nothing. They were nice and good as French common people always are. I lived with them for several days like a member of the family and I always will remember their kindness. I helped them in their work, and even as a waitress when nobody else had time. I met a lot of people in this inn and everybody told me smuggling stories, some very amusing, others tragic. The chief of the smugglers showed me a letter which he received from the office of prisoners of war in Vichy thanking him for having brought to the unoccupied zone several French prisoners who had escaped from German camps. That shows you how esteemed the smugglers were by the French people.

We soon worked out a plan how to bring Claudie over. The situation here was the same as in Mont-de-Marsan. Most of the inhabitants had permissions to go from one zone to the other, and a lot of young people from the villages around went every day to Chalons-sur-Saône to work in the factories. I understood that it was much easier to go over here than it was in Mont-de-Marsan. Chalons is a big city and the Germans could not know everybody. The river, too, gave a lot of possibilities to go over with a boat or swimming. Every night, a lot of people crossed it guided by the smugglers.

For Claudie, this was not necessary. Anyone could bring him over carrying him in his arms. For a baby, the Germans never asked for papers. Our plan was the following: a girl working in a factory in Chalons went over as usual and sent a telegram to Paris asking to bring Claudie to Chalons and to a certain address—relatives of my friends of the "I des Platanes." I made her send several telegrams to all friends in Paris, knowing that Madame L., who kept Claudie, could not come herself with her daughter sick of diphtheria. I hoped somebody else would do it. For two days I had no answer and I waited in a great anxiety. The third day, the girl came back in the evening announcing that Claudie would arrive the next day and that my neighbor, a French lady whose mother was English, would bring him. After lunch the next day, we went to the barrier. There was an inn so near that I could see everybody approaching the German barrier. And I saw that a lot of people were there speaking with friends on the other side. I was very astonished but I was told that for the last few weeks there had been a new German commandant at this place who was much nicer than his predecessors and who allowed it.

Me at the bridge at Chalons-sur-Sâone that I was smuggled across in May 1941 (the sign shows it to be the border between the occupied zone and Vichy France, at that time).

Soon, from my window in the inn, I saw a woman, the girl who had sent the telegram, carrying a baby with a well-known pink coat. I saw that the inspecting German soldier took Claudie for a moment in his arms to permit her to bring her papers from her handbag. And then the barrier rose and she went through. A few seconds later I held Claudie in my arms, crying and laughing.

The woman told me that my neighbor was waiting at the barrier and that I could speak to her. I went there and we could even shake hands, but she could not tell me very much. There were the German soldiers listening. It was hard for me to tell her goodbye—we had spent so many months together. Her apartment was just below mine in Paris and she was always nice to me and helped me a great deal in my troubles. I couldn't help crying in all my happiness. I liked her so much, and I knew it was goodbye forever. She told me how sick Claudie had been and that he still needed care.

I went back to Claudie, and a car took us to the "I des Platanes." He was a poor little baby, very pale and so weak that he could not even stay on his legs. It was only two weeks after his diphtheria. The next day, we went to Marseille where Walter saw for the first time his second son. Claudie was exactly sixteen months old. It was a Saturday, and the next Monday we got our visa for the United States. A few weeks later, we left France for our big trip, but this is another story.

THREE

COMING TO NEW YORK CITY

It was indeed another story. The exact sequence of events is not completely clear, but this much I know. In 1941, the American consulate in Marseille was besieged by people trying to obtain visas, and the situation seemed hopeless. The United States State Department was sharply restricting immigration in response to anti-immigrant—and specifically anti-Semitic—pressure in Congress. Suddenly, my father was notified to come to the consulate. When he arrived, he was surprised to be admitted ahead of the long lines waiting outside. He learned that the consulate had received a cable granting my father an emergency visa as an "endangered person."

A tall young man received me and confirmed what the letter had said. He specified that it was not an immigration visa with the right of residency but only for the emergency, and that it was for me alone. Would I take it? My answer was that I could not possibly leave my family behind. The man smiled. He was also empowered to change this into immigration visas for the whole family. Would I take that?

It took almost fifty years for us to find out what had led to that miraculous moment, a scene seemingly straight from *Casablanca*. The "tall young man" turned out to be Hiram "Harry" Bingham IV, son of Hiram Bingham III, the governor and then senator from Connecticut (and discoverer of

Machu Picchu). Young Harry Bingham, while serving as the American vice-consul in Marseille, was clandestinely working with Varian Fry, the American journalist who was managing the rescue of several thousand Jews from Europe during this time. An entry on *Geni.com* contains the following:

> Anxious to limit immigration to the United States and to maintain good relations with the Vichy government, the State Department actively discouraged diplomats from helping refugees. However, Bingham cooperated with Varian Fry in issuing visas and helping refugees escape France. Varian Fry had come to Marseille to give 200 grants to "some of the best scientists and European scholars" and help them settle in the U.S.
>
> Harry Bingham worked with him, and instead of 200, gave about 2,000 visas, most of them to well-known personalities, speaking English, not too left-wing and not looking too Jewish, among whom were Max Ernst, André Breton, Hannah Arendt, Marc Chagall, Lion Feuchtwanger and Nobel prize winner Otto Meyerhof. All the other anonymous hopefuls, waiting night and day in front of the American consulate, were not lucky enough. Varian Fry explains in his book *Surrender on Demand*: "we refuse to help anyone who is not recommended by a confident person."

Fortunately, we had a "confident person" in Paul Sachs, the husband of my father's Aunt Meta. It was Aunt Meta who, in 1938, had tried to convince my father to come to America. The cable from Washington to Harry Bingham was almost certainly the result of his influence. Paul Sachs was the son of Goldman Sachs Cofounder Samuel Sachs and his wife, Louisa Goldman, daughter of the other founder, Marcus Goldman. Paul Sachs was inclined more toward the arts than finance, becoming the associate director of the Fogg Museum and a professor of fine arts at Harvard. He became a relative when he married into my grandmother's family.

Despite the thinly veiled anti-Semitic policies of our government, Sachs was somehow able to maneuver the State Department into generating the visa that Bingham then used as a basis for his lifesaving administrative act. Many years later, during my first year at Harvard in 1957, I fulfilled a family obligation by having tea with Professor Sachs. Equipped with the arrogance of a Harvard freshman, I had little appreciation of who he was or of the role he had played in saving all of our lives.

When the State Department became aware of Bingham's collaboration with Fry, he was abruptly transferred to Argentina and resigned soon after. Bingham's courage was largely unknown, even to his own family. It was only after his death in 1988 that his family discovered documents and letters about what he had done and shared those papers with the United States Holocaust Memorial Museum and the State Department. In 2002, Secretary of State Colin Powell took up the cause to "rehabilitate" Bingham and honor him.

At that time, my brother was serving in the State Department as a career Foreign Service officer who had risen through the ranks to become consul general in both Hamburg and Frankfurt. When the word went out asking whether anyone in the State Department might have had a personal connection to Bingham, Pierre was intrigued. Fairly certain that it was Bingham who had rescued us, he described Bingham to my father, and the man he described matched exactly my father's recollection. It was deeply moving and satisfying for Pierre to bear witness and add our family's story to the file.

Back to 1941 and our pending visa. Some problems remained. In order to actually receive the visa, everyone had to be present for a final physical exam. I had not yet arrived, and in any case, I was too ill to pass such an exam. As my father's memoir then explains:

It was impossible to postpone that vital appointment and it might take months to secure another one. So, we borrowed a baby—or rather we rented it. Its mother was a refugee, too. The rental fee was Magda's treasure of knitting wool, one of the many things which had disappeared from the shelves and was worth its weight in gold. For the visa, we had to pass physicals given by an American physician. The man marveled at how well developed our son was. No wonder, given that the rental baby was three months older than the original.

When we appeared at the consulate to receive our visa, there was a last-moment glitch. Magda, because of her birthplace, fell under the Hungarian quota and the consulate had not counted on that. After a few anxious moments, a frantic scramble, and telephone calls, they then located one unused Hungarian quota spot and we walked out, visa in hand and ready to return the borrowed baby.

The next challenge was to actually find a way to get to the United States. No ships were leaving French ports and very few were departing from other European harbors. The only transatlantic commercial flights of the day, aboard Pan Am Clippers departing from Lisbon, were prohibitively expensive and booked far in advance. Then our family learned of a possibility from the American Jewish Joint Distribution Committee, an organization that had been rescuing Jews in various countries since World War I. The "Joint," as it was known, had arranged for a ship to leave for the United States from Cádiz, in Spain. The ship's name was the *Navemar*.

Tickets for the Navemar *were frightfully expensive, so somebody was making money out of our misery. I had no choice but to cable my brother for the money needed. He promptly sent it. I did not know that he had to borrow it ... It was a long, slow and hot trip to Cádiz across the whole breadth of Spain. Was it not appropriate that we should sail from the port where Columbus' first fateful crossing began?*

We arrived in Cádiz and there was no ship—even after many days. Every day there were different rumors: "The Navemar *would arrive tomorrow," "No, she would come next week," "She would not come at all." We had to stay at one of the luxury hotels, as there were no other accommodations. It was not very luxurious, except for the prices. Our money was melting away fast. Finally, a notice appeared on the hotel's bulletin board: we should all proceed to Seville and board the ship there. It did not make any sense to travel inland even if Seville was a river port. Nobody explained. We did travel to Seville—we had no choice—and there was a ship, the* Navemar.

She did not look bad—middle-sized in my landlubber's eyes, a freighter which had cabins for about twenty adjacent to the bridge. The cargo area in the hold had been converted into two dormitories of two-decker bunk beds—men on one side, women and children on the other. There were four lifeboats on board;

each could carry about a dozen people. When we had our full complement of passengers, we were about 1,200 aboard. The crew looked quite romantic, like out of a Hollywood type-B movie. They acted their roles, as well, climbing like squirrels up and down the masts and working the sails. They did not, however, have knives between their teeth like in the movies. Yes, the Navemar used its sails: was it to save fuel or increase speed? Maybe both.

Passengers on the deck of the Navemar, sleeping in lifeboats, 1941. One of the men could well be my father.
(Courtesy of the Cincinnati Judaica Fund.)

The ship carried a number of live cattle on the afterdeck, but not to provide children passengers with milk. They were part of our provisions. Every other day, one was slaughtered, for the Navemar had no refrigeration facilities. Several showers had been installed, but they provided only salt water, which did little to keep us clean. I tried the bunk bed in the hold, but could not stand the heat and stench, so I slept on the deck the full six weeks of our journey. Yes, it took a full six weeks. We were incredibly lucky, though, that these were six weeks of unchanging good weather.

After stops in Lisbon, Bermuda, and Havana, the *Navemar* finally steamed into New York Harbor—fortunately without having encountered any of the German U-boats that were wreaking havoc in the North Atlantic.

We had arrived, or almost. It was late fall of 1941. We were anchored in the Narrows, not far from the Statue of Liberty, and in front of us was the Manhattan skyline, an incredible view, exactly like the postcards all of us had seen. And an icy wind blew. Why was I always greeted by such discomfort coming from heaven when I reached a long-desired goal?

Official-looking people came on board. Some of them were from the harbor police and the health department. They shoved a thermometer into everybody's mouth, including mine. I had not known that I was running a temperature; I only knew that I had a constant toothache. They found out about my temperature and they knew about the cases of typhus, so we were not permitted to land but were sent to Ellis Island. No hardship for me, as I rather enjoyed my stay at the infirmary. I was in a clean bed and got plenty of somewhat strange-tasting food, real luxuries which I greatly enjoyed after the rigors aboard ship. I also had a neighbor with whom I played chess.

Life on Ellis Island, however, was less enjoyable for poor Magda. She had to spend her days in that large central hall with hundreds of people with nothing to do but wait and suffer the hopeless task of keeping two lively youngsters (with nothing to do and without toys) from running wild. After four or five days and a thorough examination, the authorities decided that I did not seem a threat to the health of the country and we were permitted to go on land ... At our arrival, we had but $10 and a debt of $1,600 [almost $30,000 in today's dollars!], *the money Robert had borrowed to pay for the ship tickets.*

The unsanitary conditions aboard the *Navemar* were serious enough that it made the local newspapers. Lawyers arrived to sign up passengers for a class action lawsuit. Two years later, my parents received a settlement of almost exactly the amount that my father owed his brother, and they were able to settle that debt. The *Navemar* did not fare as well. Despite flying the neutral flag of Spain, a few months after delivering us safely to America she was torpedoed and sunk off Gibraltar by an Italian submarine.

Many decades later, I was able to confirm this story, which I had long suspected might be too dramatic to be entirely true. At the time, I was the director of the New York State Maritime Museum project at Schermerhorn

Row in Lower Manhattan. One day, I found myself in the offices of an organization that had a card file of every ship that had entered New York Harbor for most of the port's history. And there indeed was a record of our voyage and the *Navemar's* grim fate. Since then I have discovered contemporaneous news coverage of our ship's arrival in America. One September 13, 1941 headline blared: "1,120 Refugees Reach New York in Horror Ship." The article went dramatically on to report:

> For the rusty old Spanish freighter *Navemar*, 52 days en route, it was the end of one of the most horror-stricken voyages since the days when slaves were shipped below-decks from Africa.[*]

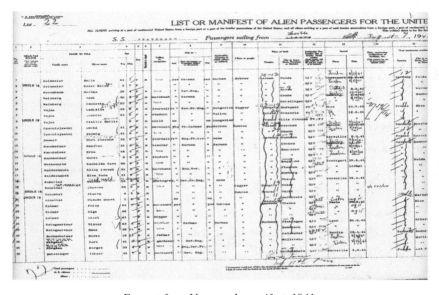

Excerpt from Navemar's manifest, 1941.

Recently, my wife, Amy, and I made a pilgrimage to Ellis Island, where I had not set foot since those days in 1941. On a beautiful fall day in 2019, we took the ferry out to the island. Chills crept up my neck as we entered the hall. I inquired at the information desk about old records. The person

---

[*] Clipping supplied by the Cincinnati Judaica Fund.

staffing the desk seemed delighted to tell me that they had recently digitized their records for that period and directed me to a nearby computer room. As Amy checked on her relatives from longer ago, I nervously entered my data. There it was: a page from the ship's manifest for the *Navemar*. Our four names were halfway down the page (see page 51).

Handwritten entries confirmed some of the details in my father's narrative. The *Navemar* had in fact sailed from Seville. "Med Hold" was penned next to my father's name, testifying to his illness and trip to the infirmary. It was duly noted that I could neither read nor write. Perhaps most remarkably to me, under "Nationality" was one ominous word: "None." We had indeed been stateless. And under the column "Race or people," was the entry "Magyar" for my mother and "Hebrew" for the rest of us. I am certain my father did not volunteer that answer.

As we wandered around the cavernous facility, I informed one of the National Park Service rangers of my history. She excitedly led us to a staircase, explaining that my mother would have carried me on it going to and from the cafeteria. She pointed up to the dormitory-style rooms facing the mezzanine balcony above the great hall. "You would have occupied one of those rooms!" she exclaimed. I was touched by her enthusiasm and moved by the immediacy of the connection.

When we were finally discharged from Ellis Island in September 1941, we moved into the Congress House on the Upper West Side of Manhattan. Operated by the American Jewish Congress, it provided temporary shelter for Jewish refugees. My father then found a job paying fifteen dollars a week at a gas station in Queens—a job for which he was totally unsuited, never having owned a car and having barely ever ridden in one. That job did not last long.

We then moved into a one-room apartment in a nearby brownstone where my father became the "super." He was laughably ill-matched for this job as well. His main responsibility was to shovel coal into the building's boiler to provide heat and hot water, a task he found challenging. My mother swept the halls and, to provide some additional income, cleaned the apartment of an aspiring opera singer for whom she also translated the German words that the singer did not understand.

My father also worked at the time as a messenger for Keystone, the European-based photo agency. This was most likely arranged by his brother, Robert, who had started the family stock photo business in New York and was struggling to get it off the ground. Here is my father's summary of our state at the time, and what came next:

We were in America. We were safe. We were not hungry. We did not suffer from cold, provided I stoked that recalcitrant boiler the right way. But I can't say we were happy. That life in our single room was far from comfortable. Mostly, there were only three of us. My mother, who, with Robert, lived only a few blocks away, mostly kept Claude with her. The two kids did not get on well together. They never played together, but when brought together were constantly rolling on the floor. Whether it was sibling jealousy or brotherly love, it contributed to making life difficult. And foremost, there was the financial squeeze. We only could afford the barest essentials. An additional subway ride was a problem, a five-cent cup of coffee a rare luxury. And there was no prospect of improvement, of a way out of it. Suddenly, out of the blue there appeared one. We received an invitation to go for a time to a strange place called Scattergood Hostel in West Branch, in the state of Iowa.

This time, my father was able to accept the lifeline held out by the Quakers. It was July 1942 when we arrived at Scattergood. We spent about six months there, allowing my parents to catch their breath and recover somewhat from the ordeal of our escape. The hostel was run on a cooperative basis, with the staff and the fifteen to twenty guests sharing in the chores. Although language instruction was held every day, my father was never able to completely lose his Germanic accent.

We were content at Scattergood. We enjoyed the peaceful surroundings, the friendly people, the relaxed mood. We were, however, also worried and tense about our future. Where would we go from here, and when would we leave? It was a strange situation; the future would not be discussed. It was kept veiled. The hostel had been operating for a few years; "guests" had arrived and left. What had become of them? They had been settled somewhere and had been placed in jobs. What kind of jobs? It was not discussed. It seemed taboo, a little like sex in our post-Victorian morality. It was not to be discussed. It was the same with our length of stay; there was a mystery about it.

The staff's attempts to place my father in a job proved fruitless. They seemed oriented to the barely schooled immigrants of a previous age, not to the well-educated refugees of World War II. My father was brought to interviews for menial jobs in Chicago and Duluth that led nowhere. He finally landed an assembly-line job in Davenport, fifty miles away, where he rented a dingy room and returned to Scattergood for weekends. Not only did he hate the work, but he was not even good enough at it to get a year-end raise. This clearly was not a permanent solution.

My mother reading to Pierre and me at Scattergood, Iowa, 1943.

From family photos, I know that we spent my third birthday at Scattergood. Shortly after that, my parents decided to return to New York. Despite the uncertainties and the lack of traction on our initial foray, we had family there and a network of refugee friends. It seemed like the best path forward. We moved back to the city at some point in the late winter of 1943.

Through a fellow refugee, my father got a job as a sales rep for a button factory. While this did not present a satisfying career path, it did provide work with a minimal basic income. And it allowed us to move into our first real home in this country: a tiny two-room ground-floor apartment with an eat-in kitchen in Kew Gardens, Queens. My brother and I shared the small bedroom with two small iron cots, while my parents slept on a pullout couch in the living room.

My father's memoir describes the next transition:

Slowly, very slowly, Robert's business prospects improved and we could envision the possibility that the agency might support two families in a modest lifestyle. In a way, Robert and I made a good team. He supplied the creative instinct, the feeling for commercial possibilities, and I contributed the steady effort and clearer vision to reach those goals.

Since we could not take great risks, our financial resources being so minimal, we had to move slowly, but my bosses at the button place were cooperative. I split my working day; in the morning I worked for them, in the afternoon I moved to my brother's office. We saw slow but encouraging improvement due to my efforts. Finally, I made the break and bid farewell to those buttons.

Our very modest life while I was growing up in Queens holds few vivid memories. One was the blizzard of 1947. More than two feet of snow fell in twenty-four hours. Pierre and I (mostly Pierre, I am sure) earned a few quarters shoveling out cars. Probably because of his exertions, Pierre came down with strep throat which led to nephritis. At the time, it was a dangerously contagious condition, so I was sent to live with my grandmother in Manhattan for several weeks. She was a rather sour person, and I hated spending time there. My bed was a sofa in an alcove. I slept under a quilt. Every night I stayed awake as long as I could by snapping and unsnapping the small metal fasteners of the quilt. The longer I could defer falling asleep, the later I would wake up and the shorter the day would be.

Back in Queens, I walked each day the five minutes to school at PS 99, just a few blocks away. I asked my friends to call me by my regularly used name, Claude, until we crossed Lefferts Boulevard. On the other side of that street, as we approached the school building, I had to be Henri, since the school insisted on using my first name. (That problem has plagued me to this day, since governments cannot seem to handle middle-name users.) One day, I casually suggested to my classmates that it would be okay if they just called me Hank. My friends just laughed. Apparently, I am just not a Hank.

One day, I came home and proudly showed my parents a jar full of valve caps which I had unscrewed from parked cars in an effort to curry favor with Kenny, the local bully. My incensed parents made me go back out and put them all back. Kenny concluded that I was a wimp. He made me hand over my precious teddy bear, and he threw it into a nearby barrel fire. I ran home crying but could not tell my parents why.

We had very limited means, but I do not remember feeling any sense of deprivation. We always had enough to eat, and my mother cooked healthy, European-style dinners for us. We rarely went on vacation, but I do recall some incidents from those few summer trips. We went to a place called The Forest House in Maine when I was five or six. Here I had my classic first encounter with the opposite sex. A little girl, who was approximately my age, announced that she wanted to watch me pee, which I excitedly allowed her to do. But then I demanded to see her "thing." She said that there was really nothing to see, but I insisted. When she bared herself, she seemed to have been right, and I was severely disappointed.

Obviously, it was an ordinary and largely uneventful growing up. During all this time, my parents tried hard to create a completely American environment at home. In addition to taking us to Sunday school, they enrolled Pierre in the Cub Scouts. They never spoke German at home except at Christmas to keep secrets or when they yelled at my brother and me for our many transgressions. By 1947, they had become naturalized citizens and my father had legally changed the spelling of our family name, dropping the "c," I suppose because he thought Shostal looked less German (and Jewish).

I became a rabid Yankees fan, and it was a great time for that. My mother even came to like Yogi Berra, but my father preferred Phil Rizzuto, perhaps because he was about the same size and even bore a slight resemblance to "The Scooter." I can clearly recall the radio announcer yelling, "Here comes the tying run—and here comes the *winning* run!" as Cookie Lavagetto's double caromed off the right field wall of Ebbets Field, spoiling Floyd "Bill" Bevens's no-hitter in the ninth inning of the fourth game of the 1947 World Series (which the Yankees went on to win, beginning their historic run of pennants and championships).

By 1949, the family business had become more stable. The Shostal Agency was one of several stock photo houses in New York that catered to the textbook, calendar, and advertising industries. Oddly, almost all were run by Eastern European Jews. The stock photo business required a reasonable knowledge of world geography and history, some imagination to figure out what the clients really wanted, and enough intelligence to make judicious submissions in response to often unfocused requests. It also required endless patience and a sharp memory to sort through files of thousands of pictures and find the right ones. My father and uncle had those traits.

To try to get an edge on their competitors, they made the strategic decision to specialize in color photography. Kodachrome had only become available in 1935, and four-color printing was on the rise in the affluent postwar years. The decision paid off, and Shostal slowly became established as one of the major suppliers of color photographs, eventually amassing a file of over 100,000 transparencies. A major boost came early on when my father and uncle secured a large file from the photographer László Willinger. They had known Willinger (whom they called Lozzi) from Paris, where he had a studio in the 1930s and was a pioneer of color portrait photography. Willinger was famous for his work with many of Hollywood's most glamorous stars, and Shostal's files included many images of Marilyn Monroe while she was still Norma Jean Baker.

Modest financial success allowed my parents to consider another step in the American Dream: a move to the suburbs. Although they had always lived in cities, they both longed for a place where they could see trees and sky, and where my brother and I could experience nature and have a more active outdoor childhood. The quandary was that my father's business was inextricably tied to Manhattan, the center of the advertising and publishing industries. Real estate in the nearby suburbs was, even then, way beyond our reach. My parents had to look farther out. After much searching, they found a small house outside of Peekskill, at the far northern edge of Westchester County. The price tag was $12,000.

The house sat on a corner lot on one-third of an acre, dominated by two huge elm trees and separated by a classic stone wall from a large lot next door where a cow munched on the grass. Across the road was a small lake (a pond, really), where we could swim in the summers and ice-skate during the winters. It had a community beach where Pierre and I would become lifeguards. Beyond the lake were woods and marshes that were destined to be developed as part of the suburban boom of the postwar years. The house came with a low-interest-rate GI mortgage that my father was able to assume. Settling us there would mean facing a commute to Manhattan of at least ninety minutes each way—but now he could afford it!

FOUR

GROWING UP IN PEEKSKILL

It was April 1949; I was nine years old. On my first night in our new house, I lay in bed looking out of the window of my partially finished but spacious (by our standards) attic room of my own, with its Mickey Mouse wallpaper. A full moon flooded the room with a light that I had never experienced. I wondered what my new life would be like in this strange environment.

I attended the Toddville School, a K-8 public school about a mile away. For the first time, I joined in the Norman-Rockwellian ritual of riding a yellow school bus. Toddville was a small school with fewer than one hundred and fifty students, and about twenty in my grade. Except for classes like gym or music, each grade was together in the same room with the same teacher for the whole day. It was a good school, presided over by Mr. Titus, a stern but effective principal. We lived in fear and awe of him. He must have worn orthotics, which made his shoes squeak rather loudly. Hearing him coming, we usually had time to correct whatever mischief we were up to.

Toddville was too small to support much of an athletics program. The field behind the school was uneven and strewn with pebbles, making the few baseball games played there into dicey propositions. Toddville also fielded a soccer team whose most singular aspect was to feature a girl at the fullback position. Gerry Brown was no Megan Rapinoe, but she could kick the ball farther than any of us boys.

Two years after moving to Peekskill, we finally got a television set of our own. Soon after, on October 3, 1951, I raced home from school to turn on the set. As the picture came crackling to life, I saw Bobby Thomson rounding third base and heading home with the winning run after hitting "the shot heard 'round the world." On the radio, Russ Hodges was yelling, "And the Giants win the pennant, the Giants win the pennant, the Giants win the pennant, the Giants win the pennant . . ." Yes, four times. It was, as has often been said, unforgettable.

My memories of my time at Toddville are generally positive, but I fell into a pattern there that was to repeat itself. My report cards consistently noted that I was underperforming but showed promise. A classic example dated from the seventh grade and read, "Claude maintains the attitude of doing as little work as possible. If he could apply himself more readily, he would show superior work. This was his attitude in the beginning of the second period, but he is improving. Claude cooperates in class very well and tries to live up to the rules which are set for the students in the classrooms. He never shirks his duties when it comes to class and school functions. He does have admirable qualities." I was apparently determined to carve a separate identity from my older brother by the shrewd strategy of being less conscientious about schoolwork.

Pierre was far more like our mother, serious and intense. He studied hard. After finishing eighth grade at Toddville in 1949, he attended the local intermediate school, Drum Hill, for ninth grade and then Peekskill High School for tenth grade. Peekskill was an economically depressed Hudson River town in those days, and its public secondary schools were woeful. My parents, passionate about education, were extremely concerned that Pierre would not get the kind of schooling that he needed and could handle.

Then a unique opportunity presented itself. The Ford Foundation had launched a pilot program to give exceptionally bright young high school students the opportunity to attend and finish college before they became vulnerable to the draft and military service. With the Korean War underway, the draft loomed over my brother's cohort. Full college scholarships were offered to those who finished with the highest scores on a competitive exam.

This was an irresistibly attractive prospect for my parents, who could not yet have managed the tuition and living costs of a prestigious university education. Pierre took the test and, of course, did very well. After a brief and agonizing stint on the waiting list, he was accepted into the Ford program and was offered a spot in the freshman class at Yale. My parents struggled briefly over the wisdom of sending a fifteen-year-old off to college, but in the end the opportunity was too compelling to pass up. Later, Pierre and my parents would regret that decision to some extent because Pierre suffered socially in his early years at Yale, and he missed out on a key part of growing up. But they also recognized that it would have been extremely difficult to have made any other decision at the time.

I felt that I simply could not compete with that level of sibling accomplishment. So I would choose a different path: indifferent student, sports nut, consumer of pop culture—all things that my parents found baffling and commonplace. As would happen again in college, I underperformed—never to the degree of courting outright failure, but enough to squander precious opportunities. I did my homework, but half-heartedly. For endless hours, I hit rocks into the lake, caught cascading elm leaves in the fall like fly balls, and fielded grounders off the stoop of the house as I pretended to be Mickey Mantle, Hank Bauer, and Bobby Brown. I played "Earth Angel" and "The Bandit of Brazil" on the record player at a volume guaranteed to annoy my parents. I would show them what I was made of!

I was building off of a previously successful strategy of distinguishing myself from my brother. When we were younger, we had fought frequently and could not be left alone together. Usually, I was the instigator. I would needle Pierre until he grew angry, which was not hard to do as he had a fairly volatile temper—his Magyar heritage. I would goad him into hitting me, and I had a precious asset: a nose that would bleed at the slightest assault. If he failed to make contact with my nose, I would give it a modest whack myself and the crimson would flow. I would wail in alarm and my parents would become furious with Pierre for causing such damage to his fragile little brother. This charade gave me inordinate pleasure. After we grew up, Pierre—to his credit—never held my old ruse against me. Throughout my life, he has always been supportive and helpful as he has cheered on my accomplishments, some of which he was cheated out of by missing those precious high school years.

The most indelible moment of this period happened when my class was practicing for our eighth grade graduation and a former teacher dropped by. Mr. Corbin had been our sixth grade teacher, so it had been quite some time since we had seen him. He was a nice and well-intentioned teacher, but he was one of those who just could not command the room. It is no secret how cruel children of that age can be, and of course, we sensed how vulnerable he was. Sadly, I was one of those who had

My eighth grade graduation picture, 1953.

helped to undermine his authority and would turn the classroom into daily chaos. He did not return after that year, but there he was at the graduation practice for what had been his class, wishing us well. He watched as they called us up on the stage, led by the valedictorian and salutatorian of the class, neither of which was I. After the practice session, he came up to me and asked incredulously, "What happened to you? How come you weren't one of the top two?"

His words came crashing down on me. He had expected me to lead the class because I clearly had the ability to do so. Here was an adult who seemed to care about me and was disappointed for me—even though I had treated him callously. I knew immediately how right he was and how easy it would have been for me to have excelled. All my shallow pretenses evaporated, and I dissolved into tears as I had never done before. I ran home and cried for hours. But something inside of me had changed just a little.

Summers in my early teen years were all about Boy Scout Camp. I had heard about Camp Read in the Adirondacks at my troop meetings, and I pleaded with my parents to let me go. I am sure this was a financial stretch for them, but they gave in. The first two summers, I went for two weeks and during the third summer I stayed for four weeks. Those were the happiest times of my childhood. The camp sprawled through a serene, forested landscape and was divided into separate troops of about thirty-five boys (each troop, of course, had a Native American name, like Pawnee). The troops were collections of large tents, each situated on a wooden platform with five or six cots, nestled into an idyllic setting. In the mornings we would sign up for an activity that would lead to a merit badge, like canoeing or orienteering. The afternoons were spent swimming, hiking, or going on nature walks. Immersion in nature, physical exercise, learning new skills, and gaining competence in hitherto unknown subjects all combined to instill a sense of wonder and accomplishment.

During the third summer, I was happy that my close friend, Frank Felleman, could join me for two weeks. Frank was overweight, Catholic, and poor, having grown up with two brothers and a single mother. He was quiet and an outsider, but he was very smart, and we spent a lot of time together. Frank lived near the Toddville School. At night, we would sneak out and meet halfway between our houses on the raised grassy berm that was the New York City water supply aqueduct. With an unobstructed view of the sky, we would lie on our backs and identify all of the summer constellations while making up some of our own. At Camp Read, we signed up for the astronomy merit badge. Frank and I completed all the requirements easily since we already knew most of what was required. The final test was to draw the Big Dipper as it pinwheeled around the North Star over the course of the night. For three nights in a row, we got up at 3 a.m. to draw the Dipper's position in the sky, but the sky was always clouded over or fogged in. The scoutmaster in charge became as fed up as we were, and he told us to just draw it as we knew it should be. We did, and we got our badges. Frank later went to Princeton, which was probably not the best place for him as he struggled to penetrate the rigid social structure of Old Nassau at the time. Later, he became a lawyer, but to my regret we lost touch and never saw each other again.

Each afternoon, as I headed up the hill to my campsite, I would perch for a few minutes on the window of the staff room, watching the counselors socialize and play ping-pong. I longed to be part of that grown-up world. By the fourth summer, I got my chance. I was accepted to be a junior assistant scoutmaster and I spent the entire eight-week summer at Camp Read. My duties were minimal, so I focused on trying to learn from what was going on around me. I sensed that the new camp director quickly alienated the senior scoutmasters. His leadership seemed erratic and inconsistent. One afternoon, I found the troop master, whom I reported to and admired, sprawled on his cot in midafternoon. Not only was this against the rules, but it was totally out of character for this mature and dedicated leader. I must have looked at him with surprise and alarm. "If our director is going to accuse me of sleeping all afternoon," he said sharply, "I guess I'd better do it." I filed that away in my mental leadership manual.

After my eighth-grade graduation, my parents were again faced with the dilemma of determining the next step in a son's education. Pierre had entered Yale in the fall of 1952, but Drum Hill and Peekskill High now awaited me, prospects that deeply concerned my parents. At Toddville, Pierre had befriended a classmate, David Leeming, whose father was the Rev. Frank C. Leeming. He was the founder and headmaster of a small Episcopal prep school nearby. He was eager to attract talented students and faculty. My parents were desperate for an alternative to public school but could not afford the tuition. This had the makings of an arrangement.

"What could you teach in exchange for Claude's tuition?" Father Leeming asked my mother.

"What do you need?" she answered.

Well, it seemed that they really could use someone to take over the remedial reading program, which had been started several years earlier and needed a new teacher. Even then, many of the school's bright young students had reading problems. That summer, my mother commuted to classes in New York City and became certified as a remedial reading teacher. She would go on to teach Latin and French as well, and even Spanish, which she did not know but managed by staying a few lessons ahead of the class.

In the fall of 1953, I entered the ninth grade—known as the first form—at St. Peter's School. Father Leeming had been born in England and brought the very High Church—very British—school model with him. Since we lived only a five-minute drive from the school and my mother was on the faculty, I was a "day boy." About a half-dozen of us commuted while the other students—roughly one hundred—lived on St. Peter's beautiful campus-like setting on both sides of Route 6 just west of Peekskill.

My time there coincided with a period of expansion and growth for the school. The property on one side of Route 6 was sold, with the proceeds used to restore buildings and construct new ones on new acreage on the upland side. During my early years, the baseball team had to share a narrow strip of land that barely accommodated a football field. A steep embankment rose along one side. When the field was used for baseball, the right fielder had to play halfway up the embankment. He was called the "mountain goat." By the time I graduated, baseball had moved to a large level area above a new gymnasium building.

Unfortunately, the school no longer exits. It was Father Leeming's creation, sustained by his passionate commitment and dogged energy. It simply could not survive without his unique vision and dedication. After Father Leeming died, the school closed in 1977. Sadly, it is now the Beach Shopping Center and a townhouse development.

I thrived at St. Peter's. Whether it was my mother's presence or the wake-up call I had been given at my eighth-grade graduation, I worked hard and committed myself to the school life. I graduated as valedictorian.

I took four years of Latin and French, and I even won the chemistry prize. I was editor of the newspaper and yearbook. I lettered in football, basketball, and baseball and was quarterback and co-captain of our undefeated football team (only 5-0). We won our last game against St. Luke's in Connecticut, 46-25, the only competitive game we had all year. Tears welled up in the locker room after the game as we sang "When the Saints Go Marching In"—our "fight song." I knew I had a precious memory.

But there was a flaw in this story, which I only discovered years later at a school reunion. Our offense was almost exclusively based on a solid running game. I would throw two—or at most, three—passes per game, just to keep things honest. My hands weren't big enough to be able to throw much of a spiral, so I would just jump up from center and fling the ball at an end, cutting across a few yards downfield. My roommate, Jack Butler, played left end, and I felt comfortable finding and leading him over the middle. Bill Murr, who played the other end, came up to me at our reunion and said, "Do you know that during the entire year you never threw the ball to me? Not once."

I was stunned and ashamed. He was obviously still hurt. He had worked hard all year, blocking and running his routes. Yet I never threw him the ball! It would have been so easy—just a couple of times, at least. But this was something I could never fix. Why had I not even been aware of it? I'm really sorry, Billy.

Our basketball team also had an outstanding season. Father Leeming had hired a real basketball coach instead of relying on one of the regular faculty. That decision paid off and we went 16-1, losing only to our rival, St. Luke's, who that year had a seven-foot-tall center. I was a playmaking guard and was not looked to for much scoring. But in a game against Peekskill Military Academy, their defense consistently opened lanes for me and I scored twenty-six points, a career high.

At the end of the season, we were invited to play in a tournament of northern Westchester private and parochial schools in White Plains. The County Center was overwhelming; it had glass backboards and stands that could seat several thousand fans. We played the New York School for the Deaf in the first round. We had a small crowd of friends and family members, but they stopped cheering when they realized that our opponents could not hear. Even the referees blew their whistles softly. The dominant sound was our sneakers squeaking against the polished wood floor and echoing through the nearly empty arena. It was an eerie experience that made us acutely aware of every movement and moment. The School for the Deaf had Westchester County's leading scorer, a young Black guy who could sink jump shots (which were just coming into vogue) from anywhere on the floor. We, on the other hand, were still throwing up one- and two-handers, and I was shooting foul shots underhand. They beat us handily, but the intensity of the competition left us more enriched than disappointed.

I was fortunate to be a fairly good natural athlete. I had excellent reflexes and was well coordinated. I was small, perhaps five foot seven inches tall and one hundred and forty-five pounds, but I would grow to almost six feet tall. I sometimes wonder whether, with sophisticated coaching and training at this time, I might have been able to compete at a more elite level, particularly in my beloved sport of baseball. I saw the result of one year of decent coaching in basketball. Nevertheless, my modest accomplishments on high school athletic fields coupled with my academic success contributed significantly to my emerging self-esteem. I could compete with the big kids and do well!

I was growing up in other ways as well. In September 1949, a few months after our arrival in Peekskill, Paul Robeson, the great Black singer-actor and one of the era's most outspoken critics of racial injustice, scheduled a concert a few miles away from our house, at the Hollowbrook Drive-In. It was very much the time of Jim Crow and emerging McCarthyism. Robeson stirred deep hatred among reactionary groups and those who continued to harbor racist sentiments. In some ways foreshadowing the Trump era and the mob attack on the Capitol in 2021, the United States in 1949 was increasingly split between Americans who were open to social change and those who were fearful of it. A racist mob attacked the audience, lynched

Robeson in effigy, and burned a cross while police stood by, forcing the cancellation of the event.

When it was reconvened a week later, the concert became a rallying point for liberal activists like Howard Fast, Pete Seeger, and others who organized a phalanx of sympathizers to protect Robeson. When the concert ended and people were starting to drive home, they were set upon. The mob had returned, shouting racist and anti-Semitic epithets, hurling rocks, overturning cars, and bloodying more than 150 concertgoers while the police again stood by. Seeger's well-known protest song, "Hold the Line," celebrated the moment. No one was killed, but neighbors who lived close to the event took in some of the injured. It became known as the Robeson Riots, and Peekskill secured its infamous place in civil rights history. Later, white-supremacist demonstrators would march behind banners proclaiming "Wake Up, America! Peekskill Did!"—a slogan seen on many local cars for years to come. Some of our neighbors responded with bumper stickers reading "Wake Up, Peekskill! America Did Long Ago!" (In 1999, on the fiftieth anniversary of the riots, Westchester County held a "Remembrance and Reconciliation Ceremony" to formally apologize to the victims of the attacks.)

My parents' experience and education made them acutely sympathetic to victims of intolerance and discrimination. Their politics ranged from liberal (my father) to sympathetic toward socialism (more my mother). My father even voted for Henry Wallace in the 1948 presidential election. In 1956, during my senior year, I led the school student debate on behalf of Adlai Stevenson against President Eisenhower's partisans. The faculty voted that we won the debate, but we lost the straw poll by the devastating margin of 101-5. It was a sign of the times and an accurate preview of the 1956 election. My political and social education was underway.

The previous winter, my family took a rare vacation to Florida. We drove the entire way in our fairly new Ford Fairlane. It was a long trip; I-95, along with the rest of Eisenhower's Interstate Highway System, was still largely in the planning stages. We offered a ride home to one of my classmates,

Johnny Settle, a tall Black student from Virginia, who played center on our basketball team. Johnny's father was on the faculty of Virginia State University. After an early start, we were passing through Delaware and stopped at a roadside diner. Although there were a few cars parked outside, my father said he would go in to see if they were open. He returned a few minutes later and reported that they were not open but that he was able to get a few rolls and donuts to go. It was a long time before I figured out that my father had actually gone in to find out if they would serve us with Johnny as part of our group—and he was turned away. And this was in Delaware, not Mississippi! I had a lot to learn about the blurring of the Mason-Dixon Line.

My best friend at St. Peter's was Norman Pritchard. "Pritch," as he was known, was one of the four or five Black students, and the son of a Brooklyn physician. He went out of his way to make clear that he was not African American but Caribbean, which he clearly felt was a significant difference. He was also our best athlete, captain and top scorer of the basketball team, shortstop on the baseball team, and an almost unstoppable halfback on the football team. In one of our football games against a fairly weak opponent, Pritch had already scored two touchdowns on long runs. I then called one of our favorite plays, the halfback option. I pitched the ball to him as he sprinted toward the sideline. He pulled up and threw a perfect spiral to my roommate, Jack Butler, our left end. Jack was cutting across the field all alone downfield and gathered in Pritch's pass for another easy touchdown. As Pritch let the ball go, I heard the opposing coach exclaim, "Oh no, the n*****can pass too!" I was stunned by the words—and thrilled to see Jack cruising across the goal line.

Since he lived at school, I would invite Pritch to our home occasionally for Sunday dinner. We would toss a football around on the back lawn, oblivious to the potential of that innocuous scene for stirring up racial antagonism. It was only years later that my father told me of the threatening phone calls he had received about it. Pritch seemed headed for a middle-class, sports-oriented future, but he instead settled into Greenwich

Village, dropped out of NYU, and adopted the lifestyle of a beat Village poet, gaining some minor notoriety. I crossed paths with him briefly many years later when I was putting together peer group arts panels for New York City, but otherwise we lost touch.

Other interests and new horizons were emerging as well. When I was eight and nine years old, I read only children's sports novels: *Backboard Magic*, *Shortstop for Sale*, and others. The summer before entering St. Peter's, Father Leeming gave me a real book to read: John Galsworthy's classic, *The Forsyte Saga*. At first, I was daunted by this forbiddingly large tome. I had never read any "serious" literature. But then, to my surprise, I got completely caught up in Galsworthy's sweeping narrative, and I was delighted to read the book again when it was assigned for our senior English class.

I was also intrigued by Richard Halliburton's *Book of Marvels*, a coffee-table book we had at home. It was full of dramatic illustrations of exotic faraway places: The Highest Waterfall, The Deepest Canyon, The Greatest Dam, Gibraltar, Carcassonne, and St. Peter's Basilica. In the introduction, Halliburton muses about his childhood, when he told himself, "I wish my father, or somebody, would take me to all these wonderful places. What good are they if you can't *see* them? . . . Well, I'm grown up now. But as yet I haven't any son or any daughter to go traveling with me. And so, in their places, may I take you?" He could, yes.

His invitation stirred in me a new craving for distant adventures that would eventually grow with time. First, it was Richard Henry Dana's *Two Years Before the Mast*. In 1950, Thor Heyerdahl's epic, *Kon-Tiki*, became a best seller and I was riveted. Then, even more significantly for me, *Annapurna* came out in 1952, telling the story of the first ascent two years earlier of an 8,000-meter (26,000-plus feet) peak in the Himalayas. As would be true for an entire generation of serious mountaineers, I was captivated by this adventure. I began to follow every expedition that set out for those distant daunting mountains. Then, of course, on May 29, 1953, a British expedition conquered Everest (albeit by New Zealander Edmund Hillary and Sherpa Tenzing Norgay), with the news reaching London on

June 1—Queen Elizabeth II's Coronation Day. How spectacularly romantic! I was totally hooked.

I do not recall when or where I first saw the movie about the 1953 expedition. I do know that, sometime later, it was shown on television on *The Million Dollar Movie*, which aired the same film twice a day for a week. I managed to watch it a dozen times. From then on, I read every account of Himalayan climbs I could find. I was an armchair mountaineer—but a seed had been sown.

For my senior year at St. Peter's, I decided to live at the school. I had felt a bit removed and insulated from the close camaraderie of campus life. The new dorm in the converted barn where I was scheduled to be housed was not quite ready when the fall term began, so for the first few months my roommate, Jack Butler, and I shared a room in the garret of the headmaster's grand house. On October 8, 1956, Jack and I, with a couple of other boys, were huddled around the radio listening to the fifth game of the World Series. Don Larsen, pitching for the Yankees against the Brooklyn Dodgers, had carried his perfect game into the ninth inning, and we were jumping up and down and howling with excitement. Hearing the ruckus, Father Leeming dashed upstairs. He was furious. "Don't you know that the bishop is downstairs for a very important meeting!" he exclaimed. We told him what was happening and he sat down with us to listen to the final two outs. Even the bishop could not compete with the drama of a perfect game.

Living at school meant that I had to attend vespers every evening and house mass once a week in the morning. It also meant that I served as an acolyte once a month at the very High Church house mass that included incense, the "*Nunc Dimittis*," and the "*Kyrie Eleison*." I was more or less immersed in the religious life of the school, but it never truly spoke to me. Father Leeming insisted that we all sing loudly and fervently, but I had a terrible voice and could not carry a tune. After vespers one evening, he pulled me aside and said, "I know I told you to sing loudly, but you're throwing everyone else off key. Please, just open your mouth and pretend to sing." I happily complied.

Music was very important to Father Leeming and he took great pride in the glee club he led. Every year, it toured the area to raise money. To my surprise, he came to me one day and said that they were doing a French song and he wanted me to try to sing a brief solo. Having heard foreign languages at home and having taken four years of French, at least my accent was pretty good. "I know you don't have a good voice," he said, "but it's a short section and I'm sure I can work with you to carry it off." I went to the rehearsal that afternoon after classes. I attempted the simple phrases two or three times while watching Father Leeming wince repeatedly. "Okay, I give up," he cried in exasperation. "You are excused."

As graduation neared, our thoughts turned to what lay ahead. I had applied to four colleges: Amherst, Swarthmore, Yale, and Harvard. While my grades and extracurricular record were admirable, my College Board scores were not—somewhere in the high 600s. Amherst rejected me, but—probably because I took the English, Latin, and French exams—I was accepted at the other three.

Swarthmore scared me as a place of Quaker austerity and unrelenting hard work. I was naturally drawn to Yale because of my brother, but New Haven was a dreary place at that time. I was standing in Harvard Yard during my exploratory visit when classes let out. I saw *girls* spilling out of the buildings! I had not known about Radcliffe. After years of all-male segregation, I was desperate to experience a life that included women, even though they were a total mystery to me. Their presence (and the attractions of the city of Boston) made me determined to go to Harvard.

One adult whom I consulted about the decision asked if I thought I was ready for Harvard. Ready? I asked what he meant. He said that Harvard did not provide a structure of fixed social expectations but allowed everyone to be and do whatever they wanted. He suggested that it took extra maturity to prosper in, and get the most out of, such an environment. He was not sure I was there yet. It was a prophetic warning.

FIVE

HARVARD AND BOSTON

I arrived at Harvard in the fall of 1957. It was the heart of the Eisenhower years—quiet, comfortable, prosperous, and reasonably optimistic. Although I gave it little thought at the time, my parents were now barely able to afford the tuition of $2,500 per year. I received a $250 scholarship from the Westchester County Harvard Club for my first year, which I promptly forfeited because of poor grades. To help financially, I took out student loans each year, contributed my savings from summer jobs as a lifeguard and waiting on tables, and I worked each semester. The minimum wage then was $1 per hour, which is what I was paid to clean students' rooms and wash dishes in the student dining hall. I would take home about $15 a week, a little less than $135 in today's dollars. That allowed me a spartan amount of spending money, some of which I saved each week by packing my dirty laundry in an aluminum case with cloth straps and mailing it home, to be returned by my mother with my clothes washed and folded.

In my freshman year I took the normal core curriculum courses. My favorite class was on the history of science from a chemistry perspective (Nat Sci IV), taught by the charismatic Leonard Nash. He was so effective at presenting the old theories and how hard it was to overcome them (what Nash called "the threshold of impressionability") that he would get complaints from parents that their sons came home describing the beauties of the phlogiston theory and the Ptolemaic universe. I loved Professor Nash's lectures and course material but could only manage a C, confirmation that I lacked talent for the sciences. In humanities, we read the *Iliad*, the *Odyssey*, the *Aeneid*, the *Divine Comedy*, and *Paradise Lost* in the first semester, followed by *Tom Jones, Don Quixote, The Red and the Black, War and Peace*, and *Heart of Darkness* in the second semester. My western White liberal arts education was moving into high gear.

I lived in Matthews North, a freshman dorm in Harvard Yard. It was a large five-story Victorian building with a central stairwell providing the only connection between floors. That configuration—and communal bathrooms—made it easy to get to know one's floormates. It also made for many raucous inter-floor exchanges. As a result, Matthews was well known as a breeding ground for pranks and generally unruly behavior. I found myself drawn to, and sometimes even becoming the ringleader of, some of those activities. I do not recall what got it started, but several of us began accumulating small spoons from the freshman dining hall. In addition to taking the single knife, spoon, and fork (which we jammed into the breast pocket of our required jackets), we would add a handful of small spoons. After a few weeks, the dining hall was almost out of spoons and we each had a laundry bag full. It was time to act. We challenged our coconspirators in Weld Hall, across the Yard, to an all-out spoon fight. At the appointed hour, we emerged and began hurling our harmless hoard of silverware at each other. It did not take long for us to exhaust our supply. We retreated to our dorms, howling with laughter. The Yard was littered with spoons, but we had left the scene before the campus police arrived. I believe the great spoon fight coincided with Mental Health Week and was part of our "Fight Mental Health" agenda.

Our next adventure did not end so well. Several of us thought it would be an inspired idea to collect water on the roof of the dorm, then set off an alarm that would draw the fire department. When they arrived, we would douse them with our cache of water. Unfortunately, we stored some of the water on the roof in glass bottles, which were discovered before we were able to hatch our plan. We were identified or confessed when angry officials investigated, and hauled before the dean of students. Although we had intended only to empty the *contents* of the bottles, not to throw them, we were severely lectured about the dangers of glass projectiles and got off with a stern warning. We felt quite chastened and very lucky, since our parents were not informed and I certainly did not tell mine.

The close community of Matthews North led to some lifelong friendships. My roommate for my three upper-class years, Tim McCaffrey, and I joined to room with Karl Phaler, a brilliant and charismatic but troubled young Matthews freshman. Karl somehow found his way to Professor James Watson's lab and got involved in the research there. Watson was in the midst of the work that would lead to him sharing the Nobel Prize in 1962 for helping to discover the structure of DNA. Karl wrote a paper about it for his freshman science course. The paper was returned by his professor, who said he could not grade it because it was too advanced for anyone but Watson to understand.

Karl had a chaotic home life. He barely knew his father, a career navy officer. His mother seemed to change partners frequently and never paid his tuition bills on time. He left after sophomore year and, perhaps not surprisingly, joined the navy, signing up for an extended commitment in exchange for the navy paying for his continuing education at another university. I did not see him again until our twenty-fifth reunion where, although a civilian, he showed up wearing fatigues and carrying a copy of *Soldier of Fortune* magazine. He was vague about what he had been doing but it seemed to involve arms sales in trouble spots around the world.

Timothy Temple McCaffrey was a more serious student than I was, and he did his best to encourage me toward more responsible behavior, to little effect. Tim headed up the Newman Club (the principal social organization for Catholic students), graduated with honors, and met and married a Radcliffe girl, Jane Russell. In our last two years rooming together in Adams House, Tim would sometimes roust me out of bed for dinner by blasting sermons by Boston's colorful Cardinal Cushing, which were broadcast over the radio around that time of the evening.

I was still inept in my efforts to understand and interact with the opposite sex, so Jane would occasionally take pity on me and arrange a last-minute Saturday night date. In the years after graduation, I stayed in touch with Tim and Jane, sometimes helping to decorate their tree at Christmas. Tim and Jane would later live in Ossining near my parents and Tim would commute with my father to the city, maintaining our connection. Despite this history, Tim and I were fundamentally different and we were both emotionally reserved, and so we never developed a deep personal rapport. Sadly, Tim died in 2019 after an extended battle with prostate cancer.

Other friendships took root from the group in Matthews North: Richard Gordon from Springfield, Massachusetts; Wayne Miller from Buffalo; and John Bing from a lot of places. These three roomed together and joined Tim, Karl, and me in Adams House (one could choose one's house then). Richard spent his career in international development at the United Nations and has long lived on the Upper West Side of Manhattan. Wayne moved to Denver, where he became a radiologist. John, after getting a PhD in international education at UMass Amherst, started and ran a highly respected cross-cultural consulting firm. We have all remained in touch and have become closer in recent times. Each year for the past five years or so, we have taken a spring hiking trip together in Arizona or California.

John became and has remained my closest friend over the years. We share a love of hiking that has been a source of joy for both of us over thousands of miles of trails walked together. John's father (a renowned research physician) was a secular Jew from Nuremberg and his mother was a Protestant from New England, giving us much common ground. His father had numerous academic appointments which led to John moving frequently from Birmingham, Alabama, to Birmingham, Michigan, to St. Louis, Missouri—making him also, like me, a bit of a displaced person. The strong bond between John and me has now lasted some sixty-five years.

At Toddville and at St. Peter's, I could lay claim to being the smartest kid in the class. At Harvard, this was definitely no longer the case. I did not feel intimidated or unable to compete, but it was sobering—even invigorating—to realize that I was surrounded by so many extremely sharp people. In retrospect, my character was formed at least as much by my fellow students as by the classroom and the library, where I spent far too little time. Each semester, I would start out determined to be a more diligent student. I would spend my first few evenings in the Adams House library, a cozy and comfortable space. But that would be my undoing. The leather chairs were too comfortable, and drowsiness would soon overcome my resolve. And an invitation to the poolroom or poker table proved irresistible. We would begin by saying we'd stay "just for an hour," but we would inevitably play deep into the night. As I skipped more and more classes (no attendance was taken then), I would fall behind. Suddenly it would be reading period, a stretch of about two weeks without classes before final exams. Panic would set in, all-nighters would be pulled, and I would squeak by. Fortunately, I had an uncanny and enviable ability to figure out what was most likely to be on those finals. I was correct often enough to get by with Cs—sometimes without even coming close to finishing the reading lists for the courses.

The poker table, where nicknames were used more commonly than our real ones, saw me for many more hours than the library. My sobriquet was "Clyde." "Ray" (Met Wilson) and "Skinny" (John Gould) were my most regular coconspirators, and we normally played in their room on the fourth floor of I Entry, where I lived as well. "Biggy" (John Bing), "Mother" (Wayne Miller), and "Hawg" (Bill Baldwin), among a few others, were also frequent participants. We played for stakes that we could not really afford, sometimes winning or losing forty dollars or more in an evening. Since none of us had that kind of cash, at the end of the game we would just swap and recalculate the IOUs among each other. None of us won or lost regularly enough to get into serious trouble. On the very rare occasions that Met lost (he was the most skilled player despite growing up in a Mormon household), he would graciously put real cash on the table and we were then able to write down some of our IOUs. It is a small wonder that we all went on to lead productive lives.

One evening during reading period of senior year, Met, Skinny, and I were downing beers at Cronin's, the local drinking venue for students. We had all turned twenty-one by then, so we were at least drinking legally, if not wisely. We compared notes on what we had scheduled for the next week and found that none of us had papers, exams, or other commitments. Both Met and Skinny were from Oregon, and we all decided that it would be a great idea to drive there. All we lacked was a car. Josh Young lived across the hall from Met and Skinny, and we knew that Josh had just been given a brand-new yellow VW Beetle as a graduation present. We ran back to our dorm, woke Josh up, and presented our proposal to him. Ridiculously, Josh agreed. We packed up a few things and set out in the middle of the night. As usual, only Met had any money.

We had reached the Rochester area on the New York State Thruway as dawn broke. It was snowing and the roads were slick. I was driving while Met and Skinny slept in the tiny rear seat. As I approached an overpass, I saw a car sticking out into the roadway; it had spun out and smashed into the abutment. I eased around it but ran over a sharp piece of debris and our right front tire blew. We slalomed between posts on the median strip and came to rest without further incident. Josh, sitting next to me, was so relieved that his new car was not damaged that he planted a big kiss on my cheek. We had to have the tire repaired at a nearby rest stop. That used up much of what little money we had. After spending several hours attending to this setback, we continued on, but by that time we had all sobered up in more ways than one. It dawned on us that Oregon was still a very long way away. Met thoughtfully offered that we should instead head for Minneapolis, where his family lived.

Taking turns, we drove all through the next day and night. My next turn came during the wee hours of the night. We passed through the small town of Menominee, Wisconsin, at something like 4:00 a.m. I was determined not to get stopped for speeding and so, despite not seeing another car, I slowed down to under forty miles per hour. The flashing lights of a police car suddenly appeared and the local sheriff pulled me over for going thirty-eight in a twenty-five-miles-per-hour zone. He obviously was fundraising. He hauled us in front of a judge who ordered us to pay the fine (I believe it was forty-five dollars) on the spot, virtually exhausting our limited cash supply. It was the only speeding ticket I have ever gotten.

We pulled into Met's home at mid-morning on the following day. It was the president's mansion at the University of Minnesota. Owen Meredith Wilson, Sr. was indeed the college's president, and he and his wife treated the ragtag, smelly group far more graciously than we deserved. A few days later, after borrowing money for a bus ticket, I returned to Cambridge, mildly chastened.

I am proud to report that there was one course in which I did get an A: History of the French Revolution. But then *everyone* got an A in that course. It was taught by Crane Brinton, a renowned scholar and author of the classic *The Anatomy of Revolution*. He enjoyed teaching a well-known "gut" course, and it was in my major field. During my reading for the course, I became enamored with Edmund Burke and his Whig-oriented critique of the French Revolution. Burke argued that the French upheaval was an assault on the Enlightenment tradition of building rationally on the past, seeking instead to destroy the social and political fabric in order to replace it with some untested new structure based on abstract ideas of natural rights. Little did I know that most of what I was reading about Burke had been written by academics who would form the base of the neoconservative movement. Most notable was Russell Kirk's biography, which made a persuasive case for seeing Burke as the father of a new spiritually-based conservatism designed to protect sacred social institutions from the radical surgery of unproven utopian critiques.

I went to see Professor Brinton with an idea about a paper showing a connection between Burke and Samuel Taylor Coleridge. He loved the idea and gave me an A+, the only one I received while at Harvard.

As I struggled to find my footing at Harvard and my place in the universe, I suffered the normal bouts of sophomore depression and junior-year angst. On my trips home for vacations, my father would normally drive me from

Peekskill to the Stamford, Connecticut, railroad station to take the train back to Boston. The drive took about an hour. Since neither of us was much given to small talk, it was mostly in silence. On a few occasions, I asked him questions that were fermenting inside.

"Dad," I blurted out once, "when do you finally feel grown up?"

He smiled wistfully and answered, "I don't think you ever do. Your mom and I still feel like we are pretending."

Coming from adults who had been through what they had, and who seemed so mature and confident, I did not expect that answer.

Another time, wrapped up in my own bewilderment, I asked, "Did you ever suffer from *Weltschmerz*?"*

His reply—"When you work fourteen hours a day, you don't have time for *Weltschmerz*"—left me feeling abashed.

During another trip, I queried, "What is happiness?"

He thought for a moment, and said, "I don't think happiness is a condition. It is an event, a moment. I remember sitting on a rock after a cold night of guard duty in the Legion. The sun came out and warmed me, and I lit a cigarette. I was happy. Was I content? No. But for that moment, I was happy."

Pretty good answers to some very naive questions.

Given my heritage, it was hardly surprising that I chose to major in European history at Harvard. I started out in the honors program, a prerequisite for graduating *cum laude* or better. Part of the honors program involved being assigned a distinguished scholar as an advisor or tutor. The student and his tutor would design one course per semester together, developing a personalized reading list. I was assigned to Stephen Graubard. He was a brilliant academic, a much-published author, and a thoroughly lovely man. During his time as my tutor, he became the managing editor of *Dædalus*, the journal of the American Academy of Arts and Sciences. Despite all the other demands on his time, he treated me with kindness, encouragement, and patience that I did not earn or deserve. His patience

---

* Weltschmerz is that quintessential German word meaning world-weariness or pain.

was not, however, inexhaustible. After I tried to bluff my way through a session when I had not read the material, he told me that since I was acting like a child he would treat me like one. From then on, I had to submit an outline of whatever I had read.

After my junior year, which I spent consistently getting Cs, or at best a very occasional B-, I decided to drop the honors program, much to Professor Graubard's relief. Still, whenever our paths crossed later on, he was always extremely friendly and seemed genuinely to enjoy my later successes. Finally, the end of my senior year approached, and with it the comprehensive exam in one's major field. I had taken "comprehensives" at the end of my sophomore and junior years and had done well enough that all I really had to do was show up in my senior year to be assured of graduating. But I had to choose a specific area for the test.

Cleverly, or so I thought, I concluded that it would be easier to pick a single country over a period of time rather than multiple countries over a shorter span. A few nights before the exam, I opted for "France Since 1415" and found a book with that title. I stayed up for a couple of nights plowing through it and reported to Memorial Hall fairly confident that I would do well enough. I looked up at the board to see where I should sit for this specialty. There was no listing for "France Since 1415"!

I asked the proctor, who replied, "Oh, we didn't have enough applicants for that, so you will have Orals." This prospect sent me into a serious panic.

I quickly looked back up at the board and blurted, "I'll take 'Europe Since1789.'"

I turned in a very scant blue book, but it was indeed enough for me to graduate. I was able to return home with my diploma, to the surprise and relief of my mother who had been convinced, with some justification, that I might flunk out at any moment.

Although it did not hurt me professionally later on, I clearly squandered the opportunity to get the most out of the rich learning opportunities that Harvard offered. I had not been, in fact, "ready" for Harvard. My friends, Wayne and John, both took a year off from Harvard to grow up and returned much more serious and dedicated. At about that time, the movie *The Hustler* came out. We all were deeply drawn to it, and not just because we had spent so many hours in the poolroom and could appreciate the scenes of 14-1 straight pool played the way it should be. Fast Eddie Felson, Paul Newman's character (for which he should have won an Oscar rather than for the second-rate sequel, *The Color of Money*), has a penchant for self-destruction and fails to appreciate what he has: talent and the love of his girlfriend, Sarah Packard, wonderfully played by Piper Laurie. In one of the many memorable scenes, Eddie asks Sarah, "Do you think I'm a loser?" Bert Gordon (played by George C. Scott), the reptilian manipulator, thinks Fast Eddie is a loser. Gordon knows Eddie has talent, but he believes that he finds excuses to lose when the pressure is on. "It's everybody's favorite indoor sport, feeling sorry for yourself," Gordon scoffs. We asked ourselves, were we losers? We seemed to be doing the same thing—not taking advantage of our talents and the opportunities we were given, and sulking about it. We would debate this deep question into the wee hours on more than one occasion.

Still, my Harvard years were not all wasteful and guilt-ridden. I had not planned on playing any college sports. As rich a part of my St. Peter's experience as they had been, I was pretty sure I was not college athletics material. But then, a week or two after arriving in the fall, I began to get the itch for football again. I wandered down to the freshman football practice field and asked one of the coaches if it was too late to try out. He asked me what position I played and I told him I was a quarterback. "What the hell," he said, "we can always use another quarterback, go suit up." I became the fourth- or fifth-string quarterback, which gave me a minor taste of a seriously organized athletic program. I even got to eat at the training table before games, dressed for home games, and played a few minutes on a rainy, muddy afternoon (as a defensive linebacker where nothing much could happen or go wrong).

I was part of a group of the freshman team called "the last eleven guys." During the final week of the season, before the game against Yale, one of our coaches sent us over to the varsity field to be fodder against the first string. There, I was put with another 150-pounder (who also happened to be from Peekskill) in the defensive line, and we were told with a smirk to rush the passer in live practice. I guess that the beefy offensive linemen were not used to blocking skinny little rushers who did not attack the way we were expected to. Several times in a row we got through to the quarterback, infuriating head coach John Yovicsin, who abruptly called a halt to the drill—not a good sign for the first string's prospects against Yale. That Saturday, I joined my brother, who by then had graduated from Yale and was at the Fletcher School of Law and Diplomacy (part of Tufts University and the premier grooming venue for those aspiring to join the Foreign Service) to watch "The Game." It was held that year at Yale Bowl. I was not completely surprised when Yale won 56-0.

After that, I happily contented myself with intramural football. I became the quarterback of the Adams House team. By this time, my hands had grown enough that I could grip a football and throw a half-decent pass. With no coach and little practice, putting together an offense was a major challenge. What little offense we were able to produce was mostly through the air. Our games, only five or six per season, were therefore very low-scoring affairs. We had an odd assortment of skill levels, from really top-flight athletes who could have made the varsity but did not want to take that much time away from studies, to some who had hardly played before, mixed with in-betweens like me. The last game of the year was against our "sister college" at Yale on that weekend. (Yale's college system of upper-class residential units was the same as Harvard's houses.) Adams House was able to win all three of the games I played in.

I had passed my language requirement before entering freshman year, but still decided to take the introductory French Literature course, French 20, as an elective. One reason I took the course was that I saw that the reading list included an excerpt from *Annapurna*, Maurice Herzog's book about the 1950 expedition. It had become a classic of French literature, particularly the last line: "*Il y a d'autres Annapurna dans la vie des hommes*" ("There are other Annapurnas in the lives of men"). I struggled through most of the course, compelled to consult a dictionary so often that I had trouble grasping—let alone maintaining—the meaning of what I was reading. Near the end of the semester, we read André Gide's *La Symphonie Pastorale*. Gide's prose was simple and crystal clear. I read paragraphs and even whole pages without assistance. It was exhilarating and deeply affecting. A blind girl discovers the beauty of nature by listening to Beethoven's Sixth Symphony. It was just the kind of story to appeal to my romantic but still frustrated yearnings.

When it came to the opposite sex, I was slow getting off the ground. At Toddville, the prettiest girl in our senior class had asked me to be her date at a dance, but insisted that I wear elevator shoes because she was taller. (I refused, she relented, and I remember feeling the hard tips of what I only later realized were her "falsies" as we danced.) While at St. Peter's, my physical development continued to be a bit behind some of the other boys. My build was slight, my face and body almost hairless, and my voice still high and uncertain. The freshman football coach could not resist making fun of my squeaky countertenor when I called signals. In any case, we had almost no time or opportunity for contact with girls outside of school. Our dances with our sister institution, St. Mary's, were awkward and had to "leave room for the Holy Ghost."

Aside from stoking unrequited romantic yearnings, reading *La Symphonie Pastorale* also helped to solidify my rediscovery of classical music. At home, my parents listened almost exclusively to classical music with very occasional detours into folk music, which was more about politics than art. The first live concert I ever attended was when my parents took me to hear the Weavers at Carnegie Hall. Classical music was a harder sell. I complained bitterly about the endless hours of WQXR (New York's classical music station) that they played on the radio. Of course, when I landed at Harvard Square, I used some of my limited spending money to buy a small sampling of classical music records in addition, naturally, to the Kingston Trio and *The Best of Harry Belafonte*. On one visit to the record store, I told the clerk, as suavely as I could, that I had heard a Beethoven violin concerto that I liked but was not sure which one it was. He looked at me with only lightly concealed contempt and replied, "He only wrote one." I survived that humiliation and WQXR now plays through my headphones as I write these words.

In my sophomore year, we lived in the older section of Adams House, part of the so-called "Gold Coast," which Wikipedia describes as "dormitories built from 1893-1902 to provide luxurious accommodation for rich Harvard undergraduates." In my days, its tiled hallways, high ceilings, and wood paneling still evoked that golden age. Across Mt. Auburn Street from our building, B Entry, was a café/coffee shop called Club 47, which featured young up-and-coming folk singers. Some of my friends urged me to come and listen to an exciting new female vocalist named Joan Baez. I did not know the name, and with typical sophomoric arrogance, I declined to cross the street—another missed opportunity.

One evening, several of us were standing outside B Entry on Mt. Auburn Street. A VW bug pulled up and a group of giggling young women asked if we knew of any good coffee shops in the area. Rather than direct them to Club 47, we convinced them that our room and a glass of wine was a far more promising venue. I found one of the women very interesting. She was blonde, very shapely, and had a familiar Germanic accent. Her name was Elisabeth Habsburg. Intrigued by her last name, I asked rather boorishly what her father did, and she said simply, "He owns land in Austria." She and her friends left, but not before I learned that Elisabeth was a student at the New England Baptist Hospital School of Nursing, and I got her phone number.

After we went out on a few dates, I went to the library and looked her up in the *Almanach de Gotha*. As I had begun to suspect, she was not your average Austrian nursing student. She was an archduchess and something like twelfth in line to the theoretical throne of the Holy Roman Empire. Her mother was a Hohenzollern and closer in the line of succession in Romania. Elisabeth and her mother lived in a fairly modest apartment in Back Bay. On their mantelpiece at Christmastime, I saw cards from an impressive cross section of European royal families. It was a glimpse into the relatively impoverished state of some continental nobility. When I went home, I proudly announced my new romance to my parents. Instead of being impressed, they cried in alarm, "Oh no, the Habsburgs were all crazy!" To my frustration, Elisabeth adhered to the strict Catholicism of her heritage, so I remained a virgin—and lost touch with her after my junior year.

Fortunately, I had other pursuits. One very meaningful and successful aspect of my Harvard career was the Harvard yearbook. Based on my St. Peter's experience, I picked this student activity over trying out for the undergraduate newspaper, the *Crimson*, which seemed a bit too high-powered for me. I joined the yearbook's editorial staff (as opposed to the business or photography units) and found a congenial, fun-loving group of capable writers. We wrote the fairly formulaic text for faculty profiles as well as coverage of student residencies and activities. The yearbook was actually a rather substantial enterprise. It published not only Harvard's annual volume but Radcliffe's as well, along with the freshman registers for both, and the staff included some "Cliffees," which added to its allure. We also launched other ventures such as the first-ever guide to nearby women's colleges. I spent an inordinate number of hours at the yearbook, working on writing assignments and enjoying the conviviality of young men and women engaged in a common enterprise with deadline pressures. There was always beer in the fridge which, particularly with access to alcohol being a problem for those of us under twenty-one, furthered the attraction of spending time there.

I rose through the ranks, becoming production coordinator in my junior year, a job that entailed putting together the editorial material and photography and creating the finished product. It was the normal stepping-stone to the top spot, president of Harvard Yearbook Publications, Inc. In my senior year, our business manager also had his eye on that prize, and an intense competition ensued. He campaigned hard among the staff of students who elected the president while I opted for a more aloof approach. After numerous ballots, we remained tied until finally one person—I've never known who—switched his or her vote to me, and I won the coveted spot. Looking at 325 (the yearbooks are named for the year since Harvard's founding in 1636) and seeing my name at the top of the masthead has always given me considerable pride and satisfaction.

One of the brightest and most charismatic of the young staffers was Tom Bethell. He came from an old New England family and his brother, John, would become the long-time editor of *Harvard Magazine*. Tom also had journalism in his blood, and he talked us into starting a general-interest magazine called *Cambridge 38* (zip codes were still in the future), an effort which he spearheaded. The magazine came out irregularly, approximately quarterly, usually focused on a specific topic of interest to us at the time. We published only a handful of issues as *Cambridge 38* did not outlast Tom's singular passion and energy—and, hot on the trail of other pursuits, he would leave Harvard without graduating. Tom and I became very close and we collaborated on one especially ambitious issue about Africa. The independence movement was sweeping across that continent at the time, and it was exactly the kind of exciting and topical subject we relished.

Tom got on the phone and set up a series of interviews. It amazed me how his persuasive self-confidence won access for a student publication. We hopped into Tom's dashing new TR3 roadster and drove to New York to see Ralph Bunche, then undersecretary at the UN and already a Nobel Peace Prize laureate. Then we moved on to Washington, DC, where, through a friend, he had bagged an appointment at the State Department with Chester Bowles, President Kennedy's special representative and adviser on African, Asian, and Latin American affairs. That interview, like others, went well beyond its allotted time, and we began to feel quite impressed with ourselves. Even better was an audience with the ambassador from the new republic of Mali, who invited us to his home. We all sprawled on the living room floor poring over a map of the region while the ambassador poured some excellent scotch and described the recently formed affiliation with Guinea and Ghana. The quality of our note-taking deteriorated steadily as the afternoon wore on, but the trip resulted in a surprisingly substantive and incisive set of articles, mostly written by Tom.

In 2011, while making plans to attend my fiftieth Harvard reunion, I sent an email to the yearbook staff asking if they were planning any get-togethers in conjunction with the graduation festivities, as had often been the case. They responded promptly, reporting that they had a big party every other year, but unfortunately, this was an off year. However, they would be honored to host a lunch for a former president. My wife and I arrived at their offices—which were much more spacious and comfortable than the cramped quarters we once occupied—to meet the outgoing and incoming presidents, who would take us to a nearby restaurant. They were both Asian American students, as were, it seemed, many of the current yearbook staff. Thinking back to our tenure, I asked jokingly if there was still beer in the fridge. "Of course," they said, "but we never drink it."

I then asked if they still inserted some fake students and faculty members into the yearbook. The two young women looked at me with horror. "What are you talking about?!" they exclaimed. I pulled a copy of 325 from the bookshelf and found Susthus Gullfilling, from Shrdlu, Louisiana, in the senior pictures of Adams House (his invention was based on some typos in the page proofs) and Paul M. Chernoff, professor of electroluminescence, in the faculty section. It had been our habit, when laying out the publication and finding ourselves with an uneven number of entries in those sections, to take the opportunity to insert a fictitious character. We were never chastised for taking these liberties and, augmented by beer, they created some of the most amusing moments of our time at the yearbook. The young women were shocked. "Oh, we would never do anything like that," they intoned soberly. It seems that going to Harvard is a much more serious piece of business now. We had a delightful lunch nonetheless.

Shortly before our graduation in 1961, we received word that, mostly for budgetary reasons, our diplomas would not be in the traditional Latin printed on large parchment sheets, but in English on an ordinary eight-by-ten-inch piece of heavy paper. We deeply resented this accommodation to modernity and fiscal prudence. Hundreds of us staged a sit-in on President Nathan Pusey's lawn and others created disturbances around Harvard Square. These minor disruptions would pale in comparison both in substance and intensity to the demonstrations soon to come, but they represented a major departure for us from the staid behavior that was the norm of the Eisenhower years. Undergraduate diplomas have been in English ever since.

Years later, John Bethell's *Harvard Magazine* carried an article on the history of Harvard's diplomas which contained this description of those events:

> When word of the abandonment of Latin came through in April, it touched off riots. Thousands of chanting students, inflamed by a toga-clad rabble-rouser on the steps of Widener Library, marched on the president's house (then in the Yard) before filling Harvard Square. Their mood was said to be jovial, the police dispensed tear gas in a fatherly way, and the rebellion came to naught. The diploma itself, the printed document, failed to stir the blood. It was said by the discerning Philip Hofer, founder and longtime curator of the department of printing and graphic arts at Houghton Library, to look "like the luncheon menu at the Harvard Faculty Club." The next year, a two-color, larger-format, more-suitable-for-framing diploma (with text still in English) replaced the menu.

I would like to think I played a small part in prompting that improvement.

My senior year, 1960-61, ushered in tangible change for us and for the country. That fall saw the election of John Kennedy, our own alumnus. The idealism and energy that swept through the campus was palpable. Though we could not know it at the time, many from our class would go on to high-profile careers in public service. Indeed, I find the roster of impressive names from the class of 1961 astounding: Supreme Court Justice David Souter (appointed by President George H. W. Bush); Representative Barney Frank; Martin Feldstein, President Reagan's chairman of the Council of

Economic Advisors; Timothy Wirth, senator from Colorado and later undersecretary for Global Affairs at the State Department; Anthony Lake, national security advisor to President Clinton; and Douglas Costle, EPA administrator under President Carter. While I was not fully aware of it at the time, the pull toward the public sector had begun for me as well.

After graduation, 1961 (looking to the future but lacking direction). (Courtesy of Thomas N. Bethell.)

With my diploma in hand, I was faced with the daunting challenge of deciding what to do next. Graduate school, the logical next step for most, did not seem to make sense for me. I was discouraged by my failures as a student and there did not seem to be a real likelihood that I would perform any better in academic environments in the immediate future. In addition, I knew all the things I did *not* want to be: doctor, lawyer, businessman, etc. But I had no idea what I wanted to do. I had no positive direction. I returned home in June and started looking for a job in New York City. Since a major in Euro-

pean history did not prepare me for any particular career path, I decided to focus on publishing, hoping that my yearbook experience would appear to offer some useful skill set. I made the rounds of the major magazines and book publishers, but mostly could not get past the reception area. It seemed that my Harvard degree was not worth as much as I had hoped. I finally landed an interview at *The New Yorker* and was offered a job—as the office gofer. They emphasized, in unequivocal terms, that I should not expect to do anything but get coffee, deliver mail, and perform menial office chores. They were persuasive, and I declined the job, failing to appreciate that this was the way many aspiring writers and journalists (such as Truman Capote) got their start. I lacked that kind of vision and commitment to writing. I have sometimes wondered what kind of life I might have had if I had chosen to run errands for William Shawn. But, since things turned out as they did, I have not spent any serious time conjuring up alternative fates.

I decided to head back to Boston, where I hoped for a less competitive and more welcoming environment. I moved in with Tom Bethell, who had an apartment in the then-dingy Central Square area. The rent was nominal. I answered a newspaper ad for a job in the editorial department of Beacon Press, the publishing arm of the Unitarian Universalist Church. Its hardcover offerings were mostly dismal, anchored by vitriolic anti-Catholic polemics. The paperback line was, by contrast, exemplary and highly regarded. Beacon issued reprints of classics in many fields, some for the general public and others oriented to the college textbook market. The job was to be the assistant to the head of the two-person editorial department—my boss and me. I was to do everything from emptying ashtrays and wastebaskets to editing manuscripts. The job paid sixty dollars a week. As I recall, the Editor-in-Chief, Ed Darling, liked the way I said "Harvard" when he asked where I had gone to college. My response seemed to strike the right combination of pride and humility. I was hired. It was a simpler world.

The job was wonderful. I did the menial tasks happily and even got to read some of the manuscripts that came in over the transom. I do not believe that I passed on any great literary works, but I doubt that the authors would have been happy to know that their fate rested in such inexperienced hands. Mostly, I researched titles for possible reissue in paperback. This entailed being given a stack pass to the immense trove of books in Widener, the library of Harvard University and one of the great libraries of the world. Even for graduate students, such passes were highly sought-after perquisites. For the titles that we were considering, I needed to find copies in good condition because we relied on photocopying rather than setting fresh type. If I could find a serviceable copy, we could then proceed to look into legal and copyright arrangements. This job responsibility had additional benefits. Whenever I was hungover, which was all too often, I could always phone in to Beacon and say I was spending the day at Widener.

My boss, Karl Hill, was a good friend of Barney Rosset, the owner of Grove Press, which was then going to court to fight the banning in Massachusetts of Henry Miller's recently published *Tropic of Cancer*. Karl was invited to attend the trial and he kindly brought me along. It was the first round of the litigation, presided over by a local Boston judge, and a negative outcome was all but certain. Grove Press called expert after expert to testify to the book's literary merit; the judge invariably disallowed their testimony, ruling that it would be "hearsay evidence."

Grove Press's attorney then raised the delicate subject of profanity. He explained that there were many words in Miller's text that some might find objectionable. He said that he would not have a problem using them in court, since those passages were fundamental to the author's artistic intent, but he understood that the judge might have a different perspective and suggested the need for some ground rules governing how the attorneys would refer to the problematic words in open court. The judge agreed and asked the attorneys to approach the bench. Several minutes of whispers—and some ribald laughter—emanated from the three as they huddled together.

As the attorneys returned to their seats, the judge announced that such words, once identified, would then be referred to by "a so-many-lettered word beginning with a certain letter." For example, he said, one might say "a five-letter word beginning with the letter 'p.'" The Grove Press attorney hesitated for a moment and then, with a mischievous smile, offered: "It occurs to me, your honor, that this may lead to some confusion. For instance, I can think of five, five-letter words beginning with 'p.'" Startled, the judge said, "I can only think of four; approach the bench!" The courtroom erupted in laughter. It was a surreal scene for a naive twenty-one-year old.

I shared a small office overlooking the grounds of the state capitol on Beacon Hill with Laurie Devlin, an extremely smart and lovely young woman. Her husband, Jim, was finishing up his law degree at Harvard. Jim and I would spend many evenings at the Casablanca, the bar beneath the Brattle Theatre near Harvard Square, listening to Édith Piaf on the jukebox, discussing the issues of the day, and then adjourning to his apartment to play poker deep into the night while Laurie served us more drinks and meals. Somehow, sixty dollars a week was ample for this lifestyle.

Jim Devlin was brilliant and unconventional, a larger-than-life character of the kind to whom I have tended to become attached. I find myself attracted to such people because I am invigorated by their assertiveness and creativity, traits that were not much encouraged or rewarded in my household. I was never made to take an art class or a music lesson. Diligently following directions seemed to evoke more parental praise than demonstrating creativity or original thinking. Perhaps as a result, my intellect has always seemed to work best in reactive mode. I am more adept at analysis and problem-solving than at setting new agendas that break old molds.

My personal agenda, such as it was, would soon be overtaken by global events. Looming over me since graduation was the prospect of military service. In May 1961, the Soviet Union shot down an American U-2 spy plane, dramatically increasing tensions between the two superpowers. In June, the Vienna summit meeting between Soviet Premier Khrushchev and President Kennedy failed to resolve the status of Berlin in Soviet-dominated East Germany. Khrushchev had previously demanded that the United States and its allies abandon Berlin and threatened to sign a separate peace treaty with East Germany that could have meant going to war over the city's status. In August, the Berlin Wall began going up to stop the escalating exodus of citizens from East Germany. The sense of crisis was palpable. Draft quotas were rising dramatically. Having eschewed graduate school, I had left myself especially vulnerable. It seemed that virtually everyone who could not get an academic or medical deferment was being called. My number was sure to come up, making my peaceful life in Cambridge both surreal and unsustainable.

SIX

THE ARMY

At some point during the fall of 1961, the Selective Service System notified me that I had been classified 1A, and not long after that, I was called for a physical. I reported to the induction center at 39 Whitehall Street, later immortalized in Arlo Guthrie's classic song "Alice's Restaurant." I passed the physical and knew that I would be called up soon.

I had thought about enlisting in the army's six-month program, as many of my contemporaries had done. This meant six months of active duty, then five and a half years in the reserves. Reserve duty involved monthly meetings and two weeks of active duty every summer for five long years. While such a commitment was not unduly onerous, a scenario of how it would probably turn out kept playing in my head. I would join a local reserve unit in Peekskill. While transfers were possible, I suspected that I would passively stay put, meet some girl, get married, and settle for a dreary, humdrum life in the suburbs. I went so far as to imagine myself buying a station wagon and becoming a Republican. Somehow I was willing to risk several years of active military service rather than face this unlikely and avoidable prospect. I wanted to force myself to leave open the possibility of a more exciting future. I still had a lot of growing up to do.

On the other hand, I was scared by the thought of being drafted without any control over where I would end up. I dreaded the idea of two years of active duty as a draftee at some bleak army post in the middle of the country. I fixed upon the idea of enlisting for three years and attending the Army Language School in Monterey, California. At least I would learn a new language and hopefully develop an employable skill.

I marched into the army recruiting office in Boston, encountered a sergeant, and told him of my plan. He assured me that there would be no problem and I filled out the necessary papers. A week or two later, I returned to the recruiting station and, to my amazement, was told that my application had been rejected. As a Harvard graduate who had taken college boards in Latin and French, I found this hard to believe. I asked the recruiting sergeant why this might have happened. He could think of only one possible reason: that I had been born abroad. He explained that the Language School was part of the Army Security Agency, which meant that I would need a security clearance in order to attend. He surmised that the army had probably decided that, given my foreign background, it would be too expensive to conduct the necessary background check while I was still a civilian.

The sergeant suggested that I should enlist for something else; he was confident that my application to the Language School would be approved once I was in uniform. That sounded plausible, so I signed papers requesting an assignment in Europe. On February 5, 1962, I reported to the enlistment center and was sworn into the United States Army. I was then sent to Fort Dix for basic training. There I suffered the standard humiliations: verbal abuse, the drastic military haircut, and the issuance of GI clothing and equipment.

After a couple of weeks of the round-the-clock initiation and exhausting drills of basic training, we were finally given an evening off. I headed straight to the personnel office to submit my application for the Army Language School. There I was informed that, in order to apply, I would have to waive my enlistment commitment. I was taken aback and extremely reluctant to do this since I had already been rejected once and certainly did not want to spend three years at some godforsaken outpost if I was turned down again for whatever reason. The personnel officer suggested that I wait until I arrived at my first permanent duty station in Europe and then reapply to the Language School. That way, I would at least be assured of keeping my Europe assignment. Again, that sounded reasonable. I left feeling sorely disappointed but still determined to seek the outcome I wanted.

About fourteen weeks later, I arrived at Combat Command A, Kirch-Göns, Germany. Stationed just east of the Fulda Gap, the traditional invasion route for armies from the east, it was the most combat-ready unit in Europe. I wasted no time going to the personnel office and telling the young second lieutenant in charge what I wanted. He looked at me sympathetically and said, "Didn't they tell you?" He pulled out a copy of Army Regulations and found the relevant sentence: "Enlisted personnel may not apply to Army Language School from an overseas command." Intentionally or not, I had been had! I had just experienced my personal *Catch-22,* and there was nothing I could do about it.

Several events from my basic and "second eight" training experiences left indelible marks. In the third or fourth week, I developed a severe upper respiratory infection (URI). With a 103-degree fever and a heavy cough, I was sent to the URI ward, where rumor had it that several soldiers had recently died. I was desperate to get out of there. Missing more than a week of basic training for any reason meant being "recycled" back to week one. That prospect terrified me, so I drank as much cough medicine as I could force down, hoping that it would loosen my chest, subdue my coughing, and help me heal more quickly. What I did not know was that the syrup was equal parts decongestant and expectorant. I promptly coughed so much that I got the dry heaves and had to be given a sedative by injection. Fortunately, I recovered just in time to avoid being recycled. I now suffer from bronchiectasis, a form of chronic obstructive pulmonary disease (COPD) that involves the pitting of the bronchial tubes. While twenty years of heavy smoking, numerous other URI infections, and several treks to high altitudes have probably aggravated my condition, I trace the respiratory problems of my old age back to basic training.

Midway through the eight weeks of basic, we spent a long, muddy day crawling under barbed wire while supposedly live ammunition screamed over our heads. We returned to our barracks late in the evening, filthy and exhausted. Determined not to flunk the next day's rifle inspection, I stayed up late cleaning and polishing my weapon to a high shine. Besides, I needed to set an example because I had been selected as a platoon leader—a dubious honor—and sported temporary sergeant's stripes.

The next day, as we lined up in formation after a training exercise, I heard our instructor call out, "Who belongs to rifle number . . . " It was my number, and I raised my hand. He said, "Step forward, soldier!" He ripped off my sergeant's armband. He then held out my rifle and turned it upside down. Sand poured out of the barrel. I had scrubbed the weapon but had forgotten, in my weariness, the most fundamental task—to run a cleaning patch down the barrel. "If you had tried to fire this thing, it probably would have blown up in your face," he snarled. "And we would have wasted our precious time and money training you." Then he confined me to post indefinitely.

I did not at all regret losing my symbolic rank, since I was no longer accountable for my platoon's bed-making and deportment. What I minded was losing my long-awaited weekend pass. My savior was our young company commander, a second lieutenant, who took pity on me on Friday and gave me the pass.

One day, in the final two weeks of basic, we went through bayonet training. We charged at sawdust-filled dummies, thrusting our bayonets into them while yelling, as required, "Kill! Kill! *KILL!*" Then, immediately following bayonet drill, we were ushered into a classroom for a session on "character guidance." A chaplain was to speak to us about moral conduct and listen to any complaints we might have. I found the juxtaposition unbelievable. Shortly before the session started, our first sergeant, who gave a pretty good imitation of John Wayne, glanced at his watch and growled at us: "Men, the chaplain will be here in about three minutes. He will ask you if you have any complaints. I don't want you bothering him. So, for the next two minutes and thirty seconds, I'm your fucking priest, I'm your fucking rabbi, I'm your fucking minister. If you have anything to say, *say it to me!*" Of course, no one said a word either to him or to the chaplain. We then received our character guidance lecture.

At some point during the latter part of basic training, I was interviewed by a personnel sergeant about my background and skills to help the army make the wisest decision about my future training and deployment.

The sergeant looked at my records and drawled sarcastically, "So, you went to college." Probably because of limited economic opportunities for young men who lacked the finances or the inclination to go to college, many white high school graduates from below the Mason-Dixon Line turned to military service as a career.

He continued, "Since you went to college, you're a teacher, right?"

I said no, I wasn't.

"Well then, what the hell are you?"

"Nothing yet, sergeant," I replied.

Turning to the form he was completing, in the space under "Profession," he wrote: "Teacher."

As we completed the final days of basic training, we apprehensively awaited our orders for "second eight"—eight more weeks of training in what the army determined in its wisdom would be our profession for the remainder of our tour of duty. I harbored hopes of receiving schooling in something useful, even interesting. My orders had me staying at Fort Dix; my MOS (Military Occupational Specialty) was 310, communications specialist. When I asked an NCO what that meant, he smiled and said, "That's where they send you if you're not smart enough for MOS 111." That was the infantry, the most dreaded of assignments.

Communications specialists were the guys with donuts of wire on their backs who had to go into a combat area *before* the infantry, to set up communication lines linking the forward units and the rear support elements. Among our exalted duties were learning how to climb telephone poles and operate a switchboard. I regularly experienced how much some of the officers and nearly all of the NCOs delighted in giving the few college graduates a hard time. This assignment fit neatly into that pattern.

The army at least lived up to one part of its commitment. I landed in Bremerhaven, Germany, on Independence Day, 1963, the irony of which did not escape me. I had had an awful crossing: eight days of very rough seas on a crowded troopship, the *USS Rose*, which would subsequently transport many soldiers to Vietnam. Most of my fellow passengers got sick. I fortunately avoided that by spending as much time as possible on deck to avoid the foul-smelling areas below (as my father had done before me). Memorably, at one meal in the mess hall, the ship was rolling back and forth heavily and rhythmically. After one particularly nasty pitch, my metal tray slid in front of the soldier next to me. He vomited into it and it slid back to me.

I was finally at my first permanent duty station, Combat Command A, and after my encounter with the lieutenant in charge of the personnel section, it looked permanent indeed. The lieutenant did, however, extend one welcome offer. He said he could use someone who could write and spell to handle the personnel records in his office. He assured me that I would be able to keep a typewriter between the enemy and me for the duration of my tour.

On one of the first evenings at my new post, I went with a couple of my new fellow soldiers to a nearby *gasthaus* for the nightly ritual of beer drinking. One soldier carried and prominently displayed a miniature ladder. He explained that he needed it because he was "so short" that he needed a ladder to reach anything. Baffled, I learned that this was army jargon for not having many days left before his tour was up and he could go home. He had only three or four days left. "How about you?" he asked.

The question stunned me since I had not thought of what lay ahead in those terms. After a quick calculation in my head, I said, "A little over 900, I guess." He started laughing so hard that he dissolved into tears. It began to dawn on me that I might have made a very big mistake.

The days started to click slowly by—ever so slowly. Most evenings were spent getting drunk in local gasthauses on very good German beer. Meanwhile, Combat Command A lived up to its name. It held frequent alerts and field exercises. During the alerts, while the line units went out into the field on combat maneuvers, my personnel section was detailed to make the rounds of the residential quarters of married officers and NCOs, knocking on doors and asking if they had their emergency kits fully stocked. It was dispiriting duty. Waiting for the often resentful and despondent wives to locate their kits, I sensed that for many families army domestic life was bleak and troubled.

I formed a close bond with the only other college graduate who had found his way into our section. Roger Long was an artist, delightful but disorganized. He had little interest in numbers, so of course he was made the payroll clerk. Roger and I spent almost every evening together, talking and drinking. We held writing contests to see who could come up with the best poem or short story in the least amount of time. Nothing memorable came from these contests, but they helped keep us sane as the depressing days dragged on.

At some point late that summer, our commanding officer asked the personnel lieutenant to put Roger and me on a special assignment. It was the turn of our unit (the 3rd Artillery, a howitzer battalion) to be highlighted at the annual 3rd Armored Division celebration. I was to write the history of the 3rd Artillery and Roger was to paint it. I remember little about what I produced, except for trying to slip in as many hidden absurdities as I could, such as: "None of the battalion's victorious battles were more significant than any other, but none was insignificant." Roger produced several large canvasses depicting some of the historic battalion's battles. I recall one in particular that depicted Civil War-era cannons shelling what Roger did his best to make look like a golden city on a hill. If you looked closely at the stacked cannon balls, you could see the holes of bowling balls.

Working with Roger on this project, I saw how passionate he was about his art. It is painful to write that he did not seem to have exceptional talent. But he had to paint. I wanted to write the great American novel, but I did not *have* to write. He had no choice. He went on to become a high school art teacher. I went on to do many things, but becoming a writer was not one of them.

In October 1962, the Cuban missile crisis began to unfold. Indisputable photographic evidence was captured by a Lockheed U2 spy plane, showing the construction of ballistic missile facilities in Cuba with the assistance of the USSR. Actual missiles were detected on Soviet ships steaming toward Cuba. When President Kennedy demanded that the Russian ships turn back, tension mounted to critical levels. For several days a nuclear war actually seemed not only possible but imminent. As the most combat-ready post in Europe, we were placed on full alert. We received shots for yellow fever, were issued live ammunition for our rifles, and then sat on our bunks with our helmets next to us as we waited for the call to ship out. Exactly what role a traditional howitzer artillery unit would play in a nuclear confrontation was not clear, but that strategic question did not concern us. We were all simply scared. The crisis passed (Khrushchev backed down when Kennedy secretly agreed to withdraw American missiles from Turkey) and the call never came. My service time is included as part of the official Vietnam War era, so I am technically a Vietnam War vet—but the missile crisis was as close as I ever came to actual combat.

Despite occasional diversions, I despaired at the thought of spending almost 900 more days in this routine. I was afraid that I would lose it at some point and do something that would land me in the stockade. Something that would be an exercise of one's constitutional rights in civilian life—like telling off your boss—could, in the military, produce a permanent criminal record. I had come to detest the military environment. I felt I could imagine just a tiny fraction of how a Black person in America might feel. One was judged purely by the color of one's rank. As an enlisted man, I was by definition a second-class citizen and, because I was well educated, I was an uppity one at that. I often felt the only slightly concealed hostility of my "superiors," whom I considered in no way superior but who seemed to derive special pleasure in making things difficult for soldiers like me.

At the same time, I understood that the military can function as it must only if rank and command are absolutes. Soldiers are being trained to do something that is fundamentally against their basic instincts and, in most cases, immoral (i.e., kill people), so the basic principles of democratic society, the rights of dissent and disagreement, cannot apply. While I had to accept this reality, it did not make day-to-day life any easier.

After yet another set of field maneuvers and another freezing night on guard duty, I became determined to do something about my situation. It was legend around Combat Command A that no one could get out of there. No Form 1049—Request for Transfer—was ever approved. One night as winter approached, after I had gotten a little drunker than usual, I drafted a letter to my fellow Harvard alumnus, President Kennedy. I described a little of my history which had led me to want to serve my country, and I expressed my sincere belief that I could do so far more effectively from SHAPE (Supreme Headquarters, Allied Powers Europe) in Paris.

The next day, sobered up, I reread and fine-tuned the letter and sent it off. Fearing that my letter might be intercepted by the military mail system, I enclosed it in a letter to my friend Tom Bethell, and asked him to send it on. This was not a spur-of-the-moment decision. In the preceding weeks, I had arranged to take an army French language exam, which I passed. My MOS now read "310.065," a French-speaking telephone pole climber, which I hoped bettered my chances.

A few weeks later, we were again on field maneuvers when a jeep roared up to our unit and I heard my name being called out. "You're wanted at Division Headquarters!" the driver shouted. I clambered into the jeep, feeling excited and apprehensive. After about an hour's bumpy ride, we arrived at a building outside the city of Frankfurt. A few minutes later, I was seated opposite a major who glared at me over an array of papers on his desk. My limited journalism experience had taught me how to read someone's papers upside down. I could see overlapped "endorsements" from the various levels of command down which my letter had traveled: the White House mailroom, the Pentagon, USAREUR (United States Army Europe) HQ, Seventh Army HQ, and finally Division. Near the top I saw the notation: "Subject Enlisted Man will not be disciplined for writing to a civilian official." I quietly breathed a sigh of relief.

After a very brief interview, the major angrily concluded, "Okay, go ahead and submit a 1049. It will go through." Lightheaded at my escape from the jaws of military justice, I returned to my unit. Back at our post the next day, the commanding officer, a captain, called me into his office. He had a smile on his face and was holding a copy of my letter. "This is a helluva letter," he said. "I wish I had known you could write like this. I would have put you on my staff." I smiled politely and left with a blank Form 1049, which I hastened to fill out.

Several weeks later, my orders came through. I was being transferred to Patch Barracks, Seventh Army Headquarters, in Vaihingen, a suburb of Stuttgart. It was not Paris, but I had escaped Combat Command A. I arrived just before Christmas and was first assigned a bed in a large room with about eight or ten other soldiers. It was true that I had gotten out of Kirch-Göns, but I felt completely downcast and lonely. On Christmas Eve, I sat on my bed opening a few presents from home and playing a record of Leontyne Price singing Christmas songs that I had found at the PX. Her voice was achingly beautiful. I felt very sorry for myself. Tears streamed down my face as I reflected on my 750-plus days left in the service of the United States Army.

I was assigned to the editorial unit, whose job it was to edit and proof-read official mail and issue the post's daily bulletin. Most importantly, we handled the final editing and reproduction of Seventh Army regulations, which covered subjects ranging from highly secret war plans to how the cooks should prepare creamed chipped beef on toast (universally known as shit-on-a-shingle, or SOS). Because of the highly classified nature of some of the material that we handled, we all had to have high-level security clearances. After a relatively brief time, I was given a top secret clearance. And because we handled NATO documents, it was called—impressively or absurdly—"Cosmic Top Secret." The final irony of this Europe-born refugee's prior failure to obtain clearance for the Army Language School had come full circle.

The editorial unit office was a distinct improvement over Combat Command A. The atmosphere, though still military, was relatively relaxed and informal. Our kindly supervisor, Major Schulz, was a devotee of 221B

Baker Street and would wear Sherlock Holmes garb during his off-duty hours. Major Schultz kept a keen eye out for college-graduate enlisted men, a prerequisite to work in his office. He had intercepted my Form 1049 as it came through the channels and he snatched me up before it could go further. Moreover, we were the only office on post that had German civilians working in it—specifically, young women who did the typing. We were the envy of all the other enlisted men. The women's presence added an incredibly civilizing element and occasionally even led to some romance.

Already ensconced in the office were John Pierce and Lester Chan. We grew to completely depend upon each other for endurance and sanity, becoming lifelong friends in the process. John, a draftee, was on the sardonic side. A graduate of Fordham, he grew up in Larchmont in a single-parent household and his mother was a teacher. Lester was Chinese American from San Francisco. He had enlisted as a way to return to Europe to be with a lovely Austrian girl whom he had met in Paris the year before. He also sought to escape the discrimination that he had endured in California, finding Europe much more welcoming. Later we were joined by Marcel Unger, who had a Harvard Law degree.

Lester, John, and I tried to inject some humor into the tedious routine of producing army regulations. Whenever an appendix contained a form to be filled out as part of whatever administrative process it was describing, we tried to sneak into the sample signature block a literary or other humorous name, much as had happened during my days at Harvard Yearbook Publications. Instead of Major John Smith, we would insert names like Captain John Yossarian, Colonel Holden Caulfield, or Major Amory Blaine. Sometimes our section chief, Lt. Col. Donahue, would catch our iconoclastic insertions and send them back, but mostly they slipped through, much to our delight. We overreached, however, when we tried to slip Eugenio Pacelli (better known as Pope Pius XII) past Colonel Donahue. He was much too good a Catholic to let that one pass. He also was not amused.

In the summer of 1963, John Pierce and I decided to make Scandinavia our next vacation destination. We brought along our army pup tent, sleeping bags, and a little more than eighty dollars apiece (our monthly army salary) for an eighteen-day trip. That left us less than ten dollars a day between us, which had to include gas for the car, which was fortunately very cheap at United States military installations. The money also had to cover the many cigarettes we consumed, which were fortunately also very cheap at the PX. We drove from Stuttgart north up through Copenhagen, then on to Stockholm and finally Oslo. We shopped for our food with a keen eye on the prices, and we cooked simple dinners like canned beans on our little army stoves and ate out of our mess kits. In luncheon cafeterias we would surreptitiously finish other people's French fries if they left them on their trays. We were hungry all the time.

In Stockholm, we decided to visit the Tivoli garden (Stockholm had one similar to the original in Copenhagen), wandering among the rides and games, mostly just looking. We met a couple of lovely Swedish girls who spoke English and who seemed to like our company. This was too good to be true. One of them spotted a sign on a marquee that announced that Dizzy Gillespie would be playing in a few minutes. The girls excitedly proposed that we all go. John and I abashedly said we could not afford it. "That's okay," they said, "we'll pay our own way." Sadly, we had to admit that we could not even pay for ourselves. The girls shrugged wistfully and went in. That was the end of our vision of a glorious vacation escapade.

Then John saw a small chalkboard on which was written: "Boris Christoff Sings at 8 pm." Christoff was one of the leading operatic bassos of his time. I did not recognize the name, but John, an opera buff, exclaimed, "We have to hear this!" I did not quite understand his enthusiasm but agreed to come along. When the hour rolled around, Christoff appeared and stood up on a several square-foot wooden platform surrounded by a small crowd of perhaps several dozen. Without any accompaniment, as I remember, he simply opened his mouth and began to sing. I had never heard such a sound: sonorous, perfectly modulated, and utterly beautiful. He sang a few Russian songs and some arias from the opera, *Boris Godunov*, which featured his signature role. I was deeply moved; but beyond that, I felt a volcanic upheaval inside. Christoff was supremely talented, of course, but at the same time it finally dawned on me that producing something as perfect as he did required not just talent but enormous discipline and years of hard work.

That epiphany forced me to face how little serious energy I had applied to my own life and how shallow was my self-righteous indignation at the world for not appreciating my talents. During all the time I had spent sitting in the corner feeling sorry for myself, I had never come to terms with the idea that I ought to start by dedicating some sober hard work to the endeavor. It should not have taken this kind of experience to drive home such a simple and obvious truth, but at least the seeds of maturity were beginning to sprout.

Lester Chan's girlfriend, Johanna, had an aunt and three cousins in Augsburg, about a two-hour drive east from Stuttgart. Soon after arriving at Patch Barracks, I used what little savings I had accumulated to buy a car for $500. It was a cute little yellow Opel that I nicknamed Clea, thanks to being deep into Lawrence Durrell's *Alexandria Quartet* novels at the time. On any weekend when we could get passes (which was quite often), Lester, John, and I would jump in the car and head to Augsburg. Tante Pepe, as Johanna's aunt was called, did not speak a word of English nor did her three delightful daughters, Helga, Monika, and Hanni. I am not certain of their exact ages at the time but they were around nineteen, seventeen, and thirteen. Despite some mild flirting on both sides, our relationship remained like little sisters to big brothers. They were a simple family of limited means, but they were warm and generous and made us feel completely part of their family.

Despite the language barrier, communication did not prove to be an issue. Tante Pepe made herself understood with body language and laughter, and we tried to do the same. Lester spoke some German; I had heard it since childhood, so I knew quite a few words. In addition, I had wisely taken introductory German as an elective at Harvard to get a grounding in basic grammar, so I was able to put together some simple sentences fairly quickly. John also began to pick it up. Those weekends—drinking beer and wine, eating familiar Austrian/German food, laughing, playing childlike games—are deeply fond memories. How desperately we needed the normality and affection of this family. We did our best to return the feelings and show our appreciation.

Johanna was a beautiful young woman with an endearingly sweet and gentle disposition. She grew up in Maria Schutz, an idyllic village about an hour south of Vienna in the Semmering, the Catskills of eastern Austria. Her father, Rudi Rumpler, ran the local gasthaus, Gasthof zum Auerhahn. She would come to Augsburg occasionally to meet Lester and he would go to Maria Schutz whenever he had leave.

Lester and Johanna were married in the charming Baroque chapel in Maria Schutz in October 1963. John and I took a few days of leave to join the festivities. It was a special time. Rudi closed the gasthaus to the public and we had the run of the place to ourselves. The village's mountain setting was magical. The attendees from near and far were colorful and interesting. (Sadly, no one from Lester's semi-estranged family came.) In accordance with local custom, we "stole" the bride after the wedding, taking Johanna to a "secret" location for an hour or so before Lester was allowed to find and retrieve her. It was a glorious interlude.

Johanna and I shared the same birthday, though one year apart; Lester's birthday was one day later but the same year as mine. Somehow, sharing this origin calendar deepened our bonds. After completing his army service, Lester settled in Austria, where he taught school and raised two sons, Dominic and Marcel. He wrote, and played a good game of chess and a great game of ping-pong. He was accepted in the community and was loved for his kind and gentle soul. He had found a good life.

In November 1963, my periodic turn of KP duty came around again. It was always a nightmare. One had to report at about 5:00 a.m. and did not finish until well after dinner, sometimes around 9:00 p.m. KP was arduous, often filthy work. The earliest arrivers got the best assignments, setting and wiping tables; the last to arrive got pots and pans. Because of my distaste for early rising, that was sometimes my fate. While on this turn of KP, late on the night of November 22, we heard the news that President Kennedy had been assassinated. I was crushed. Like so many of my generation, and particularly because of the Harvard connection, I had come to idolize the dashing young president. But our mess sergeant seemed quite pleased by the news. As did so many career NCOs at the time, he came from the Deep South and resented everything Kennedy stood for, especially civil rights. As the sergeant gloated, my rage—at him, the army, and my place in it—seethed to near the breaking point.

I feared that something would take me past that point. Fortunately, a regular correspondence with Tom Bethell, my close friend from the yearbook years, gave me an outlet and a connection to a saner and more normal world. Our letters during this time were searing in their pain and intensity, both political and personal.

Sports too provided some diversion and relief. Patch Barracks fielded a highly competitive six-man touch football team. We had a spunky, agile quarterback with a strong arm, so I played end. I was hardly a speedster, but I was sure-handed and knew how to get open. We won more than our share of games and ended up in a tournament involving army teams from a large area of Germany. We made it to the semifinals before getting knocked out by a team that was clearly better.

We had won the previous game against a team that featured an Olympic-class (or so we were told) sprinter and a quarterback who could throw a long ball. It was a lethal combination, but we had been forewarned. Early in the game, when the other team had the ball, it was obvious that they were going to run their standard long-pass play. I was playing safety and backed way up, knowing that I had no hope of keeping up with the sprinter if I tried to cover him closely. The speedster came streaking down the field and their quarterback let fly. I was so far back that I just camped under where the ball would come down. The sprinter and the ball arrived at the same time. His knee crashed into mine, but his patella struck a more solid bone of mine. I got a bruise; he was carted off the field with a shattered kneecap. We won the game.

We also had a decent fast-pitch softball team. My quick reflexes were a good fit for third base in softball, and the NCO leader of our office unit, Sergeant Harrigan, proved to be a first-rate pitcher. As I matured and filled out a bit, I found I could even hit with a little more authority.

My other army sports adventure involved coaching rather than playing. I volunteered to coach the post's girls' high school basketball team. The team I took over was disorganized and chaotic, with no grounding in the fundamentals or tactics of the game. I had to learn a new set of rules (which, fortunately, no longer exist) for a game with six players on each side: two forwards, two guards, and two rovers. The guards were not allowed in the offensive zone and the forwards could not play at the defensive end, while the rovers—the best athletes—covered both ends. We lost nearly every game at first, but we managed to become a decent team by the end of the season. The girls were too prone to take out their frustration by starting fights on the floor with the other team. I would yell at them to save their fights for after the game and told them I would hold the bus for them if they wanted. They seemed to appreciate that commitment, which I never had to live up to.

One of the secretaries in our office was Ursula, a German woman who came from Stuttgart, had married a GI, and moved to the states. She was now back taking a break from a difficult marriage. She was very attractive and spoke excellent English, and we began dating regularly. She had a close friend, Christel, who lived nearby and who had a boyfriend name Heinz. The four of us would go out together, speaking German for the most part, which significantly improved my fluency. Heinz, with whom I often went out separately in pursuit of excellent local beers and wines, enjoyed tutoring me in the Schwäbisch dialect. Having grown up hearing German at home, my accent was quite good even though my grammar and vocabulary were still limited. I could get through a sentence or two without a mistake. Heinz used to enjoy having me say a few words and then asking the people we met to try to guess where I was from. They usually guessed the Strasbourg area, since I used a French "r" when speaking, never having mastered the rolling German version. Ursula returned to the United States to her husband for a while, living just a few miles from my home in Peekskill. I saw her a few times but we then lost touch for many decades. We reconnected briefly during the early years of this century when she was again enduring a difficult marriage. Sadly, she died in 2005 from pancreatic cancer. I paid a visit to her grave with her daughter.

One of the few good features of military life was the generous amount of vacation time. We had thirty days of leave per year, plus three-day weekend passes which were precious but not impossible to obtain if applied for judiciously. For my first trip, I headed alone to Paris. As I approached the *banlieue* (outskirts) of the city, I saw a sign that we were entering the village of Courbevoie. I knew that was the place name on my birth certificate. Now it was a burgeoning suburb where the new financial district, La Défense, was being built. It was very difficult to grasp that this characterless place along the highway was, in reality, where my life began.

For my next leave, I headed toward the Alps. As I approached Grenoble in my little yellow Opel with its United States Army plates, I saw snow-capped mountains in the distance. They were the real thing, not just photographs in mountain climbing books. I headed to Zermatt to pay my respects to the legendary Matterhorn. In my little hotel, I met a Yalie on his graduation tour. He said he had done some climbing and suggested that we hire an alpine guide. I quickly agreed, filled with the romance of the idea, but having no idea what I was getting into.

The next morning, we met our guide. With his rugged good looks and flinty confidence, he could have stepped out of central casting. We took the famous Gornergrat cable car to the Rotenboden station, a short walk from the Riffelhorn, a popular climbing peak. My new friend had handled the negotiations with the guide and had intimated that we had more experience than we actually did, which in my case, was approximately none. Roped up, we ventured out onto some precipitous ledges. It soon became apparent that we were way out of our league. I was almost frozen with fear and became even more alarmed when I saw the look of concern on the guide's face. Slowly and with intense concentration, he instructed us, from one rock outcropping to the next, exactly where to put our boots. We made it back to safety and ended our ill-considered adventure. It was my first indication that, despite my romantic love of mountains, I did not do well on exposed rock walls.

That fall, I headed south, again on my own. I fell in love with the chaos and beauty of Rome with its juxtaposition of the Renaissance and ancient Rome. My favorite spot was the Campidoglio, the piazza designed by Michelangelo, the corner of which overlooks the Roman Forum. On my first visit, I stepped into the cathedral of San Pietro in Vincoli and tiptoed up to Michelangelo's statue of Moses. Almost alone and with no protective barriers separating me from that awesome figure, I stood transfixed. Kinetic energy radiated from the marble figure, seated with the tablets containing the ten commandments under his arm, mere inches away from me. I dared not look away in case I would miss the moment when he would stand up and scold the worshippers of the golden calf. I had never experienced such transporting emotion from viewing a work of art.

I would take Hanni to Rome and Monika to Paris. Even in those incredibly romantic places, we maintained our big brother/little sister relationships. And we had the tourist sites almost to ourselves. There were no long lines or reservations needed at the Louvre, the Jeu de Paume,

the Sainte-Chapelle, Chartres, the Sistine Chapel, or the Colosseum. Hotels and restaurants were uncrowded and incredibly cheap. To be a tourist in Europe in the early 1960s was a unique privilege. Hanni was extremely sweet and sunny, and probably the brightest of the three Augsburg girls. We all thought she was destined for

Statue of Moses by Michelangelo, San Pietro in Vincoli, Rome (I was transfixed by this powerful work of art).

a fine future. Tragically, it was not to be. Years later, I heard that she had married a young Serbian man who, I was told, abused her physically and mentally. In despair, she threw herself out of a window and fell to her death.

Ultimately, the most formative aspect of my military service involved, not surprisingly, my first really serious girlfriend. Lester had married and moved off post, and John had returned to the states, having served his commitment. Two years were, in fact, a lot shorter than three. By this time, I had been promoted in rank to Specialist E-5, which meant no more bed checks and KP. Army life was becoming more bearable.

In search of new companionship and stimulation, I joined the post's theater company, The Vaihingen Players. The group attracted an odd assortment of the Seventh Army family. There were officers, enlisted men, and wives. Most had little or no training, but we had two truly talented guys who had studied (if I am not mistaken) at the Bristol Old Vic Theatre School. They brought some real professionalism to our otherwise amateurish efforts. I, however, discovered that I had considerable stage fright. Despite serious effort, I found it almost impossible to invent and believe in a backstory, and thus I was incapable of truly immersing myself in another character and escaping from myself. I was therefore confined to supporting roles in *Our Town* and *Bus Stop*. I did manage to carry off, in a workmanlike way (but no better than that), the meatier role of Marco in *A View from the Bridge*.

The female lead in all of those productions was the post commander's daughter. Anne was attractive and smart, a Smith College graduate. She was self-assured and outwardly confident. She craved more intellectual challenge than she was finding among the many younger officers who pursued her. We slowly became friendly, and eventually much more. I discovered that she, too, was struggling with her identity and what to do with her life. As a peripatetic army brat, she was rootless and restless, and she felt unsatisfied by the social whirl of a high-ranking officer's family.

Anne would prod me about my lack of career focus and ambition and my self-righteous moralizing. It was the kind of push I needed. One evening, I was at her residence for dinner when her father came home. Later she said angrily, "You should have stood up when my father came into the room, not because he is a general but because he is my father!" She was teaching me manners as well. On another evening I related to her father my saga about the Army Language School. He smiled wryly and said, "Catch-22." I was impressed that he was familiar with the book, which had only recently been published and was revered by all of us who detested our military service.

Anne's parents welcomed me with genuine civility. This exposure to stability, success, and maturity helped me to weigh my future more thoughtfully as my discharge date slowly came into view. I was determined to become the kind of person Anne would take seriously. She helped convince me that I really could become a contender.

While I hated being in the army, I loved being in Europe. It felt familiar and culturally comfortable. I decided that I would apply to be discharged in Europe and then see if I could build a life there. I had to make that decision at least six months prior to my end date, and I filed my paperwork on time. This was actually before Anne and I became serious. I went to the post library and compiled a list of American companies that had more than a thousand employees in Europe. I thought they would make logical targets for job hunting. I wrote to about twenty-five of the largest companies, offering my invaluable services. I did not receive a single reply.

That experience, and Anne's prodding, made me come to the realization that I did, in fact, need more schooling if I hoped to do anything that would be rewarding and satisfying. I went back to the library and searched through college catalogs. One describing a master's degree in public administration stood out and struck the right chord. It was not one of the professions I had rejected; it was not "shallow commercialism," and it involved public service, which had positive connotations. And it seemed to cut across many disciplines: budgeting, finance, planning, urban studies, transportation, and more. I would not have to limit (or commit) myself to any predetermined path professionally or functionally. Tentatively, at least, I had found an initial direction.

In digging through my few boxes of memorabilia to support my recollections for this memoir, I came across a letter I had written in September, 1964, about a hundred days before my discharge date. It captures fairly well my mindset at the time. Since my letter to President Kennedy had produced results, I imagine I thought a similar one to his brother, Bobby (who was running for the Senate from New York at the time), might also prove fruitful. The letter contained the following paragraphs:

With agonizing clarity, my military experience has set in proper perspective those values of human decency and freedom that the army is established to defend but which unfortunately it must, to a large extent, internally deny. This experience has forged a determination and a sense of urgency to want to pursue the defense and propagation of these values and has settled in my conscience the proper means. I wish to devote my energies to public service on the highest and most meaningful levels possible. Though the aims of the American international commitment are often frustrated, and though the democratic process is often excruciatingly slow and cumbersome in battling domestic woes, I believe in them and wish to pursue them.

The rise to prominence of the new school of ultra-conservatives is another motive for my wanting to become involved in our country's politics . . . I have felt myself invariably drawn toward the liberal pole for political adherence, and I found in the New Frontier identification and agreement on the basic principles of political philosophy. The new conservatism is a force and philosophy that must be faced head-on, not simply by vituperative attacks on Senator Goldwater's rashness, but by a careful unveiling of the basic fallacies of the principles upon which it is based. The defeat of its figurehead in November will be a setback but it will not be a cure. The atmosphere of national introspection and moral awareness that President Kennedy began to create is the only proper method to establish a healthy climate of political awareness throughout the country and an environment wherein intelligent and constructive liberalism and conservatism can thrive. I want to work to improve this awareness . . .

I am, therefore, writing to offer my services in hopes that they can be used in some aspect of the congressional or federal complex . . . If, after November 3,

I can be of service to you as senator of New York, or if I can serve in another aspect on the federal or state level, I would be deeply appreciative and honored.

I actually received a signed response to this turgid expression of youthful idealism and naivete. Kennedy thanked me for my "outstanding letter" and said he would be in touch "as the need arises." That felt good, but it had exactly the same practical effect as my other unanswered letters seeking employment.

As my remaining days in the army ticked down to about sixty, I was adopting the short-timer's standard attitude: arrogant and uncooperative but just short of punishable. One morning, an exasperated Sergeant Harrigan came to me and announced, "Shostal, your attitude has gotten so bad, we're going to send your ass on TDY to Paris." I had applied for every TDY (temporary duty) assignment to Paris that had come through our administrative unit but was always told, "Sorry, you are too valuable." Now I was being sent as *punishment*—because Sergeant Harrigan was sure that the per diem allowance (which, as I recall, was twelve dollars per day) was insufficient to live decently. But this was the era of Frommer's *Europe on Five Dollars a Day*. I spoke half-decent French and could easily manage on twelve dollars. I was ecstatic.

In Paris I spent about two weeks working in the mail room for some high-level NATO conference. Because some of the material was highly classified, they needed someone with a Cosmic Top Secret clearance, and I filled the bill. I found a room in the Hôtel des Deux Continents, a charming little place on the Rue de Seine on the Left Bank that charged about $3.50 a night. I ate lunch in a NATO cafeteria for next to nothing. I was in Paris with money to spare! To top it all off, Anne managed to come to Paris, squired by some young man with a title. She would sneak away and meet me for late-night dinners and romantic walks along the Seine.

February 4, 1965, finally arrived, and with it my discharge. I was a civilian again. I moved from the enlisted barracks to the general's residence to be with Anne while we tried to figure out our futures. By this time, I was completely committed to going to graduate school in the fall, so I needed to get back to the United States to begin the application process. This did not give us much time. We took a trip to visit my brother, who was stationed in Brussels at the time, and then went on to Andermatt in the Swiss Alps. But the clock was ticking. It was time for me to go home, and I arranged for a military flight to New York. With a painful and emotional parting, we said goodbye. We sensed that this separation might well mean the end of our relationship, which proved true. It was time for both of us to go our own ways. Not surprisingly, Anne went on to great things.

SEVEN

NYU TO ALBANY

I returned home to Peekskill in the early spring of 1965. My first target was the Harvard graduate school of public administration, then called Littauer, now the Kennedy School. Its catalog made clear that the school was oriented primarily toward mid-career government officials with the grounding and promise to quickly assume the mantle of public service leaders. The school accepted only a handful of applicants directly from the undergraduate ranks, and only those with exemplary academic records. It soon became clear that I would not make the cut. I then turned to New York University's graduate program, which offered a highly respected curriculum and, to my surprise, welcomed me with open arms.

Military service and graduate school meant that I could continue to defer repayment of my undergraduate student loans. I was able to arrange for some VA tuition assistance to cover part of the cost of the NYU program and my father agreed to pay for the rest. I would work at my father's office, which was now a mature and established business but still a small family enterprise. Our agreement was that I would work about twenty hours a week, earning enough of a salary to live independently. After the forced communal quarters of the army, I craved a place of my own where I could enjoy my new freedom and privacy. I had been a captive pupa in the military cocoon, and I yearned to spread my wings.

I rented a studio apartment, with a separate kitchen, in a brownstone on West End Avenue at 92nd Street, for ninety-eight dollars a month. It was the first of several homes I would occupy on the Upper West Side of Manhattan. I enrolled in an introductory course at NYU that summer. I was a highly motivated student and things were beginning to fall into place for me. But not for my parents.

I had maintained a fairly steady and deeply important correspondence with my father throughout my time in the army. From him I knew that my mother's physical and mental health had been deteriorating. She had long suffered from migraine headaches. On a recent—and rare—vacation trip to the Caribbean, she had discovered, in the glaringly bright sunlight, that her vision was seriously compromised; she had glaucoma. The combination of afflictions led her to rely increasingly on medication. At the time, I did not know that her first love, the man who had initially helped her with her studies in Vienna and was now a doctor in the United States, all too readily kept her supplied with opioids. She became an early abuser and spent some time in a psychiatric ward at, as I remember, Grasslands Hospital in nearby Valhalla, New York. Grasslands was a county facility but was part of the state system whose scandalous conditions were so shockingly brought to light in the early 1970s, most famously regarding Willowbrook Hospital on Staten Island.

In today's climate of opioids awareness, and with proper therapeutic care and antidepressant medication, my mother might well have been able to address her issues. But not at that time and not in those places. In a letter to my father in March 1964, I wrote: "Mom described the horrors of state hospitals in such vivid colors that they really appalled me." My brother, Pierre, also recalls her citing chilling examples of the ugly conditions and her extreme unhappiness at the idea of possibly having to go back there. My father maintained that private care either inside or outside of those facilities was simply beyond his means at the time.

My father's emotional remoteness aggravated the situation. All he could bring himself to express in his brief memoir was this:

Her last years were not happy ones. She suffered from migraines and depressions. Our children had left home. Her teaching job at St. Peter's was coming to its end and our marriage was not in good shape. I cannot feel free of guilt; I should have shown more patience and better understanding.

As a matter of fact, he broached the idea of separation as early as 1963, a feeling my mother did not share. In January 1964, she came to Europe to stay with my brother in Brussels in order to bolster her spirits and reconnect with him. The miserable weather there at that time of year spurred my brother to bring her to Paris for a few days, hoping that the setting and language she loved so much would revive her spirits. I joined them there.

I subsequently wrote to my father: "She says that a pleasant turn of events would of course bring everything back to normal and to happiness, but even the worst she can face with resigned but sad determination. Her strength is admirable and I even tend to be optimistic. But of course the crux of the matter for her is whether the marriage will be able to be patched up again. She repeated often your words that it was your fondest wish to be able to find again the desire to be together but at the moment you needed separation. She recognizes that any lack of feeling on your part is not a question of malice or unconcern but of inability and exhaustion."

I had no basis for whatever optimism I felt. Early in June 1965, my father flew to Europe to attend my brother's wedding in Brussels. Pierre was marrying a French woman whom he had met while stationed there. Although I had moved into my West End apartment by then, my father and I agreed that I would stay home and try to keep in close contact with my mother as she had been very shaky in recent weeks. In conversations with her in person and on the phone, I had become increasingly concerned about her acutely sad mental state.

I called her one evening to tell her I would come out and visit the next day. She said nothing that seemed to indicate an imminent crisis, but I was troubled by her flat tone and vowed to myself that, when I arrived, I would make an urgent attempt to try to help pull her out of her terrible state of mind. It was naive of me, and I was too late.

I found her in her nightgown, sprawled on her bed. The sheets were soiled with feces; her bowels had let go. She was cool and clammy. I tried to feel for a pulse. I could not feel anything and pressed harder. For a moment I thought I felt something but realized it was only my own pulse. I called the police (911 did not yet exist). The dispatcher said they would not respond if she was dead, and they told me to call a physician. I hung up and had no idea what to do. The scene was filthy and I found half a case of whiskey in the closet. This was a complete surprise; she had been a very light drinker. I stripped her clothes and bed and threw the soiled items into the bathtub to wash them out. I carried her into the adjacent room and put a blanket over her. I called the police again and said I thought she might still be alive. The dispatcher agreed to send someone. I waited, frantic with shock and confusion.

At some point I poured out the whiskey and threw the bottles away. I suppose I was embarrassed by the clues to what had happened. It seemed clear to me that she had taken an overdose of pills along with the liquor. I do not remember if there was a pill bottle by her bedside, but I assume so. Was it intentional? Probably, but she might have just miscalculated. I had been concerned by our conversation the night before, but had not thought it significantly more alarming than other recent exchanges. There had been no threat or hint of imminent danger. She had signed off with a friendly enough closing. Was she getting back at my father through me? I will never have the answer to my questions, which makes those final images of her all the more painful.

A state trooper arrived and coolly confirmed that my mother was dead. He reprimanded me for moving the body. He said that normally they would have to investigate any unattended death, but they would not need to do so if her doctor would confirm that her death was from natural causes. I found the phone number for her doctor, who agreed to come right away. He examined her briefly and signed a death certificate indicating heart failure as the cause.

I was able to find a funeral home to come and take care of things. I also had to get word to my father and brother. I had no phone number or other contact information with which to reach them. I knew enough to contact the State Department and ask them to track my brother down. I think it took one and a half days before my message reached him and I delivered the grim news. I then had to wait another day or two for them to arrive. For support, I reached out to Al Hughes and his wife, Yvonne. He had been my Latin teacher at St. Peter's and they had remained close friends with my mother. They invited me over for solace and comfort. Then, back in my apartment, I kept listening to a record of Beethoven's "Pastoral Symphony," which has remained for me the most emotionally resonant piece of music that I know.

I tried to make sense of what had happened to my mother. Of course I could not. She had a brilliant, incisive mind. She had endured so many hardships and almost insuperable challenges and had overcome them. Finally, when the world could open up for her, when we had become relatively financially secure, when her sons were launched, when she could have pursued the dreams of intellectual and perhaps even professional fulfillment that she had deferred for so long, her marriage collapsed and with it her capacity to cope. Was it the inability of my father to respond to her emotional needs? Was it inadequate and inappropriate medical treatment and the horrible prospect of a return to a public institution? Or was it simply that her addiction and her struggle to deal with it had just overwhelmed her? It was some combination of all of these factors, I suppose, but she took the answers with her. It seemed clear to both my brother and me that it was no coincidence that my mother acted as she did on my brother's wedding day. It is an indescribable pity that she was not able to reap the rewards of a life that she had largely sacrificed for her family. She deserved so much better.

My father and brother returned and we held a very small family gathering at a Westchester County cemetery where my father had reserved several plots. My mother was buried next to her mother-in-law, who had never approved of her modest Catholic origins. My father's eyes grew moist when he placed a red rose on my mother's coffin as it was lowered into her grave.

A few weeks later, when I was alone with my father, he turned to me and asked, "Did Mom kill herself?"

I had been half-expecting him to raise this with me at some point, since we had not discussed the circumstances of her death in any detail. Still, I was unprepared for the moment. I sensed the pain and guilt in his expression.

"No," I said, "she did not."

He looked relieved but not completely convinced. He did not press me for more specifics. I mentioned this exchange to my brother shortly afterward, and Pierre strongly urged me to maintain my silence. I did, and the subject never came up again.

In the fall, I began my master's studies in earnest and pursued them seriously. I reveled in my return to the independence of civilian life. Often, I would stay up most of the night studying, setting my FM radio dial to 104.3, WNCN, an independent classical music station at the time. At midnight, I would turn on "Listening with Watson," always introduced by Mozart's "Eine kleine Nachtmusik." Occasionally, Bill Watson would stack the commercials at the front end of the program and try to squeeze in all of Beethoven's thirty-two piano sonatas without interruption. I don't think he ever managed to play them all by his sign-off time of 6:00 a.m.

I commuted from my Upper West Side apartment on the Seventh Avenue subway to Washington Square in Greenwich Village, where NYU's Graduate School of Public Administration (GPA, later renamed the Robert F. Wagner School of Public Service in honor of the former mayor) was located. I found the Village altogether too grungy and bohemian for my relatively conservative tastes. I was largely ignorant and unappreciative of the area's emerging role as a mecca for creative artists of all kinds who made it one of the most exciting breeding grounds of intellectual ferment in the tumultuous 1960s.

Working at my father's office at 545 Fifth Avenue, I was able to develop a fully adult relationship with him. My part-time job also gave me a chance to realistically test whether I should enter the business, as he (and particularly my uncle) dearly hoped. I had resisted that path, suspecting that it would not fulfill my yearning for a more consequential career. But since I still lacked a clear understanding of what the business was all about—knowing only that it offered a much faster road to financial stability than graduate school did—I felt I could not simply dismiss it.

The work of a photo agency required some imagination and intelligence to match clients' often inexact requests with the pictures we had. But it consisted primarily of the mechanical drudgery of sitting at a light table and looking through endless files of transparencies while trying to remember where that picture of the little boy walking through the woods might be. Was it filed under "Children" or "Forests" or "Hiking" or "Maine"? When we did make a sale (actually, we rarely sold a picture, only its reproduction rights for that use), there was the negotiation of a price for that use. While certain uses, such as in textbooks—which, along with calendars, were the backbone of the business—had standard fees, many transactions involved confrontational haggling, which was just not part of my nature. I also sensed that our little industry was radically changing and that our business model would not last long. Cataloging and labeling the individual photos was still done with manual typewriters. Desktop computers might have still been a long way off, but multipurpose graphic design firms were already beginning to gobble up small enterprises like ours.

Almost every day, dozens and dozens of photographs would be submitted for inclusion in our files. Some were by photographers whom we knew and regularly represented and were of known and valued subjects (western sunsets, New England villages, beach scenes with seagulls). Others, like first novels, arrived unsolicited. Sometimes the pictures came in response to needs we made known (e.g., famous buildings or places, more party scenes with people who had already signed releases, etc.), but mostly they were what the photographers liked to shoot or what they saw when traveling. All had to be evaluated for technical quality and for subject-matter value.

We did almost no advertising of our services, relying on existing clients, word-of-mouth, and our credit lines to stimulate new business. I argued that we needed to be more proactive. My father gave me a budget of $1,000 (a substantial sum for him at the time) and told me to do what I thought would work. I selected the cutest picture we had of a little boy, on the theory that everyone liked kids, and I sent out a mailer to hundreds of potential customers. I don't think it elicited a single response. Not only did I not enjoy the business very much, but it was quite clear that it would not be fulfilling for me, and I did not have the talent or vision to grow it into something that would remain competitive in the marketplace. My father's vote of confidence, however, was deeply meaningful.

During this time, I saw my Uncle Robert regularly outside of the office. He had a small but comfortable rent-controlled apartment with a Murphy bed on 72nd Street near Riverside Drive, not far from my apartment. I would have dinner with him there almost every week, prepared by a woman who knew how to cook the European dishes that he and I liked. My uncle was completely unlike my father. His cerebral palsy condition limited his physical movements but not his spirit. He liked to drink (he claimed it calmed his spasms) and had a bawdy sense of humor. He loved to tell and hear jokes. Our evenings together were lively and enjoyable. Despite his handicap, he always had girlfriends. His marriage had broken up and he seemed to have a strained relationship with his two daughters, but he was nearly always in a good humor. He loved the business that my father felt shackled by. When he died of a stroke some years later, the outpouring of affection and admiration for him from many of our hundreds of photographers genuinely surprised my father.

With regret, I made it clear to my father and uncle that I would follow the path of my studies rather than take over the business, and they began to look seriously into other options to address the agency's future and their looming retirement needs (they were fifty-eight and sixty, respectively). They entered into negotiations with a competitor, a small firm headed by two men in their forties. My father and uncle proposed a deferred compensation sale of our business to "the boys." Under the terms of the deal, all four would initially split the proceeds of the combined business evenly. Each year thereafter, for twelve years, my father's and uncle's share would diminish by one percent and theirs would increase by the same amount. After twelve years, my father and uncle would receive twelve percent whether they worked or not, encouraging them to retire. I helped my father negotiate the rather complicated terms and was pleased that he often took my advice. It turned out that I was better at that sort of thing, and his confidence in me continued to boost my ego. Regardless of the terms, however, the success of the merger depended largely on the goodwill of our partners, and they proved fair and decent men who more than lived up to their obligations under the agreement.

Having finally settled on proceeding along the public administration path with my father's tacit blessing, I focused even more sharply on my studies and, for the first time since St. Peter's, was a straight-A student. The lessons I had learned during my painful military years seemed to be sticking. I was particularly stimulated by a course in administrative law, taught by John Capozzola, and I even toyed with the idea of attending law school. A bit of sober reflection about the costs and the time involved quickly put an end to that notion. But I impressed Professor Capozzola sufficiently that he asked me and another student, Larry Bender, to serve as student researchers for a book project he was overseeing that would be written by Sterling Spero. Professor Spero was a leading scholar of public employee labor relations, and New York State was considering new legislation—which would become the Taylor Law*—to bring some order to this largely unregulated field. The assignment came with a modest stipend and could also provide the basis for my master's thesis. I would be paid to finish my degree and I jumped at the chance. This would later prove to be a watershed event.

As part of our research for the book project, Larry and I were sent on a tour of Midwestern cities that had more highly evolved public employee labor relations than New York. We were assigned to interview union leaders and government officials who negotiated contracts, tape and transcribe the interviews, and then summarize our findings. We went to Cincinnati,

* The Public Employees Fair Employment Act, more commonly known as the Taylor Law, is Article 14 of the New York State Civil Service Law, which defines the rights and limitations of unions for public employees in New York.

Detroit, Madison, and Milwaukee. Milwaukee was an historic center of socialist politics and had long focused serious attention on its public workforce. We returned impressed with the knowledge and sophistication of the union representatives we met, for whom the bargaining process was a well-known and refined exercise. Their public-sector employer counterparts, though far more experienced than those in New York, still tended to view the process with suspicion and resentment. As public officials, it was very difficult for them to accept the power of the unions and the essential validity of workers' demands. We also came back convinced that the right to strike, even if limited to nonessential services, was indispensable if the bargaining process was to have any semblance of fairness and balance. Without it, public employee unions had no real leverage to fight for decent wages and benefits for their members.

The most interesting stop was Detroit, where the Teamsters represented most of the city's workforce. The local's leader was Jimmy Hoffa. Two union representatives met us at the local's headquarters and sat with us at a table just inside the front door. It was an enclosed, secure, windowless holding area monitored by surveillance cameras. It felt like a bunker. The union officials reluctantly granted our request to record the meeting. When some other union men passed through, one of the officials we were interviewing snapped, "Watch it, we're on tape." It felt surreal. But all of the Teamster officials with whom we met were helpful and informative. Later, one of them insisted on guiding us around the nightlife of Detroit, "to make sure you guys have a good time."

I completed my coursework in the spring of 1967 and finished my thesis over the summer. It was now time to look for a job. I sent off numerous applications but received only two firm job offers. One was for a budget examiner at the Bureau of the Budget in Washington, DC. I would handle the budget of the United States Coast Guard. There was a bit of irony in this. I had actually applied for the Coast Guard Reserve program prior to enlisting in the army, because it required only two months of active duty, but had not been accepted by the time I enlisted. The second opening was with the Public Personnel Association in Chicago. On the basis of my yearbook experience, I was offered a job in charge of their library and publications. I found neither offer terribly exciting, but both seemed to offer a decent first step. I inclined slightly toward the Chicago job.

Seeking some advice and counsel, I phoned Professor Spero. We talked it through and he agreed that the Public Personnel Association seemed to offer a bit more opportunity for future growth. I was about to hang up when I heard him say, "Wait a minute. I was talking to Bill Ronan the other day." Ronan was the former dean of NYU GPA, who had followed Spero in that role and went on to serve as Governor Nelson Rockefeller's secretary (chief of staff). Ronan had just moved on to head the newly formed Metropolitan Transportation Authority. "Ronan told me," Spero continued, "that the new guy, Al Marshall [Ronan's replacement as secretary], is looking for staff. Would you be interested? It means living in Albany." I was almost dumbstruck with excitement at the thought but replied, as calmly as I could, "Sure, I would be interested in pursuing that."

The next day, Professor Spero called back and told me to contact Ed Kresky, who had moved from the governor's office to the MTA with Ronan. I phoned Ed, who turned out to be a graduate of NYU GPA, though with a PhD, and we set up a meeting. Several days later, I went to Ed's office and we had a lively conversation that ended with him saying I should follow up with a call to Ron Pedersen, Al Marshall's deputy in Albany.

This would not be the last time that Edward Mordecai Kresky would play a pivotal role in my career. He became a dear friend and mentor who inexplicably took me under his wing. Ed was one of those rare people who knew how to help younger people, and he delighted in doing so. In addition to being one of the most capable people I have ever come across, he was also one of the kindest. Ed loved to tell stories and with little provocation would spin endless yarns, often very funny, about the inner workings of New York's Byzantine politics.

A few years after I first met him, Ed would play a critically important role in rescuing New York City from the financial insolvency toward which it seemed headed in the 1970s. Ed had helped to draft the legislation creating the Municipal Assistance Corporation (MAC) and had worked to secure its passage in the state senate early in 1975. From June 1975 until June 1987, he served as MAC's vice chairman (Felix Rohatyn was its chairman and became a great friend and admirer of Ed's). MAC was the state agency authorized by the new law to borrow money and help pay the city's debts. Ed then had the unenviable task of trying to persuade potential lenders that New York City still was a good bet. He did that so well that when he died in 2013, the headline on the *New York Times*'s obit stated simply: "Edward M. Kresky, Who Calmed Fiscal Panic, Dies at 88." A fitting tribute to this very good man.

In 1982, from left to right: Felix Rohatyn, chairman of the Municipal Assistance Corporation (MAC); Eugene Keilin, executive director of MAC; and Ed Kresky. (Dith Pran/New York Times/Redux)

I made my way to Albany and met with Assistant Secretary Ron Pedersen, a laconic, laid-back upstater. It became clear during our interview that I came well recommended, and that if I was willing to move to Albany, I had a job. I would be a program assistant (later upgraded to an associate) on the governor's staff at a salary of $10,000 a year, more than was being offered by either of the other two positions that I had been considering. I was giddy with my good fortune and accepted on the spot.

I moved north to start my new job in October 1967. Albany, at that time, was a drab place. Notwithstanding William Kennedy's colorful novels about the city, it was a bleak place to live. State government dominated every aspect of the town, making for a narrow and stifling culture. Winters were brutally cold. Local politics were still in the hands of the country's last remaining Democratic machine, so vividly described by Kennedy, with such things as fixing assessed values and issuing snow-removal contracts subject to the whim of party officials.

I found a very livable one-bedroom apartment within walking distance from the state capitol for $110 a month. I bought a brand-new 1967 powder-blue Mustang, a model destined to become a classic. I had enough money for a comfortable bachelor's lifestyle and to begin paying down my student debt. Almost overnight, I had gone from the world of a struggling student with modest horizons to a new high-visibility, high-energy world with seemingly unlimited potential. I was now part of the famous "well-oiled Rockefeller machine" that operated on the national, and even international, stage. By using his vast personal wealth to augment state funding for staff and resources, Nelson Rockefeller created the perception of a uniquely efficient and expert administration.

The program staff, the governor's policy arm, was an evolving work in progress. Under Bill Ronan's direction, it had become an elite and high-powered group of fewer than a half-dozen experts who exercised considerable authority and initiative in developing and overseeing Rockefeller's activist, far-reaching agenda. Under previous governors who pursued far less ambitious programs, agencies enjoyed more direct access filtered only by the Budget Division's prism of financial impact. When Ronan left, his staff exited with him, moving on to other major positions in and out of government. At first, Al Marshall—who had come up through the Budget Division—was inclined to return more toward the historic organizational structure, in which the governor's staff played only a limited coordinating role. Fortunately for me, this meant that Al was initially willing to hire people with less in-depth substantive knowledge and experience.

The program staff was assigned a portfolio of state agencies for which we were to serve as liaison to the governor's office. Over time, with Rockefeller's insistence on leading rather than following the policies and activities of his state agencies, Al was forced to assign more and more responsibility to the program staff. The agency heads probably welcomed Al's initial budget office orientation, only to see power and control revert to the executive chamber with centripetal inevitability. We handled correspondence to and from the governor in our areas, funneled and vetted problems that required the governor's attention, managed requests from the agencies for action by the governor, helped develop the annual legislative program for our agencies, drafted press releases, and transmitted directions from the governor's office to the commissioners. Our phone calls to the heads of the agencies and their deputies were not always welcome. The seasoned heads of those departments often did not appreciate what they called "government by program associate," suspecting that the requests came from us rather than directly from the governor or Al Marshall—and, of course, they were often right. For us, it was a heady amount of responsibility.

Perhaps because the army had thought I was a teacher, I was assigned education (dealing both with the semiindependent Education Department that governed the primary and secondary school systems and the burgeoning state university system). As if this were not enough, I was given criminal justice, including state police and the Division of Military and Naval Affairs, as well as parks. I was also to help Ron Pedersen, whose plate was quite full with his deputy function, most of the public authorities, and environmental issues. It was quite a portfolio for a twenty-seven-year-old with no useful experience.

All of us were young and inexperienced but we adapted as nimbly as possible to our outsized responsibilities. I found that asking questions, honestly and seriously, and then applying basic common sense to the complex issues and decisions facing us was the formula that worked well for me.

It also seemed more palatable to the senior officials of the state agencies with whom we dealt, rather than just relying arrogantly on the weight of our position.

Barry Van Lare handled social services and John Garrison (who had preceded me by a year at both Harvard and NYU) had health and mental hygiene. Mary McAniff (who would later marry Ed Kresky) was assistant secretary for intergovernmental relations. Mary is a truly remarkable person. She matched Ed Kresky in kindness and generosity of spirit and was at least as smart. Rockefeller relied heavily on Mary to deal with other governors, particularly via the activities of the national and Republican conferences of governors. Mary served as a liaison to the Advisory Commission on Intergovernmental Relations, a panel that did some of the best work on national/state relationships and our federal structure in general. I had studied a number of its reports in graduate school. In addition, she dealt with Congress and with federal legislation, which Governor Rockefeller was always trying to shape to the state's benefit.

Mary played a major role in helping to develop the landmark federal revenue-sharing program that was implemented by the Nixon administration but did not survive the Reagan retrenchment. She coined the phrase "nickel on the dollar" to describe what we got back from Washington compared to what we sent down. Rockefeller loved that phrase so much that he kept using it long after Mary dispatched urgent memos pointing out that policy changes and further analysis showed it was really about eleven or twelve cents, or a bit more. She, too, became—and remains—a very close friend. Recently, Mary and I had a nostalgic chuckle when hearing Governor Andrew Cuomo make the same argument in very much the same terms about how much more New York sends to Washington than it gets back in federal aid. (Cuomo was responding to then-Senate Majority Leader Mitch McConnell's unhelpful suggestion that states heavily impacted by the coronavirus should consider bankruptcy rather than seeking federal assistance.)

The same week I joined the staff, Harry Albright came on board in the newly created position of deputy secretary to the governor. It was not immediately clear what Harry's role was. He had been counsel to the state chapter of AFSCME, the public employee union that represented most state employees. Although he was much closer to the center of power than I was, we became good friends. Harry was also a Democrat. The subject of my party preferences had never come up during my job interview. It was made clear that I should sign on only if I were comfortable with Rockefeller's policies. Since he was probably the most socially progressive governor in the nation at the time, party affiliation presented no problem for me.

A couple of months after I started, the garbage strike of February 1968 erupted in New York City. Trash piled up as the sanitation workers walked off their jobs, defying a court order to end the strike that also sent their leader, John DeLury, to jail under the new Taylor Law. Rockefeller and Mayor Lindsay battled publicly and privately over how best to respond. Characteristically, John Lindsay, the youthful and charismatic politician with presidential aspirations of his own, won the public relations war while Rockefeller just wanted to solve the problem. Harry Albright later told me about a phone conversation that had occurred within his earshot. All he heard was Rockefeller's end of the conversation, which ended with: "John, are you telling me you refuse to meet with the governor to try to settle this thing?" The governor, obviously hearing a negative response, slammed down the phone. It was the final rupture of a seriously deteriorating relationship. Soon after, Harry was asked by the governor to put together a white paper detailing the substance and chronology of the events and decisions involved in this agonizing situation. The governor wanted to document what he viewed as his good faith efforts and Lindsay's self-serving recalcitrance in trying to settle the strike. Harry asked me to help him. For me, it was an early glimpse into power politics and high-level decision-making. A summary of our paper appeared in the *Saturday Evening Post* several months later. By then, however, public interest had moved on, fueled by the cavalcade of dramatic events that dominated 1968.

In subsequent months, Les Mikalson, Tom Eichler, and Art Quern would join the staff, adding more depth, but it was still a remarkably small group. It was also a simpler time in some ways. The state budget for 1966-67 was a mere $4 billion, numerically less than the projected gap in the fiscal year 2020 $175 billion state financial plan, and only one-fifth of the state budget in today's dollars.

Al Marshall, as head of Rockefeller Center, in front of the Christmas tree, December 1979. (Marilynn K. Yee/The New York Times/Redux)

Presiding over the staff and operationally over all of state government was Alton G. Marshall. He was a remarkable leader. With his shock of white hair, ex-Marine demeanor, and booming voice, Al was a commanding presence. He was also the most cunning and effective manager I ever met, and easily lived up to his sobriquet of "the Silver Fox." An endless stream of paper crossed his desk but nothing stayed there; his desk was always clean. Having served as deputy budget director before Rockefeller tapped him to be secretary to the governor, he had a thorough knowledge of the workings of state government and could see through any administrative tricks that the agencies might try to pull. Behind his favorite façade—"I'm just a poor country boy from Fenton, Michigan"—was a keenly analytic and strategic mind.

Al was a graduate of Syracuse University's prestigious Maxwell School of Citizenship and Public Affairs and a serious student of government. He understood that senior public officials like himself never had sufficient time or information to make perfect decisions about the complex problems they faced. His answer to that was a life lesson for me: make the best decisions you can, and then put your effort into maximizing the outcomes—rather than second-guessing yourself about whether you could have made better choices.

In order to try to improve the quality of the knowledge base underlying the state's major decision-making, Al advocated for the creation of the Office of Planning Coordination (OPC). His government experience had taught him that if planning was left to the line agencies, it would be shunted aside by the compelling operational considerations of the daily inbox. But if it was assigned to a separate central planning entity, it would never be available within the time frame that the agencies and the governor's office needed. It would be irrelevant.

Al's answer was what he called functional planning agencies for health, transportation, etc. They would focus on large questions over longer time frames that required major investments such as: how many hospital beds will be needed in the next fifteen years, and where should they be? What combination of rail, bus, or new roads will be the best way to move people in certain increasingly congested areas twenty years from now? OPC would oversee, filter, and channel those studies so that they could be brought to bear in a timely way to help the governor make better annual capital budget decisions and handle the inevitable crises. OPC served a marginally useful function but could not resolve what is fundamentally an irreconcilable conundrum: the clash of sober, long-term planning with the press of urgent and volatile daily political business.

In addition to being a serious student of public administration, Al was the most nuanced and effective manager of people I ever worked for. My colleagues in the Program Office were first-rate and dedicated, but we were not uniquely talented. Al was able to get superb results from the brightest, and solid and serviceable work from the rest. He knew whom to yell at and whom to nudge more gently to get the best results. Most importantly, he knew how to motivate.

One of our basic tasks was to write memos for the governor when an issue had been vetted and was ready for his decision. We followed a proven formula: we had to describe the problem, summarize the options for addressing it, and make a recommendation. The memo could not be more than a page and a half. At the bottom would be two lines: "Yes" and "No." Writing such a memo was an extraordinary discipline, since nearly all of the issues that required the governor's attention were complicated and difficult. All of the memos went to the governor from Al. From our standpoint, the ideal outcome was when the governor checked the action line (usually "Yes") and scrawled "Excellent" in the upper right-hand corner.

There was one incident involving one of those memos that I drafted, which I will not forget. I no longer recall what the subject was, but I do remember that I was not sure of a certain aspect or fact and I lazily fudged the matter, assuming that Al would know and would fill in the necessary detail. Instead, Al initialed the memo and sent it on, knowing full well the memo's shortcoming. It was returned by the governor with the offending portion circled and a notation from Rockefeller along the lines of: "Al, this is sloppy work; redo." Al sent it back to me without comment. I was horrified. He had taken the heat to teach me a lesson. It hit me with far more force than if he had initially returned it for correction before sending it in or stormed in afterward and reprimanded me for the embarrassment I had caused him. Needless to say, I never did something like that again.

The year 1968 was an incredibly turbulent but compelling time to serve in such rarefied political air. The Vietnam War was intensifying, widening the already bitter divisions within the country. The Tet offensive by the North Vietnamese early in the year had made clear that no end to our military involvement was in sight, and it galvanized the opponents to the war. The assassinations of Martin Luther King, Jr. in April and Bobby Kennedy in June caused numerous cities to erupt in violence, and many

Americans questioned whether our social contract was still valid. It was no secret that Nelson Rockefeller wanted to be president. He had failed in 1964 when he was booed and heckled at the Republican convention by the triumphant Goldwater contingent. He was running again in 1968. National implications colored our responses to what would have been otherwise limited state issues.

While Governor Rockefeller spent time in Albany, the true center of the action, both politically and governmentally, was the New York City office, a pair of brownstones he owned at 22 West 55th Street. I found excuses to spend as much time there as I could. Henry Kissinger prowled the building providing advice on foreign affairs for Rockefeller's presidential campaign. Jackie Robinson, whom the governor retained on a part-time basis to help him with the Black community, could be spotted in the hallways. Rockefeller's commitment to alleviating the plight of Black Americans was genuine and deep. His closest advisor on racial matters was Rev. Wyatt T. Walker, King's chief of staff, who was a board member of the Southern Christian Leadership Council (SCLC) and a founder of the Congress of Racial Equality (CORE). When tragedy struck, Rockefeller quietly paid most of the costs of King's funeral.

As the presidential effort heated up, much of our staff went over to the campaign and transferred to the campaign payroll. I was reassigned to help staff 55th Street and took up residence in an Upper West Side hotel that accepted the state reimbursement rate. One evening, several of us were unwinding in the office. I was chatting with Mary Kresky, Sarah Deland (who would eventually marry Al Marshall), and Nancy Maginnis (who was dating Henry Kissinger and would later marry him). Obviously, professional and social lives overlapped. Nancy was waiting to go out to dinner with Henry, who as usual was working late.

The question for the campaign at that moment was deciding when Rockefeller would announce his position on Vietnam. We knew that this was the subject of the meeting that was going on while we waited, and that a public announcement was imminent. The elevator door opened and Henry stepped out. Mary asked, "Well, Henry, what is the governor going to say?" After a brief and portentous pause, he replied—in his now well-known gravelly voice with its thick German accent—"Okay, here is what we are going to say. First, we will dig a ditch across Vietnam and make it into an offshore island. That will solve the military problem. And then we will send everyone in this country who does not have a job to dig the ditch. That will solve the unemployment problem. Good night. Come on, Nancy." With that, the two of them left, leaving the rest of us uninformed but laughing. Henry's public face was that of a dour intellectual, but he could be very funny.

In 1971, Mary, Nancy Maginnis, Nancy Shea (another staffer), and I used hockey tickets made available by Henry to go to a New York Rangers playoff game. It was the classic triple-overtime game against the Chicago Blackhawks that was won by Pete Stemkowski's sudden-death goal. It was the most exciting sports event I ever attended, slightly surpassing Chris Chambliss's ninth-inning home run against the Kansas City Royals in 1976, which I saw from a box right behind the third base dugout, courtesy of Al Marshall.

The spring, summer, and fall of 1968 and the year of 1969 were an intense and dramatic time. On March 31, 1968, President Lyndon Johnson, facing growing opposition to the Vietnam War and the prospect of defeat in the Wisconsin primary, suddenly abandoned his reelection campaign. After King was killed in Memphis on April 4, riots broke out in Baltimore, Chicago, Washington, and scores of other cities. College campuses were tense and spawned protests; most immediate and worrisome for us was Columbia. When Robert Kennedy, vying with Eugene McCarthy for the Democratic nomination, was assassinated in Los Angeles on June 5, the nation's social and political turmoil escalated still further. Then the Democratic convention in Chicago in late August became the scene of unprecedented confrontations between police and angry anti-war demonstrators. Some of the extreme rhetoric on both sides struck me as calling into question our basic social compact, and America's democratic institutions seemed more fragile than I could ever have imagined possible (until

Trump!). The Democrats nominated Vice President Hubert Humphrey as their standard-bearer. It was a thankless task for Humphrey who, despite his progressive credentials and history within the party, came to stand for the defensive centrist wing of the Democratic Party because of his dutiful service as Johnson's vice president.

The Republican convention had already taken place in early August, again dashing Rockefeller's hopes. In the weeks leading up to that demise, I was meeting with public interest and protest groups of all kinds regarding state issues, trying my best to respect and respond to their concerns, nearly all of which were legitimate. Many of the meetings were about education and school funding. Representatives from minority communities sought more aid for inner-city school districts while Catholic groups argued for financial support for parochial schools. In the meetings, which were intense and emotional, I did my best to communicate and defend our record of support for education and civil rights. When the meetings were with minority groups, I was usually joined by Sam Singletary, Wyatt T. Walker's assistant, who added some credibility to our rhetoric of concern. Nevertheless, I came away from these sessions feeling drained and convinced that we should have been doing even more.

In 1968, presidential primaries still played only a minimal role in the selection of the party's candidate. Gaining the nomination was all about securing the commitment of delegates, who tended to be party regulars. While the delegates were mindful of polls, obtaining their votes was more about building up party loyalty than winning the hearts of potential voters. Rockefeller never toiled in the vineyards of party activities and activists, relying instead on his popularity with voters to gain traction as a viable national candidate. No one on his campaign staff was schooled in the trench warfare of delegate hunting. Since 1964, the party had clearly drifted more and more toward the right. All of Rockefeller's barnstorming, media attention, policy proposals, position papers, and personal warmth could not overcome the deep distrust and even outright animosity of the conservatives who were more and more dominating the GOP.

When Rockefeller's presidential campaign collapsed at the convention, I returned to Albany, where responding to the upheavals all around us remained our office's overriding concern. Al Marshall asked me to staff two cabinet-level committees to coordinate our efforts. Typical of Al's irreverent sense of humor, he named them "The Bleeders" and "The Beaters." The Bleeders were the human services agencies: Social Services, the Office of Economic Opportunity (OEO), and the state university system. The Beaters were, of course, the law enforcement types: state police, criminal justice, and military and naval affairs.

The Bleeders worked on facilitating a number of service delivery programs. The issue I remember most clearly was responding to the unrest among college students that was testing the viability of our higher education system. City University's answer was launching the Open Admissions initiative. Among Rockefeller's signal and most lasting achievements was the expansion of the state university (SUNY) system from a fragmented array of teachers colleges when he became governor in 1959 to a sprawling but unified system of more than a dozen top-notch university centers, four-year colleges, and medical centers. Rockefeller was profoundly committed to preserving this legacy, as was his friend Sam Gould, whom he appointed chancellor in 1964. Rockefeller had brought Gould to SUNY to help build a world-class university system. Gould had served as president of Antioch, chancellor of the University of California at Santa Barbara, and head of educational television for the metropolitan area (at Channel Thirteen) and was known for bringing nontraditional and innovative policies to higher education. But both viewed Open Admissions as a potential threat to the quality of education they had done so much to improve. They recognized, however, the social imperative involved; minority students accounted for only 1.5 percent of CUNY's enrollment at the time.

The colorful Julius C. C. Edelstein was CUNY Chancellor Albert Bowker's deputy, leading the Open Admissions effort. "C. C." stood for Caesar Claude. He was an alumnus of Franklin Roosevelt's White House staff and understood how to navigate political minefields. He lobbied hard and effectively for the state approvals needed to move ahead with Open Admissions. We decided not to oppose his plan and felt that SUNY needed some sort of initiative of its own. Al Marshall directed me to come up with a state program. "But it can't cost much money," he barked.

Working with the supremely capable and personable deputy chancellor, Ernest Boyer, who would follow Gould as chancellor and later served as secretary of education under President Jimmy Carter, we invented SUNY's Full Opportunity Program or FOP—admittedly a less than inspiring acronym. I no longer recall the details, but FOP consisted mostly of administrative actions to facilitate entry of minority and other disadvantaged students to the SUNY system. It did, however, contain the seeds of Empire State College, which Boyer formally established in 1971 when he became chancellor. Today, Empire State is a major component of SUNY, offering individualized, experience-based learning opportunities to thousands of students whose family obligations or job commitments would otherwise put higher education beyond their reach.

The Beaters, on the other hand, focused on maintaining order on the urban streets and college campuses of the state. Our meetings consisted mostly of reviewing reports from the Bureau of Criminal Investigation of the state police concerning potential threats. I remember distinctly one report delivered by a fresh-faced young lieutenant with a blond crew cut. He soberly detailed their concerns about certain activities at SUNY New Paltz, explaining that they were led "by a known [Eugene] McCarthy supporter," as if that proved their explosive potential. I had to bite my lip hard to suppress a sarcastic guffaw.

A serious and ongoing concern was New York City. John Lindsay was doing a superb job of keeping a lid on the city. In shirtsleeves, he walked the streets of Harlem and other Black neighborhoods and established "Little City Halls" in some of the most troubled neighborhoods to demonstrate his personal concern and provide genuine outreach to minority communities. His efforts were working, but we had to prepare for the day when they might not. Tensions were running high on the urban streets of the country's Black communities, and the threat of violence seemed imminent.

One of the historic dynamics of New York politics is friction between the mayor of New York City and the governor. Oddly, it seems worst when they are of the same party. When they are from different parties, clashes tend to be partisan and not personal, and the ground rules are fairly well understood. When the two are from the same party, policies and party affiliation are not the problem—but egos are. Both are almost by definition national figures, often with national political aspirations. Who controls the state's party machinery, who gets credit for successes and blame for failures, and who gets national recognition in the party hierarchy become highly personal and frequently bitter flashpoints. All of these factors came into play in full force in the relationship between Rockefeller and Lindsay.

Despite the fact that the governor and the mayor were not on speaking terms, Al Marshall was able to maintain an effective relationship with Deputy Mayor Bob Sweet, and I worked well with Lindsay's aide, Jay Kriegel. Jay and I were tasked with negotiating a protocol in case the city blew. Our biggest hurdle was the long-standing mindset among state officials that if they were called in, they would be in charge. After all, according to the state constitution and legal structure, cities are "creatures of the state." It did not take me long to become convinced that it would not be a good idea to have the all-white, upstate, sunglasses-wearing state troopers (although excellent in their realm) patrolling New York City streets and telling the NYPD what to do. Al fully agreed, and we were able to override the inclinations of our colleagues. Jay and I put together an agreement that would have us playing a logistical and man power-supporting role to the city. Jay gave me a tour of the command center where we would all convene if worse came to worst. Fortunately, we never had to use it.

With our agreement in place in early 1969, Al, Bob Sweet, Jay Kriegel, and I boarded a state airplane and flew to Washington to meet with the Feds. We wanted to be sure to have clear procedures in place for their assistance "if the balloon went up." We went to the Department of Justice and met with newly appointed Deputy Attorney General Richard Kleindienst, later of Watergate fame. As we entered the room, he greeted us with a superficially friendly but decidedly stern demeanor. He announced proudly: "Before you guys say anything, I want you to know that we are ready and we are behind you 100 percent. If this phone rings and you need help, in hours we'll have our tanks, armored personnel carriers, and the 82nd Airborne on the streets of New York." I watched as Al's and Bob's faces turned ashen. That kind of reaction was exactly what we most feared and had come to DC to head off. I do not recall much about the rest of the meeting except that we devoted our time to ensuring a much more muted federal response focused on social rather than military assistance.

For contrast, the year 1969 also brought the "Summer of Love." By July, we slowly became aware that something extraordinary was about to happen in the Catskills. It was on-again, off-again as permits for a music festival were accepted and then denied. Prospective sites, first in Wallkill and then in Saugerties, fell through before the promoters received approval to hold the event at Max Yasgur's farm in the town of Bethel in the southern Catskills. A gathering that was initially planned for between 10,000 and 20,000 people had grown to an estimated 150,000. In the end, as is well known, more than 400,000 actually showed up. And this was before social media!

In the days leading up to Friday, August 15, the opening date, the switchboard routed a call for the governor to me from H. Clark Bell, a local assemblyman. Concerned about the impact of the event on his constituents, but mostly engaging in a bit of grandstanding designed for media attention, he demanded to talk to the governor about the crisis. I assured him that I would personally speak to Rockefeller and convey his concern. Sensing that the assemblyman had gotten what he wanted, I managed to end the call. In reality, I communicated with the governor only on paper, and through Al Marshall. Had I actually approached the governor, I might have looked vaguely familiar to him but he would not have known who I was.

The next day, Al called me into his office and showed me a copy of the *Middletown Record*, a Hudson Valley newspaper. "I wish you would tell me when the governor appoints you to something," Al said with a half-annoyed smile. "Governor Rockefeller Appoints Festival Coordinator," blared the front-page banner headline. The article read something like: "Assemblyman Clark Bell announced today that, responding to his demand, Governor Nelson Rockefeller has appointed one of his top aides [a wild exaggeration], H. Clyde Schliestel, to be the Woodstock Festival Coordinator . . ."

On behalf of Mr. Schliestel, I apologized to Al. He took my explanation well, and I went back to my desk, not thinking or doing much more about the festival for the remainder of the day. That evening, I drove down for the weekend to New York City to see my girlfriend, Cita. The next morning, hearing the radio news reports, I said to her, "Why don't we drive up there and see what's going on?"

Driving up Route 17 toward Bethel became increasingly difficult as we were beset by mounting congestion and confusion. Using my governor's office shield, which looked like a police badge, I was able to talk my way through several barricades. Making our way around cars that had been abandoned by the roadside, we finally arrived at the state police command post about a mile from the actual event stage. The troopers had commandeered a sportsman's lodge—a large, plain, one-room log building—as their headquarters. A sergeant sat at a typewriter in the middle of the room. On benches along the walls of the room sat twenty or so scruffy, disheveled-looking young men in tattered clothes. I introduced myself and asked if they had arrested those men. He looked around and said gruffly, "Yeah, those three," pointing to one group. "The rest of them are our guys." Then, warming up a bit, he added, "We can't let our undercover guys out of the building. They get twenty yards down the road and someone offers them a joint and we have to arrest them. We don't want to do that. There's a really good feeling out there and we don't want to disturb it. We're trying to stop the hard drugs at the perimeter, but other than that we are just trying to leave things alone."

I did not make much of his comment at the time, but in hindsight I am amazed at how accurately and strategically the state police were tuned in to what was going on. I am unaware of any direction they received from our office or elsewhere. I believe it simply was a case of competent and sensitive leadership by those directly involved.

A few minutes later, the senior officer in command, a state police major, walked in. The sergeant introduced me, and the major said, "Do you want to go for a ride in a helicopter and take a look around?"

I said, "Sure!" and then added, "Mind if I bring my girlfriend?"

"No," he replied, "bring her along."

We clambered into the waiting aircraft and took off. As we ascended, a surreal scene of utter chaos unfolded below. Scores of cars were abandoned along the approach roads, some of them blocking access to large fields that could have accommodated hundreds of vehicles if there had been anyone directing traffic and parking. Approaching the event area itself, we saw an unimaginable mass of people set against the reddish-brown backdrop of a sea of mud. It had rained heavily the night before and the entire area occupied by the attendees was a gooey quagmire. We dodged some of the other helicopters circling the expanse, mostly medical personnel attending to emergencies. We then landed and returned to the lodge, and I thanked the major and left. I did not think to do anything further. As a governmental problem, it seemed under control. As a cultural phenomenon, it was part of another universe.

On Monday morning, I walked into my office in Albany and found myself summoned by Al Marshall. "Where the hell were you?" he roared.

"I was there, Al," I proudly retorted.

"A lot of good that did me!" he answered. "I had to handle all the phone calls myself."

He did not mention, and it did not occur to me to ask him, about any other instructions or directives he or others might have given that helped lead to the legendary outcome of "Peace and Love." The Wikipedia entry states that on Sunday, the governor offered to send in 10,000 National Guard troops but the festival organizers convinced him not to. If that actually happened, I never heard about it. I feel certain that Al, with his exquisite sense of timing and strategy, played a meaningful part in the state's restrained response, but I do not know any of the details.

By late 1969 and early 1970, the modern environmental movement was beginning to gain serious political traction. The publishing of Aldo

Leopold's *A Sand County Almanac* in 1949, and especially Rachel Carson's *Silent Spring* in 1962, provided environmentalists with powerful and popular semi-sacred texts. Young staffer Art Quern argued to us that the proposal for an Earth Day in April was an important development and that we should pay attention to it. More bemused than convinced, Al told him to run with it. Art was more than prescient, as he would prove repeatedly throughout his remarkable career. He became one of our group's most valuable members, was tapped for the White House staff when Rockefeller became vice president, and took over responsibility for the Domestic Policy Council. Art went on to serve as chief of staff to Illinois Governor James Thompson, then chaired Aon Risk Management Services and the Illinois Board of Higher Education. His life was cut tragically short when he died at age fifty-four in the crash of a corporate jet.

Governor Rockefeller was characteristically determined to lead rather than follow state governments in responding to the surge in environmental awareness. A few other jurisdictions had created new agencies in this blossoming field and he was determined to do the same. Al and the governor were both very receptive to ideas for restructuring and reorganizing the state's agencies to more effectively handle the ever-evolving challenges. At the time, we had a rather limited and hidebound Department of Conservation, which administered the "forever wild" areas of the Catskill and Adirondack Forest Preserves and regulated fish and wildlife programs throughout the state. The Health Department housed state activities related to water supply and air and water quality. We decided to put those two elements together to form a new agency consisting of two components. It would be a regulatory entity overseeing the permitting required by the new 1969 National Environmental Policy Act, administering the provisions of all water- and air-quality-related statutes, and handling hunting and fishing licenses and regulations. It would also be the state's planning and policy arm recommending programs and implementing legislation relating to all activities concerning the protection of air, water, and land resources.

This initiative also offered Rockefeller an opening to complete the consolidation of the state park system that he had already begun. State parks had long been administered by separate independent commissions for each part of the state. Previously, New York governors appointed the members of the ten regional commissions, but they elected their own chairmen (they were all men in those days) and operated largely independently. A council of the chairmen, the State Council of Parks, held executive authority over the regions. A division housed in the Conservation Department staffed the council and coordinated rather than oversaw its activities. Rockefeller had managed to wrest appointment authority of the chairmen away from the commissions and secured that power for himself. He then appointed his brother and closest confidant, Laurance, to chair the council. Laurance replaced Robert Moses, who chaired the body from 1924 to 1963, as part of Rockefeller's successful effort to dismantle the empire that the legendary Moses had amassed over the state's parks, transportation, and construction infrastructure. Laurance was an early convert to—and leader of—the environmental movement, and he chaired the Palisades Interstate Park Commission. But these changes still did not constitute effective gubernatorial control over the policies and operations of state parks. Since parks were part of my portfolio, I joined the task force working on the restructuring and took the lead on this part of the effort.

A major figure in our deliberations was Henry Diamond, a suave Southerner from Chattanooga. Henry was a brilliant attorney who served as Laurance's principal staff assistant for environmental matters. He became the new environmental agency's first commissioner. The first, if hardly critical, issue we faced was what to call the entity. Clearly, it had to have the word "environment" in it. Many of the other jurisdictions included "protection" in the title, but this seemed too limiting and proscriptive for what we had in mind. At one meeting, the incumbent commissioner of the existing department, the staid Stewart Kilbourne, a Republican politician from Westchester County, warned that if we did not include the word "conservation" in the title, we would lose the "conservation lobby." Someone brightly volunteered, "Well, how about the Department of Environmental Conservation?" Thus was the cumbersome name birthed.

My major focus was working with the counsel's office in drafting the legislation to create the new parks agency. A key member of our group was Alexander Aldrich, universally known as Sam. He had been head of the Hudson River Valley Commission and, not by coincidence, was the governor's cousin. State parks were clearly a family affair. Sam was a lawyer and also a graduate of NYU GPA, and a delightful and capable man. We worked extremely well together. Sam would become the first commissioner of the Office of Parks, Recreation and Historic Preservation when the agency came into being in 1971. It became an "office" in the executive department rather than a full-fledged department on its own simply because the state constitution limited the number of departments to twenty, and the roster was full. The governor would appoint the commissioner. The regional commissions would continue to exist but would become advisory, as would the state council. The governor would appoint the chairmen and the regional managers who would report to the commissioner. Gubernatorial control would be clear if not explicit, a textbook public administration solution.

One of the first things a new entity seeking identity and credibility needs is a logo. Sam wanted the classic maple leaf. We informed the various regions, which balked but had no effective way to object. The Palisades Region objected, and had the clout to do so. Palisades was, in fact, an interstate compact, created by agreement between the states of New York and New Jersey and formalized via federal legislation. We could not impose our decision on the representatives from New Jersey. Moreover, Laurance Rockefeller was still chairman of the Palisades Interstate Park Commission and conveyed its concern. We had to find a compromise. In a classic Solomonic gesture, Palisades would be granted an exception; it would be allowed to keep its existing oak leaf but it had to be displayed *within* the state maple leaf. Today, as you drive along the Palisades Interstate Parkway, the jumbled logo you see along the roadside is an oak leaf inside a maple leaf! Certainly not a triumph of graphic design.

Another major program launched by the governor in which I was heavily involved was a significant overhaul of the criminal justice system. Having absolutely no background in any aspect of this complex discipline, one of the first things I did was to tour several of the state's prisons to see them firsthand. The most upsetting of these visits was to Dannemora, the maximum-security facility in the far north of the state near Plattsburgh. The feeling of barely contained violence in the yard was palpable. The noise and dust in the cotton factory where inmates made their underwear were almost unbearable. Hard-boiled cynicism among the guards fueled anger and resentment. At lunch in the cafeteria, I heard the guards telling obscene death row jokes inspired by the gruesome fact that the execution facilities had just been transferred that very day from Sing Sing to Dannemora.

Despite my lack of grounding, I had the privilege of working with a profoundly talented, committed, and progressive array of professionals. They maintained their devotion to enlightened policies despite their much greater exposure to what I had seen and to what so many of us have, in a very limited way, experienced in jury duty or other exposures to the system. Leading Governor Rockefeller's reform effort was Richard J. Bartlett. In 1961, Rockefeller had appointed him to head one of the many blue-ribbon panels that the governor was fond of creating to provide him with the solid academic and policy foundation for difficult or unpopular reforms. This one was the Temporary Commission on the Revision of the Penal Law. Dick Bartlett was a Harvard Law graduate who had been a Republican assemblyman representing the Glens Falls area. In the Assembly, he had risen by 1966 to the post of minority whip. Dick distinguished himself and was admired in every endeavor he undertook. He went on to be a state Supreme Court justice, chief administrative judge of the new Unified Court System, and finally dean of the Albany Law School.

Dick became a valued friend and mentor. He invited me to the New York City Harvard Club in 1968 to watch the celebrated Harvard-Yale game of that year. Yale, led by Calvin Hill, who later starred in the NFL, was undefeated and even nationally ranked. Harvard was also undefeated, but not nearly in Yale's class. With two minutes to go, Yale led comfortably 29-13. Then, capping a miracle finish, Harvard tied the score with a two-point conversion as time ran out. The legendary headline the next day in Harvard's newspaper, *The Crimson*, declared: "Harvard Beats Yale 29-29."

The other members of our team were almost as impressive as Dick Bartlett. Peter McQuillan, the Commission's special counsel, took the lead in drafting the comprehensive revision to the Penal Law, which initially took effect in 1967 with final amendments and provisions added in 1971. Wikipedia's description[*] of that legislation is that it modernized "the entire criminal procedure law, ensuring consistency and fairness in sentencing guidelines, and eliminating the many archaic provisions of the existing law that went back to the previous century." Peter headed up the new state Office of Crime Control; Mayor Lindsay then appointed him to the criminal court in 1971. He became a justice on the state Supreme Court, serving for twenty years. He was also named administrative judge of the criminal branch of the state bench.

Archibald Murray had worked in the counsel's office and was brought back to state government as counsel to the New York Crime Control Council. Arch became the first commissioner of our newly created Division of Criminal Justice and then led the Legal Aid Society for twenty years, and he was the first Black president of the New York City Bar Association.

Peter Preiser, perhaps the most intellectual of the group, became the state's director of probation and then succeeded Russell Oswald as corrections commissioner. He also served on the faculty of Albany Law School for over thirty years.

Nelson Rockefeller had recruited Russ to be a member of the state Parole Board and then commissioner of corrections after Russ built a national reputation for progressive parole and prison reform in Wisconsin and Massachusetts. The tragedy at Attica in September 1971—when prisoners' demands for reform led to rioting and hostage-taking that ended with the

* "Peter J. McQuillan," Wikipedia, last modified December 16, 2020, https://en.wikipedia. org/wiki/Peter_J._McQuillan.

deaths of forty-three prisoners and guards—forced Russ to resign and destroyed his prior legacy as an enlightened thinker and practitioner.

Rockefeller assembled this array of talent, uniformly committed to liberal and humanitarian approaches to criminal justice. He seemed personally committed to this philosophy, pushing—mostly unsuccessfully—for more funding to improve prison conditions and rehabilitation programs. Each year around the Christmas holidays, the Capitol Building became an art museum, displaying paintings done by inmates of what are now called correctional facilities rather than prisons. This annual exhibition was a personal favorite of the governor's, who firmly believed in the therapeutic and rehabilitative power of the arts.

Sadly, however, Attica and his later embrace of the harshly punitive legislation that became known as the Rockefeller Drug Laws of 1973 permanently defined his criminal justice legacy as that of a brutal reactionary rather than as a visionary reformer. There can be no denying that the drug laws had a devastating impact, destroying the lives of countless Black men from New York and their families. Why did Rockefeller move in that direction? One thing I can say with reasonable certainty is that his motive was not intentionally racist. With high-level and influential members of the administration like Dick Parsons, Arch Murray, Wyatt Walker, and Evelyn Cunningham—an outspoken Black journalist who led our office on women's issues—and given Rockefeller's close personal relationship with leaders of the Black community, respect for African Americans was a core value that permeated our offices. There were no snide inside racist jokes or sneering superior glances. It was understood that such behavior was simply not what we were about and would not be tolerated.

From my personal vantage point, the drug laws in particular seemed to be the product of an unfortunate collision of influences. First was Nelson Rockefeller's relentless passion to solve problems. Faced with the intractable scourge of the drug epidemic and its impact on public safety, his initial inclination toward liberal policies and solutions did not seem to be working. He had championed the use of methadone, and devoted major state resources to progressive demonstration programs and prison reform. Still, violent crime kept climbing and recidivism rates stubbornly refused to decline. Second, his equally relentless presidential aspirations pushed him to the right in a vain effort to court the growing conservatism of the Republican Party. Nixon had declared the "war on drugs" in 1971. Rockefeller did not want to be outdone. Frustration and ambition, in some combination, pushed him down that disastrous path.

My only personal, in-depth experience dealing directly with Nelson Rockefeller involved my criminal justice responsibilities. In the fall of 1968, Rockefeller was scheduled to testify before Congress on the Omnibus Crime Control and Safe Streets Act. I had drafted the background briefing memo for the governor, tapping into the wide array of expertise that I had at my disposal. On the day before the hearing, I got a call that Al Marshall, who would normally brief the governor and accompany him to the hearing, was sick and could not go. I would have to fill in. Nervous and apprehensive, I tried to imagine what questions the governor might ask me. It finally dawned on me that he would focus on the big picture while most of my memo dealt with details—important facts, but still details. He would want to know what was really at stake. What percentage of our total criminal justice expenditures might the potential grants to New York State make up? What impact might they actually have? I made some hurried phone calls to find the answers.

Seated opposite him on his private plane, a Fairchild F-27 named *Wayfarer*, I held my breath as he started his questions. He opened with exactly what I had guessed; my talent for figuring out the questions on final exams still held. For an hour he grilled me, and I experienced directly the forceful and restless probing for which he was well known. His may not have been the most incisive or profound intellect, but he was persistent and relentless in his pursuit of information and practical answers. By the time we landed in Washington, I felt he knew more about—and had a better grasp of the topic—than I did. I sat behind him during his testimony and provided a few whispered answers to questions posed by members of Congress. I neither starred nor stumbled, but I had survived.

Sometime during this period, I was asked to meet with Peter Sanford, who was seeking state support for his vision to create a maritime museum in the Fulton Fish Market area of Lower Manhattan. Passionate and charismatic, Peter was a superb salesman and I was deeply impressed by his proposal to create a South Street Seaport Museum. I was determined to become the advocate for the project within the administration. In Sam Aldrich I found a willing collaborator to make the project part of the agenda for the new parks agency we were creating. There would be much more to this story in the years ahead.

EIGHT

RETURN TO NEW YORK CITY

The summer of 1970 saw Nelson Rockefeller's campaign for a fourth term as governor move into high gear. Most of the Program Office moved over to the campaign staff, which was based in New York City, and we were transferred to the political payroll. I asked Al Marshall if I could stay in the city after the election and work out of the 55th Street office. To my surprise, he agreed. (I did not know then that he had already decided to leave his post at the end of the year.) I worked mostly on what we called "promises and performance," cataloging the governor's many campaign commitments and what we had done about them. He had amassed an extraordinary record. That led to our clunky but accurate campaign slogan: "He's Done A Lot; He'll Do More."

The campaign had the kind of intensity and camaraderie that is unique to this singular American political ritual. For several months one is totally immersed in what feels like a combination of all-out war and the World Series. The laughter is unbridled and the heartache profound.

We anticipated that Arthur Goldberg, the Democratic candidate, would be a formidable challenger. He was a former Supreme Court justice, appointed by President Kennedy, who had surprisingly resigned from the Court to serve as Lyndon Johnson's representative to the United Nations. He had more impressive credentials than Rockefeller's previous opponents.

He proved, however, an inept campaigner. Trying to appear vigorous and appeal to New York's outdoor constituency, he went on a well-promoted trail hike. When reporters noted that he had brought a ham sandwich for lunch, he was ridiculed by the Orthodox community. Goldberg's campaign went downhill from there, and Rockefeller won easily.

Early in the campaign, George Humphreys, an intriguing member of the advance staff with a mild southern accent, would wander periodically into our area. Nelson Rockefeller's advance team, under the unflappable leadership of Joe Boyd, was a legend in political circles. Fueled by Rockefeller's personal finances, it operated with unmatched efficiency and confidence, even arrogance. No obstacles to the governor's movements and logistics were allowed to stand in the way of his seamless public, political, and private appointments. The advance men tended to be colorful, even outrageous. A young George Pataki, who would become governor himself twenty-five years later, was among them. George Humphreys was probably the most swashbuckling of the crew, but he yearned for involvement in the policy and program matters that we in the Program Office, doubling as the issues group of the campaign, were handling.

George was the next larger-than-life character to whom I was drawn. We became and remained close friends until his death some twenty-five years later. George's closest friend from childhood was Henry Diamond, who brought George up from Atlanta to work on the campaign. Henry and George both attended McCallie, a small prep school in Chattanooga. Henry was fond of saying that every year the school admitted one poor boy and one Jew, and that they really didn't need George because Henry could fill both slots. Although George was small for a fullback, he had played big-time college football for famed coach Bobby Dodd at Georgia Tech, even winning MVP honors in the Cotton Bowl in the mid-1950s. He was the best raconteur and games-player I ever knew. A competitor to his core, he wanted to excel at everything but devoted much of his time and extraordinary talent to the card table, bars, and chasing female company.

I spent much of my social time for the next dozen years with, first, George and Maxine Paul, his long-time girlfriend who worked in the governor's press office, and then with George and Grace, his lovely wife, who sadly passed away as I was writing this reflection. I contributed significantly to George's children's education fund by reliably losing money to him at gin rummy and the board-game version of Jeopardy that we played for not insubstantial stakes. George was also one of those people who stirred the pot and set the agenda for others, sometimes to a maddening degree. He commanded and freely returned fierce loyalty. At the reception after his funeral, which occurred all too soon because of his dissolute lifestyle, I was chatting with Joe Persico, Governor Rockefeller's head speechwriter, who went on to be a distinguished historian and biographer. A keen observer of human nature, Joe looked around the crowded room and remarked, "I bet half the men in this room think George was their best friend."

With the successful campaign behind us, I moved back to New York City and the Upper West Side. I found a little rent-controlled one-bedroom apartment with a tiny balcony on 87th Street between West End Avenue and Riverside Drive. My salary had soared by this time to over $20,000. A rule of thumb for me and my peers was that if we made our age (I had just turned thirty), we were close to being wealthy. The rent was less than $250 a month, allowing me to maintain a very comfortable lifestyle. I was thrilled to settle back into bachelor life in New York City, and to be out of the dreary atmosphere of Albany.

I had an easy commute to 22 West 55th Street, where I shared a small office with Mary Kresky and Sarah Deland. We found that our routine and responsibilities had undergone a subtle but significant change. Bob Douglass, who had served as counsel to the governor, took over Al Marshall's job as secretary, with Mike Whiteman becoming counsel. Bob Douglass had a much closer personal relationship with the Rockefellers than Al had ever managed to achieve. He was almost a member of the family. Bob's management style was also very different from what we were used to. Al was all about structure, order, and discipline. Communication was efficient and often done in writing. Bob's style was highly personal; he liked direct contact to convey his instructions. If you wanted guidance or direction, you needed to talk to him face-to-face. One-on-one meetings in his office were frequently interrupted while he took phone calls, albeit important ones, which could last for many minutes. A meeting that could have taken ten minutes might last an hour or more. His time was certainly more valuable than ours, but our frustration level was substantial.

More significantly for us in the New York office, Bob spent much less time at 55th Street, preferring Albany and time with his family. In addition, T. Norman Hurd, Rockefeller's long-time budget director, was assigned to the newly created position of director of state operations, further reducing the purview of the Program Office. The enormously capable Dick Dunham, Norm's deputy, took over as budget director.

As a result of these changes, we in the New York City office were called upon less and less, and our input and involvement dwindled. Recognizing reality, after a few months my lead responsibilities for criminal justice and education matters were formally transferred to assistant counsels Howard Shapiro and Lew Stone, respectively, who were used to working with Bob and who lived in Albany. Mary, Sarah, and I found ourselves doing a lot of crossword puzzles and spending more and more time at the Italian Pavilion, the restaurant next door, for long lunches or early cocktails. Sometimes the former seeped directly into the latter.

The Italian Pavilion was in many ways the center of our social life. We would inform the 55th Street switchboard that we were "heading next door to the library to do research." They could patch any important calls in to the restaurant. The round table and banquette in the bay window next to the front door was always reserved for us, and the restaurant's owners—as well as the two bartenders, Marsan and Paul—took very special care of us. Several times a week after work, some of us would gather there and would see who came in and what might happen. If George Humphreys or Warren Gardner, the deputy press secretary, showed up, they often had interesting and attractive people in tow. The evenings could unfold in any number of entertaining ways.

For me, there was one very providential outcome of the shuffling of duties. In September 1971, the Attica prison riot erupted. Instead of being the principal staff person involved, and probably the one directly on-site, that fate fell to Howard Shapiro. The tragic outcome profoundly affected all those who were drawn in, most particularly Russ Oswald. I have always been struck by those two historic events—Woodstock and Attica—that I saw from relatively close up, the first in August 1969 and the second in September 1971: only two years apart, with some of the same people involved, and two completely different legacies.

What was it like working for Nelson Rockefeller, and what did I think of him? I will leave it to his many biographers—the best, in my opinion, being Cary Reich—to catalog his achievements and failures and to judge his final legacy. I was both too close but not nearly close enough for an objective critique or an insider's knowledge. I can only address what the experience of proximity meant for me. I was most struck by his relentless pursuit of solutions. He had grown up politically as an aide to Franklin Roosevelt during the New Deal, and that heritage was unmistakable. Rockefeller felt deeply that government could—and should—try to address society's problems, and he felt a personal obligation to be a leader in that effort. He seemed to me to be a complete pragmatist; ideology played no role. He was only interested in what worked. He would put in more hours than everyone else, burning out most of those around him with his impatience and drive. He would bring in and listen to whatever expert seemed to have the best ideas and the most proven track record, but on rare occasions could fall victim to quackery or following the last piece of advice he heard.

Rockefeller truly enjoyed the rough and tumble of politics and campaigning. He was invigorated by the endless pressing of flesh and kissing of babies, activities that most of us would abhor. Having served as a staff person in FDR's White House, he understood better than most the difference between the assigned power of staff and the real power of elected office. He thus had special respect for, and paid deference to, those who had succeeded at the ballot box.

From what I saw, Rockefeller was more than color-blind; he believed profoundly in the civil rights cause, and his convictions infused the atmosphere around him. He also fully embraced the cause of organized labor and enjoyed the company of labor leaders and working people. He was the genuine "Rocky" of the popular political cartoons. Working on his staff allowed one to participate in some of the most exciting political initiatives of that era and to meet the most knowledgeable experts available, as well as a few eccentrics with quirky ideas. For those who hold that a unique feature of our federal system is the role that states can play as experimenters and incubators in the laboratory of government, Rockefeller supplied the richest source of research and leadership.

To my mind, more even than State University of New York or the State Council on the Arts—stunning achievements in their own rights—nothing captures Nelson Rockefeller's ambitions better than his effort to address the decaying of the state's cities. Urban America in the late 1960s was the domestic crisis of the time. Housing, jobs, race, economics, health care, crime—all were involved. The initial approach of massive clearance and renewal had soured. As Lizabeth Cohen describes in her acclaimed 2019 biography (*Saving America's Cities: Ed Logue and the Struggle to Renew Urban America in the Suburban Age*), Rockefeller avidly recruited Ed Logue, the boldest and most progressive practitioner in the country, to head the New York State Urban Development Corporation (UDC), the most powerful public authority ever created for the purpose. It took brass-knuckles politics and creation of a few new judgeships to get UDC through a skeptical state legislature, but get it through he did.

For seven or eight years, UDC built more affordable housing and other civic improvements than anywhere else in the country, sometimes with enthusiastic community support, other times over bitter local opposition. As Cohen reports: "Despite these many challenges, the UDC nevertheless exceeded its goals for diversifying communities. By 1975, 33 percent of UDC residents were low income and 42 percent were minority." The virtual elimination by the Nixon administration of direct federal subsidies for low-income housing and the fiscal problems of the state and city of the early 1970s both contributed decisively to UDC's financial problems. But, as Cohen makes brilliantly clear, Logue, with Rockefeller's full backing, placed the idealism of his mission above the business of keeping UDC solvent. In the end, the hubris of the endeavor—if such it was—succumbed to fiscal realities. Its financial house of cards collapsed, but no one could fault the UDC experiment for lack of passion or progressivism.

While those of us on the governor's staff were primarily concerned with state problems and issues, Rockefeller's presidential ambitions played as a leitmotif to everything that went on in our world. As the country divided during the Vietnam War, Rockefeller followed the Republican conservative drift. His movement to the right was again partly a matter of political calculation and partly reflected his frustration with the ineffectiveness of some elements of the liberal agenda he had previously championed. He would in all likelihood have made an excellent president, but his path would have been far easier as a Democrat. In any case, that phone call with Sterling Spero in 1967 changed my life both professionally and personally, and it set me on a path I otherwise could never have even dreamt about.

Some years later, Mary and Ed Kresky were at my apartment to help celebrate my forty-ninth birthday on January 26, 1979, when the phone rang. It was Hugh Morrow, Rockefeller's communications director, reporting that Nelson had just had a heart attack and died in very compromising circumstances. Could Mary please help with handling the fallout? That world had come to an end.

But back to 1972. After a year of sitting around and doing very little, it was clear to me that my governor's office career was over and I needed to think about next steps. It was difficult to leave the prestigious cocoon of the governor's staff. There is an intoxicating quality to the power and stature of a position like that. It is particularly seductive when one is serving such a dynamic national figure with presidential aspirations as Nelson Rockefeller, who was willing to commit his own seemingly unlimited private resources to supplement state efforts to address important public policy issues.

One intriguing option presented itself through Abe Levine, Al Marshall's closest personal friend and an important figure in the administration. Abe had just taken over the new state office to administer the recently enacted Taylor Law, overseeing labor relations with state employees. Abe was aware of my studies at NYU and asked if I would be interested in joining the new office. Had I been interested in a career in labor relations, it would have been a terrific opportunity. But, both because of my student research trip and from watching some of the state's recent labor disputes, I had gained some insights into the realities of the life involved. As a practical matter, it seemed to me to mean too many endless nights of negotiations in shabby hotel conference rooms, eating stale sandwiches and drinking bad coffee. My idealism ran headlong into the realities of everyday life. I thanked Abe, but declined.

A more appealing prospect emerged. The South Street Seaport project had been progressing slowly but was still in its infant stages. Negotiations were inching toward a structure that involved the state, the city, and the banks, who held the mortgages on the historic properties of the Seaport area. At the core of the proposed transaction, the state would acquire the most important set of historic buildings, the Schermerhorn Row block, bounded by Fulton, South, John, and Front Streets in Lower Manhattan. The state was the only player in a position to add actual cash to the deal.

Sam Aldrich approached the UDC. Ed Logue had been responsible for the highly successful Faneuil Hall Marketplace in Boston, so was familiar with and sympathetic to historic preservation projects as part of his urban revitalization strategy. Sam asked Logue to take a look at the Schermerhorn Row project to see if it could be undertaken as a self-sustaining, revenue-bond project by the UDC. Logue agreed, and it was arranged that I would go over to UDC to coordinate that analysis.

UDC had a special excitement and aura of its own. Logue shared Rockefeller's hard-driving style and impatience with bureaucratic and political obstacles. He had brought some of his dedicated staff from his Boston and New Haven days and hired others who soon became acolytes to his liberal idealistic vision of urban renewal. His chief of staff was John G. Burnett, a brilliant lawyer who had clerked for Justice William O. Douglas. I would work for John in another capacity in the years ahead.

Logue felt strongly that first-rate architecture contributed far more to the success of his civic undertakings than its incremental costs. His longtime chief of architecture, Ted Liebman, who was trained at Pratt and Harvard, brought in Italian architect Giorgio Cavaglieri to work on the Schermerhorn Row project. Cavaglieri was one of the leaders of the emerging field of historic preservation in New York City. He had headed the Municipal Art Society in the mid-1960s when it was involved in the Penn Station and Grand Central Terminal battles. He had earned accolades for his work on the successful conversion of the old Calvert Vaux/Frederick Withers Jefferson Market Courthouse to a new branch of the New York Public Library. Cavaglieri was an advocate of sensitive adaptive reuse to ensure the economic viability of repurposed historic buildings rather than adhering to a rigidly strict vision of preservation.

While Cavaglieri was finishing work on our glossy report on how the buildings might be used and what the exteriors and interiors would look like, UDC's financial staff was crunching the numbers to determine what it would cost and how much revenue it could produce. That task took several months and involved a lot of massaging of the numbers, but the conclusion was clear: the project just did not pencil—real estate jargon meaning that it was not financially feasible for UDC to pursue.

Sam Aldrich and I were unwilling to see the state abandon its participation in the Seaport. Indeed, its participation was crucial to the deal that many people—bankers, lawyers, and city officials—were trying to hammer out. The outline of the complex and multilayered transaction was as follows:

The city, under the leadership of the mayor's Office of Lower Manhattan Development (OLMD), was rezoning the area into a special district, which would strip the several blocks of the Seaport historic district of their air (development) rights. Those air rights above the buildings in the district would be donated to, and reside in, a central pool totaling over two million square feet of potential office space.

A consortium of banks led by Chase Manhattan would own that pool in exchange for writing down the mortgages they held on those properties, allowing those buildings to be transferred free and clear to the nonprofit South Street Seaport Museum. The provisions of the new special district would allow the air rights to be transferred more widely in the district to receiving parcels, which would offer sites with better potential for later high-rise commercial use. This would make the air rights more usable and valuable so that the banks might have a better chance of recouping the money they had forgone by writing down the mortgages. Lastly, the state would acquire the Schermerhorn Row block, which contained the best-preserved examples of nineteenth-century warehouses, and would pay for their restoration.

I learned later from the lead attorney, John C. "Larry" Nelson of Milbank, Tweed, Hadley & McCloy (now Milbank LLP), who was handling the negotiations on behalf of the banks, that they did not really expect to be made whole. They named the air rights holding entity Seacape. That stood for "Seaport Caper," which indicates how speculative they considered their prospects to be. The banks were acting under the auspices of Chase CEO David Rockefeller, who was the leader of the business community of the Financial District, an area that was severely depressed in the 1960s and '70s. The new Chase Manhattan headquarters had been built downtown in 1961 at David's insistence, reflecting his commitment to the revitalization of the area. He also established and headed the Downtown Lower Manhattan Association (DLMA), an organization of the area's business leaders advocating for the area. The Seaport was seen as part of the long-range goal of creating a twenty-four-hour downtown community, a vision that would take thirty more years to fulfill.

State participation was crucial to the deal structure. Since UDC could not be the vehicle, Sam Aldrich agreed that State Parks would take over our involvement. Supporting David Rockefeller's commitment to Lower Manhattan was almost certainly central to Sam's and Nelson's willingness to assume this obligation, but I was only dimly aware of those considerations. In any case, Sam asked me to join the state Office of Parks, Recreation and Historic Preservation as its general manager for the New York City Region. Our office would assume responsibility for the state's role in the Seaport project. At age thirty-two, I would be the executive in charge of a significant state operation. I would be responsible for *doing,* not just analyzing and advising. It was a thrilling prospect.

I made the move in late 1972. State Parks' New York City Region was a relatively new creation. It had been established in the late 1960s in response to the new emphasis on urban recreation. In 1969, pursuant to a recommendation by Regional Plan Association (much more about RPA later), the first urban National Park, Gateway National Recreation Area, was established in the New York Harbor area. Rockefeller created the new state office to be at the forefront of this growing interest. I have also suspected that Rockefeller's bitter competition with John Lindsay added an incentive to his existing inclination to take aggressive action in this field. He must have relished the prospect of stealing some of the spotlight away from the high-profile mayor and his blue-blood parks administrator, Thomas P. F. Hoving, by launching new state initiatives in their backyard. Much more would follow: there are now eleven state parks and historic sites in the five boroughs of New York City.

At the time, one new state park—Harlem River State Park, later renamed in honor of sports hero Roberto Clemente—was under construction. Planning was underway for Riverbank State Park along the Hudson River in Harlem, and the state had acquired the Empire Stores in what is now trendy DUMBO (the acronym for "Down Under the Manhattan Bridge Overpass") on the Brooklyn waterfront, and was trying to figure out what to do with it. Schermerhorn Row would be added to that list.

My first concern was to see to the completion and opening of the Harlem River Park. Some twenty-five acres of derelict waterfront land were being reimagined by leading landscape architect M. Paul Friedberg into an exciting mix of swimming pools, gyms, and open spaces adjacent to a UDC affordable-housing project and school. The day-to-day oversight of construction was being handled largely by an engineer and architect on our staff while I focused on how we would operate the park in the challenging area of the West Bronx. After an extensive search, we hired Richard Ortiz to be the park director. It proved a fortunate choice as Rich served for many years as a capable and effective manager who had the key ability to relate to the community he served.

Ensuring public safety—at a time when urban parks were almost synonymous with crime—was our primary concern. We would need armed security personnel. State Park police were authorized to carry weapons, but I had the same concern that I had had in 1968 with having all-white police officers from rural upstate areas, trained at the state Police Academy, patrolling a park in the Bronx. In addition, there was a height minimum (I believe it was six feet) for state troopers, which applied to State Park police as well. This would not do. I decided that we needed to create a new civil service title—urban park patrolman—with no height requirement. Getting that through the skeptical bureaucracy took many months, but we finally succeeded. I also fought hard to have the new officers trained at the New York City Police Academy rather than upstate, and secured approval for that as well. Finally, we were able to hire a retired New York City police captain to head our security force. He interviewed candidates, made the final hiring decisions, and we assembled a solid group of ethnically diverse young urban park patrolmen.

But we did not want armed police officers to be our only interface with the visiting public. We secured a federal grant (under the legislation which I had briefed Nelson Rockefeller about several years previously) to hire a crew to be the welcoming face of the park. Dressed not in police-type uniforms but in casual slacks and sports jackets, they would greet visitors, provide information about the rules and regulations, and be the first to respond to inappropriate behavior. They would call in the armed officers only when absolutely necessary. All of these precautions worked well and we did not have any serious incidents during my tenure.

With the opening date fast approaching in the summer of 1973, we had to scramble to get the park ready. We stayed up all night before the opening, stamping the tags for the metal baskets that visitors to the swimming pool would use, but we got it done.

A photograph of the inaugural ceremonies features me at the podium, with 1970s-length hair. Robert Moses was in attendance, having been invited as a gesture to his legacy by Governor Rockefeller after having effectively dismantled—and gained control over—Moses's empire.

The park's new director, Rich Ortiz, later told me that after the ceremony Nelson Rockefeller searched out Ortiz's parents and spent ten to fifteen minutes with them, chatting in Spanish. He put them completely at ease and provided a lifelong memory for them. Moments like that almost never happen unscripted, but neither Rich nor I could recall having played any part in bringing it about. However it came to pass, it was Rockefeller at his best.

My work on Riverbank State Park was far more preliminary. Rockefeller had struck a deal with Percy Sutton, borough president of Manhattan and the most prominent political leader of the Harlem community. If Sutton would support the construction along the Harlem waterfront of a critically needed sewage treatment plant to handle all of Manhattan's waste, the state would build a magnificent park on top of it.

I should note that one of Rockefeller's most significant and lasting achievements was cleaning up New York's waterways. His aide, Dick Wiebe, one of the high-powered team under Bill Ronan, wrote what became the national Clean Waters Act (formally entitled the Federal Water Pollution Control Act Amendments of 1972). New York State used nearly all of the first year's federal appropriations to fund facilities, such as the North River Wastewater Treatment Plant, all around the state. True, Pete Seeger sang and the *Clearwater* sailed, definitely helping to create public awareness and support for government intervention, but those unpopular sewage treatment plants were, in fact, what cleaned up the rivers.

With Sutton's backing, the Riverbank project proceeded. We surveyed the adjacent Harlem community on what facilities the residents wanted in the new park and began very preliminary engineering. Since construction of the sewage treatment project had already begun, we needed to act quickly to allow the park to be a feasible part of the plan. We secured funding in the state budget to strengthen the caissons (the plant's underwater foundations) in order to bear the extra load of the park. My friend, George Humphreys, was then heading the state's Environmental Facilities

Corporation—another of Rockefeller's many special-purpose authorities—which was in charge of constructing the plant. George and I never tired of arguing whether I was building a park on top of his sewage treatment facility or he was building a sewage plant under my park. Riverbank State Park was finally completed in 1993, enhanced by an imaginative design by the talented architect Richard Dattner, and has become a popular and treasured community asset. It emitted a noxious smell for several years following construction, but that problem was finally remedied.

Empire Stores presented a very difficult challenge. Built in the early nineteenth-century as warehouses for coffee, tea, and tobacco, they had been empty since World War II and were in disrepair. Compromised roofs and foundations and windowless interior spaces made renovation costly and reuse problematic. What would eventually become DUMBO was still a grim, largely abandoned waterfront area. We thought about trying to include the warehouses in plans for the South Street Seaport across the river, but nothing seemed to make sense. It would be forty years before the neighborhood became transformed enough to support the costly conversion of the Empire Stores and enable them to become a key component of Brooklyn Bridge Park (which I will discuss later).

Another potential target for State Parks involvement in New York City emerged briefly. UDC approached us about the possibility of taking over the open space component of Roosevelt Island. I had gotten to know Bob Litke, head of the Roosevelt Island project, while I was at UDC. I toured the island with Edward Hallam Tuck, our commission chairman; commission member Marian Heiskell of the *New York Times's* Sulzberger family; and William vanden Heuvel, who was leading the advocacy effort for a memorial to FDR at the southern tip of the island. Louis Kahn, the renowned architect who had developed a preliminary design for the memorial, also joined us. Initially, nothing came of this visit (and Kahn died not long after our tour), but the stunning Four Freedoms State Park was completed in 2012, having been built very much according to Kahn's design and including a dramatic bust of FDR by the great sculptor Jo Davidson.

Ed Tuck, an admiralty lawyer at Shearman & Sterling, was another of those remarkable leaders and mentors who provided me with unstinting understanding and support. Marian Heiskell, a hugely influential force in conservation and philanthropy, would prove an invaluable friend later at Regional Plan Association.

Opening Harlem River (later renamed Roberto Clemente) State Park, the first state park in New York City, 1973 (from left to right: not shown, Robert Moses; Ed Logue, president of Urban Development Corporation; Richard Clurman, New York City commissioner of parks; Governor Nelson Rockefeller; Sam Aldrich, New York State commissioner of parks; Richard Ortiz, director of Harlem River State Park).

An amusing incident from my time at State Parks stands out in my memory. Laurance Rockefeller, in his capacity as chairman of the State Council of Parks, invited all of the regional managers to his home on upper Fifth Avenue for a New Year's reception. I was one of the first to arrive and Laurance asked a couple of us to help him with a problem on the upper floor of his apartment. We climbed the stairs to a room that contained several large ship models. For whatever reason, he wanted to move one of them to another room. I do not remember the physical constraints, but it was clear that we had to remove the tall Plexiglas case enclosing the model that he wanted moved. Laurance turned to us and asked if anyone had a screwdriver. That is not the sort of thing that one brings to a holiday party, but Rockefellers had long been used to having people around them having whatever is needed to solve any logistics challenges they faced. I recalled that CBS had just aired a TV special narrated by Walter Cronkite about the Rockefellers. In it, John D.'s penchant for handing out dimes was highlighted. I reached into my pocket, pulled out a dime, and handed it to Laurance. "This might work," I offered. "I think it is in the best family tradition." He gave me an icy stare. I had crossed an invisible line that did not allow outsiders to make jokes about the family. The dime did the trick—we unscrewed the top and moved the model—but Laurance failed to appreciate the gesture.

Work on the Schermerhorn Row project continued to command much of my time. The point man for the city on the negotiations was Richard Weinstein. An architect by training, he was part of the elite group of urban designers that John Lindsay and city Planning Commission Chairman Donald Elliott had brought into city government. This supremely accomplished group included Jaque Robertson and Alex Cooper, and was led by the guru Jonathan Barnett, author of *Urban Design as Public Policy,* their sacred text. Richard, who would become dean of the UCLA Graduate School of Architecture and Urban Design, was brilliant and difficult, but we managed to forge a good working relationship around the common goal of supporting the Seaport project. Facilitating the process was Richard's extremely capable attorney, Edgar Lampert. We finally agreed on the terms of the state's acquisition of Schermerhorn Row, particularly the price. It is important to remember how depressed the New York real estate market, especially Lower Manhattan, was in the 1970s as the city sank into fiscal distress. We had to come up with enough state money to meaningfully contribute to the overall project but not exceed what had to pass muster as an "arm's length" transaction. The purchase of the block took the form of a state contract, which required the approval of the state Comptroller's Office. We settled on $1.1 million and hoped it would fly.

I went to Albany with Ed Lampert and Marilyn Friedman, his very sharp assistant, and met with a deputy comptroller. After a long and tense meeting, he indicated that he found our evaluation reasonable and that he would approve the deal. This was the culmination of years of hard work and we were ecstatic. We decided that a fitting celebration was in order. On the way home, we stopped off for dinner at the Depuy Canal House in High Falls, possibly the finest restaurant in the Hudson Valley. We enjoyed one of the great dinners of our lives, augmented by liberal amounts of very good wine (at our own expense, of course).

During the winter of 1973, I attended a black tie gala dinner with Al Marshall. I no longer recall the occasion, but as president of Rockefeller Center, Al attended many such functions and sometimes had an extra seat to fill at his table. Mike Burke, the CBS executive who was president of the Yankees at the time, was at our table. I took the opportunity, emboldened I am sure by several glasses of wine, to tell him of my prowess on the baseball diamond. I volunteered that I thought I could fill the hole they had at the time for a new third baseman. He thanked me but said they had just traded for a guy named Graig Nettles.

Since playing for the Yankees was now foreclosed, I set out on one of the great adventures of my life: my first trip to the Himalayas. Over the twenty-odd years that had passed since the initial climbs of Annapurna and Everest, I had continued to follow the expeditions to the Himalayas and the exploits of the premier climbers. Often, I would exasperate my friends during happy hour by drawing Everest climbing routes on the backs of envelopes and cocktail napkins. One evening in the summer of 1973, Maxine Paul—George Humphreys' girlfriend, who worked in the press office—walked into the Italian Pavilion and threw down on our special table a fairly crude brochure that announced: "Trek to the Base Camp of Everest, No Experience Required."

"Okay, Shostal," Maxine declared, "put up or shut up!"

I was taken aback. It had never occurred to me that something like this would be possible for a pure amateur. Himalayan trekking, much less guided climbs, was virtually unknown. I *had* to check it out. A few weeks later, I attended a reception for those interested. The trip was sponsored by Buddy Bombard, a rather effete tour operator who specialized in balloon trips, not high-altitude trekking. Nevertheless, he was reasonably persuasive; it was only a fifteen-day trip and it was not very expensive. I signed up.

Still smoking close to three packs of cigarettes a day, I made a modest effort at getting in shape. I assembled the required clothing and gear, packed my army duffel bag, and boarded Pan Am Flight 001 (the then-famous "'round-the-world flight"). I had no idea what to expect. After some twenty hours and multiple stops (London, Frankfurt, Rome, Damascus, etc.), I arrived in sweltering Delhi in the middle of the night. Following a six-hour layover in that chaotic airport, I boarded a Royal Nepal Airlines flight to Kathmandu, Nepal's capital. From the left side of the airplane we caught glimpses of the soaring white peaks of the great range of the Himalayas. None of us had ever seen anything like it; we all gasped.

Landing in Kathmandu in 1973 was like entering another world, another century. Only the main streets were paved. There were no access highways, so there was very little traffic and the few vehicles had been carted in. Sacred cattle wandered the streets. We assembled at the Blue Star Hotel, a fairly dreary accommodation. It turned out that there would be twenty-eight of us, a group twice the size now considered to be an acceptable maximum. At our welcome dinner, we were greeted and briefed by a Colonel Anji, a Bhutanese former military man who headed the local service that would manage our trek. Colonel Anji started off by announcing that Buddy Bombard had canceled at the last minute because of allegedly pressing business at home. This was discomforting news.

We had a couple of days to tour this exotic city on our own, visiting its magical sites: the temples of Patan, Swayambhunath and Boudhanath, and Durbar Square. The ancient buildings, dusty streets, and colorful people enthralled us. We saw extreme poverty but did not experience the despair that we had felt in Delhi. The official photograph of the King of Nepal, which adorned the walls of almost every public space, bore a striking resemblance to Peter Sellers. We felt that we were in a magic, mountainous Duchy of Grand Fenwick. In the distance we could see the snowcapped peaks of the front range of the Himalayas.

I spent most of the time with Jim Berger, another bachelor from New York City. A few years older than I, Jim was the only one of our group who had been to altitude, having previously climbed Kilimanjaro. He would also prove to be a tireless hiker. I felt comfortable with Jim, who was a lawyer with the Air Line Pilots Association, and we decided to share a tent on the trek. Sharing a tent on such an extreme adventure is a good way to forge a deep bond. Jim and I have remained friends for more than forty years and have shared many more climbs and hikes together. When we get together, we still relive the dramatic days of that unique experience.

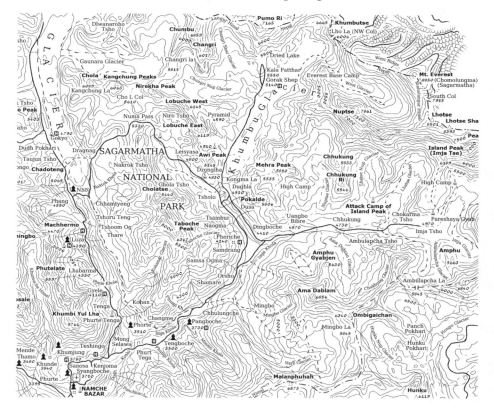

Trekking Map of the Khumbu: The Everest Region

Map highlighting the main trekking route from Namche Bazaar to Kala Patthar above Everest Base Camp. The Lukla airstrip is off the map, below and to the right of Namche Bazaar, one full day's trek away. Island Peak, which I climbed in 1978, is in the upper right-hand quadrant. Mt Mera, which I climbed in 2000, is also just off the map at the lower right-hand corner, above the Hunku valley. The spellings of some of the place names vary slightly from my text, which adopts more widely accepted usages.

The next morning, our large contingent boarded several classic Pilatus Porter STOL (Short Takeoff and Landing) aircraft at Kathmandu's Tribhuvan International Airport, a fairly primitive facility then. Each plane could carry about eight of us at a time. Despite the aircrafts' legendary versatility, very favorable weather conditions were required for landing at our destination. Lukla, perched at 9,400 feet in the foothills below Everest, is often regarded as the scariest landing strip in the world. It was built in 1964 at the initiative of Sir Edmund Hillary, who had bought the land for it. Tragically, both his wife and daughter died in a crash there two years after our trip. It is now called the Tenzing-Hillary Airport.

It took several hours for the planes to ferry us to Lukla, a flight of forty-five minutes. Landing, we could see the wreckage of various aircraft strewn along the grass runway, which disappeared over a precipice. A large contingent of Sherpas, porters, and yaks met us as we landed and began loading up our gear. We were really underway. Two days later, we arrived at Namche Bazaar, the main Sherpa village at 11,350 feet. It had been a long, hard hike up from the Dudh Kosi River, which drains the Everest region. The air was crisp and cold, and I had my first experience with altitude headaches. Our leader, Colonel Anji, abruptly departed, after telling us only that important business required his immediate return to Kathmandu. Our large and inexperienced assemblage was left completely on our own with only the Sirdar (head Sherpa), whose English was quite limited, to lead us.

We were furious but could do nothing. We decided that we needed to designate one person to deal with the Sirdar, and the task fell to Sid Wein, the one physician in our group. Sid was affable but proved indecisive. Instead of moderating and channeling our concerns and questions, he would dither and delay, inadvertently compounding the chaos and confusion.

After a rest day, we headed up and caught our first glimpses of the Everest massif, with the summit poking up behind the wall of Nuptse. We camped below the new, and indeed barely completed, Everest View Hotel at around 12,000 feet. While we were enjoying a beer on the not-yet-enclosed terrace facing the mountain, a party of Japanese climbers arrived. They were coming down off of Everest and one of their group had made it to the top! We gawked with awe as he approached, his face ravaged and sunburned and his fingers wrapped in gauze. He had severe frostbite. Too excited for niceties, we asked for his autograph. He obliged, clutching the pen in an awkward, bandaged grasp. Somewhere in my boxes of memorabilia is my trip diary with his signature, next to which he had scrawled, "Success." It seemed a bittersweet expression given that he would probably lose several of those fingers and some toes.

We trekked farther. I was feeling in good shape and exhilarated. After descending to about 10,000 feet and crossing a river, we climbed back up and arrived at the monastery of Thyangboche, above 12,500 feet. It is one of the most beautiful and magical spots on Earth—in good weather. We stepped through the arch at the entrance to the grounds and stared at a 360-degree scene of soaring peaks of 20,000 feet or more with the Everest massif looming in the distance, perhaps another fifteen to twenty miles away. I said to myself that Ronald Colman must be here, it felt so much like Shangri-La. We camped in a field which I recognized from the pictures in John Hunt's book, *The Conquest of Everest*. The Hillary expedition had used the exact same site in 1953. We had the scene to ourselves. This would change: when I made my last trip to this spot in 2000, Thyangboche had become a small village dotted with numerous lodges (teahouses) housing hundreds of trekkers.

But that evening in 1973, the Sherpas built a bonfire (which is now strictly prohibited)* and they entertained us with singing and dancing. I was struck by how perfectly the slow, rhythmic chanting and shuffling fit the setting and their stoic but cheerful lifestyle. The Sherpas then asked us to do a dance typical of our culture. After some consultation, we fixed upon the bunny hop. Just a few minutes of our spasmodic lurching and lyrics left the Sherpas rolling in laughter and us collapsing in the thin night air. The

---

* Decades of trekking have left much of the forest cover in the Everest Region denuded, prompting the creation of Sagarmatha (the Nepali name for Everest) National Park, where there are strict penalties for cutting any of the remaining protected timber.

bunny hop, as with so much of our way of life, is not relevant to existence in the shadow of the Himalayas.

Our next stop was Periche. Located at 14,000 feet and surrounded on all sides by mountain walls towering over it, it was a dark, chilly, gloomy place. Several of us arrived before most of the others. Jim, of course, was first; I followed and soon was joined by three remarkable women in their forties who were traveling without their husbands and who had already become our climbing buddies: T. Jewett, Nan Cullman, and Gerry Harris. The latter two were close friends prior to the trip. The five of us, often including their husbands, would go on hikes and outings together in the Adirondacks and elsewhere for years to come.

Our gear and tents had not arrived, which was a bit unusual. We were stomping our feet to keep warm and staring across a flat plateau hoping to spot our porters as the rest of the group began to trickle into camp. Suddenly, Gerry, who had a dance and theater background (and whose husband was a Broadway producer), pointed and began to sing: "Over there…over there…the yaks are coming, the yaks are coming." It was a hilarious moment for those who knew the classic World War I song. The last of our group to arrive, perhaps an hour later, was Ed Wallerstein, a colorful seventy-year-old Jewish "Kentucky Colonel," who drank Jack Daniel's and flew a rebel flag from his tent.

The trek, and especially the altitude, had proved far more challenging than many had anticipated. Almost half the group opted not to go any farther, rather than face the dramatically higher altitude, thinner air, and colder temperatures ahead. Ed, who was suffering from the stark conditions, said wistfully and memorably, "Whatever happens, I can die a happy man because I've seen the two most beautiful sights in the world: the sun on Mount Everest and the moon on the lawn of the University of Virginia." (Ed did not die; he made it back in fine shape.)

About fourteen of us made it to the next stop, Lobuche, at 16,000 feet, for an icy night, and the next day went on to Gorak Shep, next to a small glacial pond near Base Camp just above 17,000 feet. These were short but extremely demanding days. The stress of uncertainty was as taxing as the physical exertion. Climbing at altitude is as much a mental as a physical challenge, and we had no one to tell us whether what we were experiencing—headaches, nausea, confusion, and sleeplessness—was normal and survivable or life-threatening.

Atop Kala Patthar, 18,500 feet, with the summit of Mt. Everest behind me, 1973.

T. Jewett, whose face was puffy from water retention, a common symptom of altitude sickness, confided into her tape recorder that night that she did not know if she would wake up in the morning. She did—we all did—after what felt like a sub-zero night.

The next morning, after a breakfast of instant coffee and oatmeal, we picked our way up a rocky mound above us called Kala Patthar. As we ascended, the summit pyramid of Everest became visible, towering almost 11,000 feet above us. After about two hours, we arrived at the top of Kala Patthar, spent but supremely proud of what we had accomplished with almost no leadership. I pulled a postage-stamp-sized American flag out of my pack and posed for photos holding up the flag with the summit of Everest looming behind me, a treasured memento.

We then made our way down, retracing the route we had ascended and rejoining the rest of our group at Periche. The others had spent the three days killing time there and wandering a little way up the adjacent valley. On the return trek back down the Khumbu (the area around Everest), we vowed to never again put ourselves through such discomfort, complaining bitterly to each other about how the trip had been mismanaged. We muttered about getting together for a lawsuit against Buddy Bombard. Of course, by the time we were back in Kathmandu, all we could talk about was what a spectacular adventure it had been and how soon we would come back. I would return to the Himalayas four more times, reaching significantly higher altitudes twice, but none of my later trips could quite match this first experience for sheer drama and intensity.

An incidental feature of the trip left a different but significant imprint. Among our large contingent of trekkers were three couples. The husbands, former IBM managers, were in their late fifties or early sixties, but had been able to retire at an early age and were looking forward to decades of active travel to remote parts of the world. At the age of thirty-three, this was a future prospect that resonated deeply with me.

NINE

CITY GOVERNMENT DAYS

In 1974, Abraham Beame had become mayor. Not long after, I received an unexpected phone call from Richard Weinstein, the head of the mayor's Office of Lower Manhattan Development (OLMD), with whom I had been negotiating about the Seaport project. He said that with the change in administrations, he had had enough of city government and wanted to return to the practice of architecture. He asked if I would be interested in taking his job. "In order to leave," he said, "I first have to find a replacement, and then I have to convince two people—Abe Beame and David Rockefeller—to approve of it. You're the only guy I can think of."

I was flattered, intrigued, and tempted. OLMD was one of five urban design offices that John Lindsay had created, charged with encouraging, in key areas of the city, development projects based on sound urban planning and innovative design concepts. To give the development offices more political clout, they were administratively part of the mayor's office, but to give them access to planning and zoning expertise and resources they were physically part of the Department of City Planning. In addition to OLMD, there were offices for Midtown Manhattan, Downtown Brooklyn, Queens, and Staten Island. All were headed by accomplished architects and urban designers—which I clearly was not.

While I had thoroughly enjoyed my time at State Parks, OLMD seemed sexier, more exciting, and likely to open more avenues for the future. After mulling it over, I called Richard Weinstein back and said I would like to pursue it. Naively, I did not take into account the fiscal disaster that was beginning to roil the city. I met with Jim Cavanaugh, the crusty first deputy mayor, and John Zuccotti, then chairman of the city Planning Commission. Finally, I had my audience with David Rockefeller at his office on the 17th floor of One Chase Manhattan Plaza, and I met Roland Peracca, his assistant for such matters. I survived their review. In the spring of 1974, I resigned from State Parks—Ed Tuck graciously threw me a wonderful going away party—and moved into the OLMD offices at 2 Lafayette Street.

Some extraordinarily smart and competent architects and designers staffed OLMD, committed to the progressive principles of Jonathan Barnett, who had been the director of the Urban Design Group at the city Planning Commission and had published *Urban Design as Public Policy,* the influential book that was their bible. They viewed me a bit warily at first, as a possible philistine from the Rockefeller camp, and made a point of giving me Barnett's book to read. But Weinstein had been a prickly and difficult boss, so they were inclined to give me the benefit of the doubt and soon went further, offering their full and generous support. They had created the innovative South Street Seaport Special Zoning District, which enabled the flexible transfer of air rights using the same policy tools that were proving successful in Midtown's Theater District. They had also developed the master plan and zoning changes for Manhattan Landing, John Lindsay's grand scheme for the East River waterfront that was supposed to include a new home for the Stock Exchange. Lindsay had secured David Rockefeller's support for this mammoth project (which was to be constructed on platforms over the river but never got off the ground) in exchange for Lindsay's agreement to back Battery Park City, Nelson's megaproject (on landfill from the World Trade Center excavation) in the Hudson River.

In another part of the city under our purview, the early 1970s had seen the phenomenon of artists moving into SoHo's spacious lofts, and the city was now trying to adopt catch-up zoning measures to recognize and regulate the new reality of mixed-use, live-work spaces in other districts. OLMD was determined to get ahead of the curve in the next area to undergo similar change, the industrial neighborhood between Canal and Chambers Streets. Jack Freeman and Jeff Bliss, two of the brightest young members of the office, were studying and surveying every block to understand what was going on, and to create new plans and regulations that would promote better, safer development outcomes. What to name this area? It was south of SoHo, but "SoSo" didn't seem to have the right ring to it. Instead, the "Triangle Below Canal" (TriBeCa, or simply Tribeca) won out, though the area looks more like a trapezoid than a triangle. Anyone visiting dynamic Tribeca today can see that Jack and Jeff did remarkably prescient and effective work.

Jeff Bliss's restless mind and creative energy would lead him into other pursuits. He renovated a building in Tribeca and moved on, with his business partner, the colorful Jerry Kretchmer, to co-develop numerous other properties and open some of New York's best-known restaurants, including the Mesa Grill and the Gotham Bar & Grill (neither of which, sadly, carries on today). Jeff still keeps my mind challenged with his interest in philosophy and political theory—and beats me regularly at pool.

In 1966, the Downtown Lower Manhattan Association (DLMA), the business group that David Rockefeller had formed in 1958, released a long-range plan for Lower Manhattan. There were serious doubts about whether the area would survive as the center of finance or even as a viable business district despite David's commitment to build Chase's new headquarters there. The DLMA plan centered on creating a twenty-four-hour community—mixing residences, retail, parks, and cultural amenities—as the key to halting the area's decline and creating a truly vibrant urban center. These were laudable objectives, but they faced an increasingly moribund real estate market and business climate. Nevertheless, these goals became our lodestar and we were determined to pursue any strategy that might move us, even microscopically, in the right direction. The traditional public tool for economic development is government money to invest in amenities and to prime the pump for private investment. But as the fiscal crisis loomed ever closer, the city's capital budget, increasingly raided to meet operating expenses, was almost nonexistent. There was no public money to work with.

Michael Bailkin, our office's attorney, had a restless and highly creative mind. He came up with the idea that we establish a special assessment district encompassing the core of the Financial District. Businesses would be assessed a very minor supplement, just a few cents, to be applied to their real estate taxes, with the proceeds going into a fund to underwrite amenities and improvements to the area. These projects, although modest in themselves, would inject a sense of progress and positive movement and would, we hoped, begin to reverse the negative psychology that enveloped Lower Manhattan. The projects would be agreed upon in advance and prioritized. It was a heavy lift but seemed to have promise. John Zuccotti signed off on the idea, and Mike and I began to shop it around. Sylvan Lawrence, a civic-minded supporter of our work and a major downtown property owner, agreed to support the idea. We went to the Port Authority, owner of the World Trade Center (which made payments in lieu of real estate taxes), which would have to be willing to join in. We met with the august Bill Ronan, who had moved from the MTA to chair the authority at the time. He, too, agreed that it was a viable concept. "At least," he said, "it isn't another one of those empty bag proposals that Nelson and I used to dream up."

Encouraged, Mike and I felt that we really had a chance to pull this off, so we arranged a meeting with Harry Helmsley—the single most critical player. Harry owned more downtown real estate than anyone else. He also had a well-deserved reputation for responsible civic involvement. But when we met, Harry shook his head and said, "I just can't do it. I think it is a really interesting idea, but I can't agree to what amounts to an increase in my real estate taxes, however small, when I'm complaining all the time about how high my taxes are."

Our plan was dead. It just was not its time. A few years later, with a recovery in market conditions, it would revive in the form of the highly popular Business Improvement Districts (BIDs), which now exist all over New York City.

With the Bicentennial celebration on the horizon, we tried to take advantage of this major anniversary that was to be focused on our purview, the historic downtown. Lower Manhattan lacked a historic trail of the kind that attracted tourists to Boston and other older cities. Seeking to remedy that, we went to American Express, which was headquartered downtown. The company agreed to be the principal funder. We had only about a year to put a trail physically in place by July 4, 1976. Several of our staff members—I remember Janet Peña and Jack Fahnestock, in particular—dove into the research needed to accurately describe the most important of the many historic points in "ye olde New York."

We retained the outstanding graphic design consultant, Sam Lebowitz, to come up with a prototype of a historic marker that would be both attractive and durable enough to withstand the abuse of city sidewalk locations. We decided on directional signage affixed to lampposts rather than embedded in streets and sidewalks, which tend to get torn up regularly. The DLMA agreed to hold and administer a maintenance fund. We did manage to have most of the historic markers and directional arrows fabricated and—most challenging of all—to gain the cooperation of the myriad city agencies involved in permitting their installation, in time for the Bicentennial celebration.

The ravages of weather and street traffic, the lack of sufficient ongoing funding, and the absence of a permanent operating sponsor all combined to make this first version of the Heritage Trail fairly short-lived. Several years later, under Richard Kaplan's leadership and with renewed funding from the Kaplan Foundation, an effort—which I was invited to join—was launched to put in place a revised and improved incarnation with new signage. For many of the same reasons, it too gave way to what exists now: a mélange of historic markers and signage scattered throughout the downtown area.

Also, as part of the Bicentennial effort, we decided to publish a glossy brochure highlighting about a dozen major historic preservation projects that needed funding. We secured sponsorship for printing and reproduction costs from Scott Printing, Chase Bank, Morgan Guaranty Trust, and the

DLMA. The idea was to create an enticing menu of options for individuals, businesses, and foundations looking to fund Bicentennial-related initiatives. The booklet included the United States Custom House, the Battery Maritime Building, Fraunces Tavern, Hanover Square, and other potential projects, all of which eventually found sponsors (although for some it took years, for others decades). I also insisted to our staff that we continue to help the Seaport in any way we could.

In 1975 and early 1976, a very young and raw Donald Trump started visiting our offices looking to take advantage of the depressed market. He would drive us around Lower Manhattan in his limo, asking about various potential sites while placing calls to Governor Hugh Carey (was it really the governor on the other end of the line?) to impress us. He finally focused on renovating the old Commodore Hotel at Grand Central Terminal. Although this was not in our geographic bailiwick, John Zuccotti had tasked Mike Bailkin with dealing with Donald and trying to structure a workable deal. The city was desperate for any kind of real estate development. Even though Donald (yes, we called him Donald then, too) had brought in Sandy Lindenbaum, a savvy and highly respected real estate attorney, I did not take him seriously.

I told Mike, "This kid will never build anything. His father has given him a million bucks to play with [the rumor at the time], and as soon as he burns through it, he'll disappear."

Mike just smiled and said, "We'll see. But John wants me to do it, so I have to stay with it."

I underestimated how creative Mike could be. He invented the UDC pass-through for this transaction. As previously noted, the New York State Urban Development Corporation had been created in 1968 with extraordinary powers, which Mike was inventive enough to recognize and tap into. UDC would acquire the property and lease it back to the developer, making the project eligible for favorable public financing and significantly enhancing its feasibility. This technique would be used many times by many entities in the future. The outline of Donald's deal was completed in late 1976 and the Grand Hyatt Hotel opened in 1980.

Later, Mike told me about a conversation he had had with Donald at some point during the negotiations. Outraged by something Donald had said, Mike exclaimed, "Donald, that is the shallowest thing I have ever heard!"

Without missing a beat, Donald replied, "Don't you realize that I am probably the shallowest person you will ever meet?"

During the long years after 2016, I often thought back on that prophetic claim. He may well have meant it as a boast, already sensing his talent for connecting with people on the most primitive level.

Even while overseeing OLMD's exciting professional agenda, I kept thinking about getting back to the Himalayas. I was determined to try even more demanding trips, which required at least some basic technical training. In the summer of 1974, I signed up for a week at the Palisades School of Mountaineering (PSOM) in the Sierra Nevada range of California to learn the basics of rock climbing. I managed to survive the initial sessions and prepared for a final test climb. Having rediscovered my extreme discomfort with the exposure of vertical rock faces, I was miserable. I dreaded the upcoming trial.

In preparation, we hiked up to a plateau below the peak of 14,400-foot North Palisade. This highly technical climb was not our objective, but its verticality warned us of what might be to come for us. As we set up camp, we heard that some climbers on the main peak were in trouble. One had fallen and broken his pelvis. He could not urinate and would die if he could not be brought down soon. Our experienced guides were drafted onto the rescue team. On a beautiful summer night, under a brilliant star-studded sky, we watched the pinpricks of headlamps as the rescuers worked their way up and then down the stark silhouette of the summit pinnacle. As dawn broke, a helicopter arrived and ferried the injured climber and his companions to a hospital and safety. Our guides were exhausted from their danger-filled mission and our climb was called off. I was doubly thrilled to have watched a dramatic mountain rescue and to be relieved of having to attempt a climb that filled me with panic. Better yet, I received my qualifying certificate.

To further bolster my climbing résumé, I signed up for a snow-and-ice-climbing seminar on Mount Rainier in 1975. Rainier is the most Himalayan-like peak in the United States, outside of Alaska. It is the same 14,000-foot-plus height as many of the mountains in the Rockies, but because it is further north and in a wetter climate, it is much more heavily glaciated. Rainier guides are often trainees for the 8,000-meter Himalayan expeditions. We spent a week learning techniques to ascend ice walls and execute crevasse rescues. The class was a self-contained, self-supported miniexpedition, which meant carrying all of our gear and doing camp chores like pitching tents and melting snow. On the final night, we camped in the summit crater and smelled the sulfurous gas seeping out of the quiescent but still potentially active volcano. The next day, we descended from the summit to the Paradise Inn lodge at 5,400 feet. As climbers know, going down can be tougher on the body than going up. Descending 9,000 feet in one day with over fifty pounds on my back was a new experience for me, especially for my legs. The next day, I could barely walk, and I seriously considered asking for a wheelchair to get on the plane home. Back in New York, it was nearly a week before I could walk down the stairs to the subway without clinging desperately to the handrail in excruciating pain.

The staff at OLMD was young, energetic, and passionate about work and play alike. We did quite a bit of socializing together including highly competitive evenings of squash and darts. One weekend in the early spring of 1975, my amiable and capable deputy, Ric DuPuy, suggested we go whitewater canoeing, which I had never done. Ric and I, along with two others from the office, headed north to western Massachusetts and the Westfield River. We rented two aluminum canoes and put in on a quiet section. After managing a few rapids, we pulled up to the shore to rest and eat our lunches. Some guys living in a house nearby invited us in to share a joint (this was the 1970s, after all). Refreshed and relaxed, we set off again. It is within the realm of possibility that our rest stop played a part in what happened next.

We came upon a set of serious white water. I was in the bow and probably did not give sufficient warning to avoid a boulder. We hit it head-on and were thrown from the canoe into the icy water. The canoe filled with water and careened uncontrollably away from us, carried by the swift current. I emerged from the waist-deep water and felt my right leg give way. I had not felt any pain, but when I looked down at my leg, I saw that the skin behind my knee had fallen away, revealing much of my calf muscle. I must have sliced the back of my leg on the metal strut against which I had been kneeling. I slapped the flap of skin and tissue back up, and knelt down to compress it. I was shaking badly from cold and shock.

Ric called out, "Are you okay?"

I replied, "No!" emphatically, but that seemed to be all I could say.

Startled, he came up to join me and turned ashen when I showed him the wound. My companions flagged down a passing motorist and were able to call for help. An ambulance arrived about a half hour later. On the way to the hospital, the talkative young EMT told me he was new on the job. He said he had had CPR training but not "cuts and bleeding." I was not bleeding badly but was hardly comforted by this bit of information. The ER doctor sewed me up with what seemed to be countless stitches and told me I had been very lucky. I had just missed having an artery cut and the gash stopped micrometers short of the fascia covering the calf muscle. I was bandaged up, given crutches, and released. I was able to heal without consequence.

We were not too far from Albany. My almost-ex-girlfriend, Cita, who had been with me at the Woodstock Festival, had a home near Chatham, about an hour away. She agreed to pick me up and take me in. I stayed several days to recuperate. One evening, Cita invited me to accompany her for dinner at a local restaurant with an "interesting Australian couple" she had met, who also had a house in the Chatham area. The couple turned out to be Rupert Murdoch and his wife. It was a pleasant enough evening, but unfortunately I remember nothing about the conversation.

Cita and I had had an intense on-again, off-again relationship for several years, and were at times close to getting married. We even agreed at one point to become formally engaged. Yet we could never seem to get our emotional clocks fully synchronized. Initially I was completely smitten, but she was still recovering from a collapsed marriage and was unwilling to attempt another "permanent" commitment. By the time she was ready, my ardor had cooled sufficiently that I retreated behind my characteristic emotional reticence. We finally parted company soon thereafter.

Meanwhile, by the fall of 1975, the city's fiscal crisis was full-blown. Major layoffs and budget slashing were in the offing. In October, President Ford rejected the city's request for federal assistance to stave off default, prompting the immortal New York *Daily News* headline: FORD TO CITY: DROP DEAD. At the time, I had been planning another trip to the Himalayas, but I did not dare leave. I felt I had to try to do whatever I could to minimize the fallout of the impending disaster. By that time, John Zuccotti, our highly regarded boss, had taken over as first deputy mayor at the insistence of the banks, who respected his competence and unmatched credibility with the financial community. The Municipal Assistance Corporation (MAC) and the Emergency Financial Control Board (EFCB) had been created in June, and John was the principal city liaison with their activities. The EFCB was given unprecedented oversight powers to monitor and manage city expenditures.

Development offices were becoming hard to justify at a time when there was no development. We heard that press releases had already been drafted announcing the elimination or consolidation of the five development offices into a single entity. I knew that at least one other development office director—Rick Rosan of the Downtown Brooklyn office—had more political traction than I did and would probably be the one to survive (which turned out to be the case).

As the months of the early winter and spring of 1976 ticked by, I waited for the ax to fall, eliminating OLMD and my job. In the late spring, my phone rang. It was Martin E. Segal. I did not know him but recognized the name as the mayor's confidant and guru for cultural matters. He asked to meet with me. I innocently asked why. He said, "I would like to speak with you about possibly becoming the new commissioner of cultural affairs." I was stunned. Where had *this* come from? I mumbled that I would be happy to discuss the position.

I met with Marty a few days later. As always, he was impeccably dressed and sporting his signature small red rose pinned to his lapel. He was strikingly short, just over five feet, about the same height as his friend, the mayor, about whom he was fond of joking that they saw "eye-to-eye" on everything. Born in Russia in 1916, he had immigrated to Brooklyn as a five-year-old. In his teens he began selling insurance, and in 1939 he founded the actuarial consulting company that still bears his name. His speech bore no trace of his foreign origins. Early on, while amassing a considerable fortune, he became a devotee of the arts. He had founded the Film Society of Lincoln Center in 1968 and had persuaded Charlie Chaplin to come to the United States from Britain to headline its first annual gala. Marty loved galas (Fred Astaire headlined the Film Society's second, Alfred Hitchcock the third). Now, at age sixty, he was determined to use his wealth to become an even more important figure in the cultural life of the city. Marty had talked the mayor into letting him produce a study on the importance of cultural activities to the future of the city and on how the city should best organize itself to support the arts. Not surprisingly, the study concluded that the arts were a critical and indispensable part of New York's economy and that the city's current financial and administrative support was inadequate. At the time, the only agency specifically charged with supporting the arts was a small office within the Department of Parks & Recreation that had a minimal budget, mostly for a few summer programs.

The report recommended the creation of a new cabinet-level Department of Cultural Affairs charged with prioritizing, advocating for, and administering the city's financial assistance for cultural institutions and programs. Given New York City's fiscal distress, the only argument that had any hope of gaining traction was economic: that the new agency was fundamental to the health of one of the remaining cornerstones of the city's economic base. The department would be headed by a commissioner and advised by a prestigious commission, which Marty—naturally—planned to lead. As he would later say to me, "It is far better to be a patron than an employee of the arts."

I had a good discussion with Marty about the challenges of starting a new government agency for the arts while the city was teetering on the edge of financial collapse, and about what our respective roles would be. Marty seemed comfortable with our chemistry and said he would recommend me to the mayor for the job. No other sign-off was needed. If it was okay with Marty, it was okay with the mayor. John Zuccotti was visibly relieved when I told him. He could never have sold the mayor on me for this job without Marty having taken the initiative. Now he did not have to fire me. But how had this happened? I had no idea. It was only later that I heard that Marty had supposedly offered the job first to Tom Hoving (the genteel head of the Metropolitan Museum) and then to Joe Papp (the creative genius behind the Public Theater), and that both had turned him down when it became clear that Marty intended to be the one to speak to the mayor and to be the new agency's principal public face. Marty was mostly looking to the new commissioner to set up and manage the infant organization. Apparently a subordinate role did not appeal to those major figures—and egos—of New York's cultural scene.

At the time, Marty was also a partner at the investment house of Wertheim & Co. Wondering where he could find someone to fill the role he had in mind for the new commissioner, he consulted the occupant of the office next to his. That was none other than Ed Kresky, who had joined the firm to pilot its recent entry into the municipal finance sector. "Ed," Marty said, "you must know somebody who knows how to run a government agency." That's when my phone rang.

It was in late April 1976 that this transpired. The press release went out and the *New York Times* responded to the announcement with a "Man in the News" profile of me on May 5. Although the *Times* reported that I described myself as "close to" John Zuccotti, I am sure I did not use those words. I got along well with John but he would not have appreciated the implication that my professional future was of personal concern to him, as the piece lightly implied. The article also stated that I was Martin Segal's "personal choice," which was technically true, but I certainly had not been his *first* personal choice.

I was still the commissioner-designate when the Bicentennial Fourth of July rolled around. The city council had not yet voted to approve my appointment. I was assigned the task of escorting Brooke Astor, one of the city's leaders in society and philanthropy, to the day's festivities. She was seventy-four at the time, but I had trouble keeping up with her as we raced from event to event. One of my few clear memories of the day is of sitting behind Bella Abzug's enormous hat at a ceremony and being able to see little else.

In Mayor Beame's private office, at my formal swearing-in ceremony as the city's first commissioner of cultural affairs, 1976 (on the left, my father and my stepmother, Ilse; at the far right is Martin E. Segal).

The Council voted a few days later. I was sworn in, at age thirty-six, to head a new high-profile agency with a purview that would be the envy of anyone connected with the cultural life of the city. The public ceremony was held in the Blue Room of City Hall and I invited a few close friends. It was a brief and innocuous affair, and I gave a short speech. Beforehand,

I was ushered into the mayor's private office accompanied by my father, my stepmother, and Marty Segal. As I took the formal oath of office, I was filled with a sense of validation that my father could witness this moment and accept it as justification of my decision to pursue my own life path. He was clearly proud although uncomfortable in that setting.

The next Monday, I reported to my new office in the Arsenal, the headquarters of the Parks Department in Central Park near 65th Street. I found myself in a situation somewhat akin to what I had experienced in the governor's office. I was young and without substantive grounding in the portfolios for which I was responsible. I would be dealing with mature and prestigious experts who had professional stature and constituencies of their own. Previously, I had simply been the conduit for the flow of information and decisions. Now I had actual executive authority and operational accountability. Again, I relied on asking questions openly and honestly, trying to work collaboratively, and hoping to be guided by prudence and common sense.

Our offices had the standard dingy appearance of the impoverished municipal offices of the time, but I had a bright room with a bay window at the back of the first floor that looked out onto the park. Before taking over, I was able to recruit the beginnings of a staff. It was a skeleton operation: a deputy commissioner, an assistant commissioner, and an administrative chief. I inherited a few program people who had long dispensed the meager program funds almost at their sole discretion. This was as much staff as I could get budgetary approval for at a time when the cash-strapped city was laying off police officers and firefighters. (Today the department has some sixty employees.)

I brought Mike Mehlman, my reliable finance guy from State Parks, to handle the bookkeeping and administration. I selected a young African American woman, Cheryl McClenney, to head up what I hoped would be a growing and more professional program operation. Cheryl had a degree in fine arts from the School of the Art Institute in Chicago and was managing partnerships with community organizations for the Museum Collaborative.

In addition to these impressive professional credentials, she had the passion and personality to relate credibly to the neighborhood and ethnic arts communities and organizations that the city had so woefully neglected for so long. As Cheryl McClenney-Brooker, she would go on to create a distinguished career in the arts, notably as director of external affairs for the Philadelphia Museum of Art.

I had met Richard Bader, a deputy in the Parks Department who headed its design and capital construction operations. I thought he would be the ideal person to be my deputy and liaison to the eighteen large cultural institutions that commanded over 90 percent of our $28 million annual budget, down from almost $50 million prior to the fiscal crisis. (Today, DCLA, as it is now known, has an operating budget of $156 million and a capital budget of some $822 million that supports thirty-three major arts organizations.) We dubbed that original roster the Cultural Institutions Group (CIG), a name which I believe still survives.

Marty informed me, however, that the mayor wanted to see the deputy post go to Janet Langsam, a protégé of Queens Borough President Donald Manes. I bitterly objected, having had a previous deputy forced on me at OLMD. Although I argued with Marty, he pleaded with me not to force him to say no to the mayor. I reluctantly relented and Janet was hired. She turned out to be capable and committed to the arts and we forged a solid working relationship.

The large institutions had been very comfortable dealing directly with the mayor's Office of Management and Budget (OMB). With their prestigious boards and track record of political access, the major arts organizations had little use for another layer of bureaucracy standing between them and the city's coffers, particularly an agency charged with passing independent judgment on the merits of their requests. Most of the public funds went to supporting the operations of the city-owned buildings: the heat, light, power, and guards for the Metropolitan Museum, the Museum of Natural History, and the zoos and botanical gardens. (The city's libraries, because of their unique history and legal structure, were not included in our portfolio.) Tom Hoving, in particular, had little use for this uncredentialed newcomer. He would look down his long patrician nose at me with undisguised disdain as he allowed the phrase "Of course, Commissioner," to roll slowly past his lips.

The lion's share of programming money went to the New York Philharmonic, the Metropolitan Opera, and the Public Theater for their summer-in-the-park activities. Whatever their feelings about dealing with us, each institution responded to our requests for data and information respectfully, helpfully, and often cordially. Slowly, we established good working relationships. I was an ex-officio member of the boards of all of those organizations and periodically attended meetings to show our interest and concern. It was an extraordinary privilege to be exposed to this array of talent and civic commitment. I made a point of calling upon the leaders of the cultural entities on their turf in order to introduce myself and put a personal face on the new agency.

I also visited organizations in the outer boroughs, which received little or no funding, in order to try to acquaint myself with what was going on. I was astounded by the vibrancy and creativity that I found there. For example, I went to a concert of the Queens Symphony (a community orchestra), which was held in a high school gymnasium. At the dinner beforehand, held at the West Side Tennis Club in Forest Hills (not far from where I had lived in Kew Gardens), I found myself seated next to the rising young pianist who would be the evening's guest soloist; his name was André Watts. In the minority communities of Harlem and the Bronx, I encountered bitter and justified anger at how little support their groups had been receiving from the city. I was determined to at least begin the slow process of addressing these inequities.

I spent considerable time in the early months working with Carnegie Hall. The city owns the building and leases it to the nonprofit entity at very favorable terms in exchange for free programming provided for young people and special populations. The lease was expiring and a new agreement had to be negotiated. Early on, I paid a courtesy call to Isaac Stern, the famed violinist, who headed Carnegie Hall. Stern was far more than a figurehead. He was one of those rare individuals who could be both a world-class performer and an effective manager. When I arrived for the interview, I was told that Maestro Stern was up in the balcony, listening to a practice concert by a youth orchestra. I was ushered into the darkened theater and sat down quietly next to him as the music rose from below. As I was about to say how wonderful the playing was, he turned to me and said, "I can't take it anymore. Let's get out of here."

In his office, after a few minutes of pleasant conversation, it occurred to me to say to him, "Mr. Stern, I am new to this job, and the job is new. What should a commissioner of cultural affairs do?"

He thought for a moment and replied, "The city will never have enough money to satisfy everyone. Right now, the big boys get almost everything, and the minority and other communities are going to besiege you to get a fair share. As you weigh these competing demands, keep one thing in mind: insist on excellence."

I was struck at how perfectly he summed up my challenge. I treasured his sound, succinct advice and tried hard to live by it.

My next experience with those in high places was less inspirational. I received a call from the office of Bill Paley, the legendary CEO of CBS. It was an invitation to lunch in his private dining room. I could not help being aware of his stature, in part because of my family's fascination with the role that CBS and Edward R. Murrow had played in bringing down Senator Joseph McCarthy. I learned that Blanchette Rockefeller, the wife of Nelson's older brother, John D. III, would join us at lunch. At the Museum of Modern Art (MoMA), she was a long-serving board member and major supporter. The lunch was delicious and the wine even better, and I had a glass more than I should have. They argued that MoMA deserved city support and that it had been denied unfairly for too long. I meekly—and possibly with a bit of a slur—responded that the city provided operating assistance only for institutions whose buildings or land were publicly owned, and that given the city's fiscal problems I did not see how that situation could change for the foreseeable future. They quickly concluded that I was in no position to help, and I never heard from them again. It would take MoMA many years and a different economic climate to turn that situation around.

My job allowed—actually, required—me to attend the opening night of the Metropolitan Opera in the mayor's box, address tens of thousands of people at a New York Philharmonic concert in Central Park, attend a gala at MoMA honoring Alexander Calder, share a stage with Joanne Woodward to present an award, and attend many other events and ceremonies. But I think my meeting with Isaac Stern remains my favorite moment from my days as commissioner.

A close second was getting the second or third Bammy Award ever presented by the Brooklyn Academy of Music (BAM). Over the Fourth of July weekend in 1977, a water main burst outside BAM, completely inundating the main auditorium. Water rose above the seats and the place was a gargantuan mess. Over the ensuing months, I managed to muster—with enormous help from the deputy mayor for operations—an array of city resources to clean and repair the damage on an emergency basis. BAM was able to reopen in time for its first fall event. Through the process, I became good friends with the remarkable Harvey Lichtenstein, the founder and prime moving force behind that wonderful institution. I was proud to accept the award on behalf of all the city workers who had rescued BAM, and my Bammy still occupies a prominent place on my bookshelf.

I was determined to expand our support for arts programming while also insisting on excellence. I felt that the best way to do this would be to professionalize the process in order to boost the agency's credibility and justify larger appropriations. Cheryl McClenney was just the person to lead such an effort. We were able to set aside about $250,000 for a competitive grant program vetted by peer-group panels, a process patterned on the structure of the successful and respected State Council on the Arts. It was a pathetically small amount for the entire city, but it was a start. By 2017, program grants had grown to almost $60 million and supported almost 1,000 organizations.

The other major program initiative I undertook was to try to tap into the recently enacted federal Comprehensive Employment and Training

Act (CETA) program. Co-sponsored by New York Senator Jacob Javits, CETA was signed by President Nixon in 1973. Loosely patterned on the Works Progress Administration (WPA) of the 1930s, it was designed to help combat the high unemployment of the 1970s by providing public service jobs for low-income workers. The WPA had financed a lot of great art; why not CETA?

We were able to get a million-dollar grant to hire jobless artists to undertake specific projects, something we could not legally do with city funds. Again, we set up a peer review process to evaluate the merits of the applications. We had to agree to certain borough-by-borough allocations to get the program through the Board of Estimate, which consisted of the three citywide officials (the mayor, the comptroller and the president of the city council) and the five borough presidents, and was the all-powerful approver of city contracts under the old city charter.* Even with these constraints, we managed to preserve the integrity of the process. And we hired Rochelle (Shelly) Slovin to direct the program, which she did with superior wisdom and skill. Shelly would found and then direct the Museum of the Moving Image for thirty years and had an acclaimed acting career as well.

I had what one could easily argue was the best and most fun job in New York City, and I was enjoying it immensely, but I found the powerful draw of the Himalayas still exerting itself. I had felt cheated out of a trip in the waning days of OLMD and was determined to go back. In September 1976, only a few months after assuming my exalted post, I announced to Marty Segal that I was taking a month off to go trekking in Nepal. He was furious with me but did not forbid it. Ed Kresky was appalled by my hubris. But I was young and stubborn.

It was an extremely demanding trip, a thirty-day circuit around Dhaulagiri, the seventh highest mountain in the world at 26,795 feet. The mountain is in western Nepal, near Annapurna. Dhaulagiri had been the original target of the Herzog expedition in 1950, but the climbers could not find a

* The Supreme Court of the United States unanimously declared the Board of Estimate unconstitutional in 1989.

route to the summit in what was then an unmapped and largely unexplored region. The romance of going there was for me irresistible. The days were long and arduous, requiring us to cross two 17,000-foot passes, but the trek did not involve any technical climbing. The scenery was again stupendous, particularly along the Kali Gandaki river gorge. The sheer face of Dhaulagiri rises up some 18,000 feet from the valley floor to the summit, perhaps the greatest vertical distance on Earth. I was too exhausted to join a few of the stronger trekkers on an optional climb of a 19,000-foot peak, but still felt I had seen and done what I came for. Of course, I was completely out of contact with my office the entire time, but remarkably there were no serious consequences.

Because I was a mayoral appointee, my tenure was winding down as the year 1977 ticked by. I began to wonder what would come next. The Bicentennial had been a boon for New York, but the fiscal crisis—much of which Beame inherited from Lindsay—had sealed Beame's political fate. He was challenged by five other Democrats and finished third in the September 8 primary. Ed Koch and Mario Cuomo competed in a runoff election eleven days later, which Koch won, and Abe Beame's days as mayor were soon to be over. I recognized that it would be a long shot to be held over. But I knew several people on the arts committee of Koch's transition team and I decided to give it a try. I did not look for another job, thinking naively that sending out my résumé would weaken my chances of being kept on.

My strongest advocate on the committee was Betty Chapin, Schuyler Chapin's wife and an established figure in her own right on the cultural scene. Schuyler had been the general manager at the Metropolitan Opera and engaged in his own political fight for survival there. He was superseded as chief executive by Anthony Bliss, who was brought in with the new title of "executive director." Schuyler had taken me under his wing and introduced me as much as possible to the ins and outs of cultural politics in New York. Schuyler would later assume my job in the Giuliani administration.

I was told that the transition committee recommended that I be retained, but it was just too plum a job. Early in January, Koch announced that he had selected Henry Geldzahler for the post. Geldzahler was a well-known and influential curator of twentieth-century art at the Metropolitan Museum with visibility and stature in the cultural scene. The *New York Times* mentioned me in an editorial about outgoing Beame appointees and opined that New Yorkers owed me a debt of gratitude for a job well done. That was considerable solace, but I still had to find another job.

Early in the new year of 1978, my phone rang again. The caller was Fred Rath, deputy commissioner for historic preservation at State Parks. Fred was an early leader of the emerging movement to restore and repurpose historic buildings. He had led the National Trust for Historic Preservation and had joined our new state office in 1972. Fred was my main contact at the agency regarding the Seaport project while I was running the New York regional office, and he continued to shepherd it while I was at OLMD. We had gotten along well and stayed in touch. Fred was a wonderful person and was widely respected. "Would you be interested in coming back to State Parks," he asked, "and heading up the state's part of the Seaport project?" The plan was to put a new state Maritime Museum in a restored Schermerhorn Row. The state now owned the block and had the funding to proceed. The title would be "director of the New York State Maritime Museum." I had never thought of myself as a museum director, and once again I would be taking on an assignment without bringing to it any significant amount of professional expertise. Although the offer felt like a bit of retrogression, I had no other leads.

This was early in February. I called Fred back and said yes, I would take the job. "On one condition," I added. "I can't start until May 1." Fred was somewhat taken aback, but he agreed. My reason for delaying was that I had been mining the Mountain Travel catalog and found two trips, back-to-back, that I really wanted to do. One was a climb of Mt. Kilimanjaro along with some wild-game viewing; the second was the ascent of Island Peak, a 20,305-foot mountain in the Everest region and the second highest "trekking peak" in Nepal. It often served as a training ground for climbers who had their eyes on the 8,000-meter giants.

I set off in late February for Africa and joined our group in Nairobi at the rustic but comfortable Stanley Hotel, which reeked of its colonial heritage. Almost equally divided between men and women, our group included about fifteen trekkers of varying ages and fitness levels. This time I would prove among the youngest and strongest of the group. We headed first to Mount Kenya, about one hundred miles north of Nairobi. Our objective was Point Lenana, a subsidiary peak of 16,350 feet. The main summits, at over 17,000 feet, were highly technical and out of our league. Lenana was a "walk-up," albeit a demanding one. I got furious headaches from the altitude but otherwise had no problems. After the climb, we headed a bit farther north to the Samburu National Reserve for several days of game viewing. We camped in relative luxury, discovering—in addition to the magnificent animals)—HP sauce and Kenya Cane, a highly potent, rum-like distilled spirit.

Kilimanjaro, at 19,300 feet, was our main goal. It straddles the border between Kenya and Tanzania and is normally climbed from Arusha on the Tanzanian side. It is not very far from Nairobi, but at the time there was a political dispute between the two countries and the border was sealed. The only way we could get to Arusha was to fly from Nairobi, not directly but via Ethiopia. We flew into Addis Ababa and found ourselves in an eerie and unreal world. Ethiopia was then under a radical communist dictatorship. Armed militias accompanied us everywhere and political speech, much less critical joking, was not permitted. We stayed at the Addis Hilton, where we were the only western guests. We had a wonderful dinner of superb Ethiopian cuisine at a local restaurant but were much relieved to depart the next day without incident.

Our plane landed at the Arusha airport, and we spent the night in a lovely lodge as we prepared for the challenge. Perhaps the most remarkable aspect of climbing Kilimanjaro is the kaleidoscope of climates that one passes through. The mountain sits almost directly on the equator. One sets off through a tropical environment where elephants graze. We were told that if we saw a pile of elephant dung, we should stick a finger in it and, if it was still warm, to get the hell out of there. This advice was not completely serious, but it got our attention.

As one ascends, the vegetation changes. First, one passes through a rain forest, then starker grasslands, and then into a barren moonscape. Finally, one slogs up the ash hill of the summit cone and into snow and ice to reach the crater rim. Reaching any point on the rim is sufficient to say, in mountain ethics, that one has climbed it. But the ultimate goal on Kili is Uhuru Peak, the highest point on the crater rim.

In 1978, the conventional wisdom was to try to climb the mountain as quickly as possible and to get down before altitude sickness could set in. Today, the climb takes a few more days, with acclimatization and rest days built in, resulting in a much more manageable experience and a much higher success rate. Starting at around 3,000 feet, we took three days to arrive at our high camp at the base of the main volcanic cone at about 15,500 feet. We were awakened at about 1:00 a.m., given just a few candy bars to eat (in order not to upset our queasy stomachs), and led out wearing headlamps for the summit climb. Our guide put the slowest climbers just behind him at the front. His idea was that they would not lag behind and become discouraged, and that everyone would make it at least to the rim. This strategy worked but prompted much grumbling from the stronger members as we made our way very, very slowly in the cold thin air.

We made it up to the rim at about 9:30 a.m., and after a thirty-minute rest, half of us continued on to Uhuru. I was competing with another strong hiker to be the first one up, but he beat me by a few minutes, arriving at about noon. The view from the summit is not what one comes for; there is nothing to see but the plains of Africa stretching endlessly to the horizon. It was cold and getting late. We headed down, covering in minutes what had taken hours on the way up. I stumbled into our camp at 10,000 feet at 6:00 p.m. At something like seventeen hours, it was one of the longest, hardest days I had ever experienced in the mountains.

After the climb, we spent another couple of days in beautiful lodges, recuperating and game viewing, but after Kilimanjaro, it was a bit of an anticlimax. From Arusha, we drove to Mombasa, arriving at a luxury seaside resort, unfortunately in the middle of the night. We were unable to enjoy it because we had to catch an early flight to Dar es Salaam, the termination point of our trip. From there, several of us flew on Air Madagascar to Cairo, arriving in a sandstorm. The intense winds and swirling dust made for the scariest landing of my life.

Two days later, I made the journey to Delhi and Kathmandu, extremely happy to be back. I checked into the Malla Hotel, a lovely oasis near the Royal Palace. It offered excellent food, charming rooms, and a peaceful interior garden. Mountain Travel definitely made better arrangements than Buddy Bombard! There were only about ten in our group, all men, ranging in age from two in their twenties to Bernard, a seventy-year-old British man determined to get to 20,000 feet. We were a fairly experienced lot. When our leaders sorted out our climbing gear in the hotel yard, the sight of all the ropes and hardware made clear that we were in for something fairly serious.

Instead of flying in to Lukla, a distance of roughly 150 miles, our itinerary called for us to land at an airstrip perhaps halfway there. We would trek in from that spot. The ten-day approach march would ensure that we were in good shape for the climb. We hiked up and down ridge after ridge, through tiny villages and endless terraced plots of barley and potatoes. It seemed that almost every usable inch of land—none of it flat—was used for subsistence farming. The methodology and implements used for tilling the fields and planting the crops appeared to be unchanged from the Middle Ages. Along the way, our sherpas bought a goat. He was nicknamed Din Din, signaling his imminent fate. The goat was our companion for several days. One evening, we were invited to witness or even participate in his demise. I demurred but thoroughly enjoyed the chops and stew that followed.

We marched through beautiful forests of rhododendron trees festooned with brilliant red spring blossoms. A couple of days before getting to Lukla, we were ascending yet another ridge. I stopped to rest and put my precious Yashica camera on the rock wall beside me. I treasured the camera because it took 2¼-inch-square transparencies, which made for dramatic slideshows that I loved to inflict on my friends. I resumed the climb and discovered after only a few minutes that I had forgotten the camera. I raced back, but it was gone. I was devastated. Proudly sharing the pictures when I got home represented a major part of my total experience. The most dramatic scenery lay ahead, and I would have no record of it or the climb. When I reached our camp for the night a little while later, I mentioned my loss to our Sherpas. They were mortified that one of their people would steal a valuable item. Four of them sped down the mountain, querying the locals and following leads in search of the missing camera. Hours later, they returned, proud and smiling. They had recovered the Yashica. I was ecstatic and tipped them generously.

Passing Lukla, I was again in familiar territory. From the valley below, I started the 2,500-foot climb from about 8,500 feet up to Namche Bazaar, which I dreaded, remembering my previous struggle with it. After several hours, I was about to stop for a rest when I saw the roofs of Namche around the next corner. After Kilimanjaro and the trek in, it proved to be a piece of cake.

We followed the route up toward Everest again, stopping at Thyangboche. This time, we encountered a late-winter snowstorm. It turned this magical spot into an icy fairyland, but the snow quickly melted away. At Periche, instead of heading left, up toward Base Camp, we turned right, passed Dingboche, and caught the intimidating sight of Island Peak a few miles ahead. The Sherpas set up our camp at about 16,500 feet amid some boulders at the base of the steep incline leading up to the mountain itself. We spent a rest day airing out our clothes and sleeping bags and acclimatizing to the thinning air. I was free of headaches and felt strong.

Early the next morning, we began the serious part of the ascent. We picked our way, agonizingly slowly, up the severe slope. We were straining for every breath, yet we were far below the altitude where oxygen can even be considered. (Given the weight, logistics, and expense of bringing, using, and disposing of oxygen canisters, they are almost never employed below 25,000 feet except in emergencies.) We reached our high camp, which was perched on a few rocks at about 19,000 feet, at about noon. Despite the vertiginous setting, I was not uncomfortable. I was probably too mentally compromised by the altitude to notice. We spent the afternoon getting our gear sorted and preparing for the next day's summit push. No matter how many times I laid out my gear in my tent, my brain was too fuzzy to retain where things were.

We again got an early start the next morning and made our way up through the rocks until we emerged onto a snowfield just below 20,000 feet. There were ominous lines across the snow, indicating crevasses. Bernard could go no farther; he would not reach his goal. The rest of us roped up and put on our overboots and crampons. I was on a rope with Jonathan Calvert, an easygoing and congenial Texan in his early fifties. As we were about to set out, I saw Jonathan begin to sink slowly in the snow. Instead of doing what I had learned—dropping into a self-arrest position to provide an anchor in case he fell farther—I simply watched, frozen in befuddled fascination. Fortunately, his descent halted and with the help of our Sherpa guide he was pulled up and regained his footing on firm snow.

We began our ascent up an almost vertical ice wall, one hundred feet or more high. We had a fixed rope to hold on to that the Sherpas had gone ahead to install, but we needed the front points of our crampons and an ice axe to pull our way up the ice wall. Part of the way up, my left overboot came loose and I was reduced to one effective foot. (Overboots are a cumbersome relic of the past that have since been replaced by sleek plastic mountaineering footwear.) By the time I clambered to the top of the wall, I could feel my left foot beginning to freeze up. I stared up at the summit, now tantalizingly close. I knew that I probably should go down and not risk severe frostbite. But, like so many others in such moments, I thought to hell with the consequences. I had come this far, and I was not about to make a cautious decision.

One more half-hour across a precipitous knife ridge, and up still another incline, and I stood on the summit. The afternoon clouds had built up, depriving us of some spectacular views of the surrounding Himalayan ridges and summits, but the overcast sky could not rob us of our exhilaration. Better still, the feeling returned to my feet as soon as I started down and I suffered no ill effects. Four or five days later we were back at Lukla to catch our flight to Kathmandu.

I had had two demanding adventures in a row and had not had a decent shower in weeks. My boots had deteriorated badly but still had some useful life left, so I gave them to a porter at the airstrip. Still, I was not anxious to go home and resume my normal life. I would have headed back up into the mountains in an instant, given any plausible excuse. But none was available and I headed home.

With my climbing Sherpa, on the summit of Island Peak, 20,305 feet, 1978.

There was one development that did draw me back to New York. Late in 1977, I had started going out regularly with Marilyn Russell. I had met Marilyn a year or so before, of course at the instigation of my gregarious friend, George Humphreys. George had arranged for Marilyn to pay me a call at my office at OLMD, ostensibly for career advice. I liked her instantly and we had a couple of dates. I quickly concluded that she was someone to be taken seriously. She was smart, determined, and directed. I, on the other hand, at age thirty-six, was still avoiding major emotional commitments in my romantic attachments. *Alfie* was still one of my favorite movies and I identified with Michael Caine's portrayal of an anchorless existence. I did not call her again.

One evening many months later, I wandered into the Italian Pavilion and found George, Henry Diamond, and Marilyn ensconced at our usual table. Marilyn had been Henry's secretary for a number of years but had recently moved to a high-powered sales and marketing job at NBC. I joined them and was reminded how delightful, smart, and interesting Marilyn was. After a few drinks, I dragged first George and then Henry to the bar to privately ascertain if either of them was dating her or had a prior claim on her attention that evening. They both said no and encouraged me to take the next step. They tried to interest Marilyn and me in watching them as they adjourned next door for one of their frequent games of gin rummy. Neither of us found that a very appealing offer, and we went out to a nice dinner by ourselves. We went back to her apartment and played Mastermind long into the night, and we were together most of the following week. We dated regularly for several months after that, before I had gone off on my trip to Kilimanjaro and the Himalayas.

I had told Marilyn that I would be at the Italian Pavilion at 6:00 p.m. upon my return from Nepal in mid-April. I went straight there from the airport, arriving at the appointed hour, but she did not show up. When I caught up with her a day or two later, I asked why she hadn't come. She was not impressed with my *Around the World in Eighty Days* punctuality, pointing out that she had received exactly one postcard during my two-month absence. My lame protest—that I had actually sent two but one had failed to reach her—did not go very far in mollifying her. Fortunately for me, she soon relented and we picked up where we had left off, becoming very much a couple.

A week later, I reported to my new office on John Street sporting a beard but feeling out of place carrying an attaché case instead of wearing a pack. The beard was probably supposed to help me adopt the persona of a museum director. I set about to learn the basics of maritime history and to think about what kind of collection we should aspire to. The history of the port of New York was rich and offered many fruitful possibilities. Walter Lord, the noted author of *A Night to Remember,* about the sinking of the *Titanic,* served on our advisory board and had an intriguing collection of memorabilia from the disaster. I toured established maritime museums at Mystic, Connecticut; Salem, Massachusetts; and Norfolk, Virginia. I learned the difference between a bark and a brig. I read Robert Albion's classic, *The Rise of New York Port, 1815-1860.* I had a lot to absorb and knew I was just scratching the surface.

However, most of my time was spent on the physical buildings for which I was now responsible. Giorgio Cavaglieri's design of adaptive reuse of Schermerhorn Row was too modernistic for the state's more conservative approach, which emphasized exactingly researched preservation. We therefore decided to hire Jan Hird Pokorny, whose firm was an early leader of this unique branch of architecture. Jan was born in Prague in 1914 and had immigrated to the United States in 1938. His accent and demeanor were very familiar to me, and I immediately felt comfortable with him. Working with Jan and Bud Moskin, his extremely able assistant, was a delight for me and for Fred Rath.

The block was a mélange of different building types, the oldest dating from the second decade of the nineteenth century. All had seen modifications to storefronts, rooflines, and fenestration. What date would we pick to restore to? The most controversial issue was whether we would keep the mansard roofs that had been added in the 1850s to the main façade of the row of circa-1811 warehouses on Fulton Street. These warehouse buildings, erected by the merchant Peter Schermerhorn, were the crown jewel of the block and the best surviving example of that architectural period in the city. Since the commercial history of New York is all about change and evolution, we decided to restore to the approximate time of the mansard additions and to incorporate some of the other modifications that had accreted by then.

Fenestration was another major challenge. Few elements of an old building are more central to its character than windows, or as critical to a structure's integrity. Windows are also the most subject to deterioration and most likely to be in need of replacement if modern uses are to be accommodated within. Our agency had a highly regarded historic resource center on Peebles Island, at the confluence of the Mohawk and Hudson rivers, among whose specialties was constructing replicas of historic windows. The conservators set about fabricating windows typical of that era to our exact specifications.

Schermerhorn row in the South Street Seaport area of Lower Manhattan, 2021.

The brick façades needed to be repointed using historically appropriate mortar and to be cleaned of their accumulated grit, grime, and more recent overpainting. But we wanted to save as much of the historic signage as possible. The best answer, I learned, was to blast the surfaces with ground walnut shells. That was expensive, but it was the most effective and least abrasive cleaner. Every aspect of the research, design, and construction processes was intricate and demanding—and exciting. The end result would meet with considerable praise from the historic preservation community.

While we were immersed in the physical restoration process, I was also the buildings' landlord. In addition to housing a variety of eclectic shops, the block was home to two well-known restaurants: Sloppy Louie's and Sweets Seafood House. I came to know the owners of these two New York institutions, which always had operational issues that needed attention. But most significantly, several artists had established themselves in the upper floors of the buildings, which were among the first live/work spaces for artists in the city. The state's first response to the situation was that the artists were simply squatters in landmark structures and would have to be evicted. The artists felt strongly that their "sweat equity" had helped save the buildings and that they deserved to remain. They did not intend to be kicked out. Among their number was Mark di Suvero, already a well-known sculptor, who gave them significant visibility and clout.

Their cause was taken up by Manhattan Borough President Percy Sutton, who was represented in the negotiations by Wilbert Tatum, his deputy, who would follow Percy as publisher of the *New York Amsterdam News*. Sutton's support and Tatum's effectiveness in the political arena were formidable assets for the residents. Finally, the artists themselves were represented by Brian and Anita O'Neill. Brian could be blustery and difficult, but Anita was gracious, whip-smart, and strategic. Anita later remarried, becoming Anita Contini; she became one of the nation's most highly regarded arts advocates and administrators. I spent many long and difficult evenings in discussions and negotiations with the artists and their advocates seeking to resolve the conflicts between my responsibilities and my considerable sympathy for their position. Not surprisingly—and quite appropriately—they eventually won the right to stay, and the renovation took place around them.

As I continued to explore how best to create and operate a major new maritime museum in those buildings, I was in regular touch with John Hightower, who headed the South Street Seaport Museum. John was an amiable and competent arts administrator and we got along well. He had been a highly successful executive director of the New York State Council on the Arts (NYSCA) and had served a brief and turbulent stint as director of MoMA before falling victim to the highly political protesting and infighting of the time.

It slowly occurred to both of us that it was ridiculous to have two maritime museums operating on Fulton Street. I also doubted that the state would step up to a long-term commitment to the ongoing operation of a fledgling museum. Based on my experience with cultural institutions in New York and John's at NYSCA, we both concluded that a different but proven model would make far more sense. The two institutions should merge. The state should cover the basic operating costs for heat, light, power, and guards, as the city did for the institutions whose buildings it owned. The nonprofit Seaport should assume responsibility for the programming and funding of the museum, as the city's nonprofit cultural groups did. We knew, of course, that it is much easier to raise private money for exhibits than for rent and utilities. A merger seemed to both of us to be in everyone's best interests, and we tried to sell it. We traveled to Albany to meet with Orin Lehman, the State Parks commissioner, among others. Orin was a gracious and effective public servant, serving the longest stint ever in his job, from 1975 to 1993. He found our proposal, however, a bit too complicated and controversial for him to adopt without considerable reflection. He did not veto it and said he would think about it. But I never received any further guidance from him, and without his active support the merger could go nowhere.

I had been in the job for just over a year. The physical restoration project was proceeding well and had been a source of great satisfaction. The museum aspect seemed pointless and frustrating. I could see no viable and rewarding long-term future there. I became aware that the job of executive director of the NYSCA had become available. I was not sure that I was best suited for a career as an arts administrator, but it seemed to me to be one of the few senior government positions that I might enjoy and that my résumé might fit. I spoke to John Hightower, who had held the job, and he encouraged me. I also turned once again to my friend and rabbi, Ed Kresky.

Ed, a devotee of the arts himself, was vice chairman of NYSCA. Its chair, Kitty Carlisle Hart—who had taken over in 1976 and would serve for twenty years in that capacity—relied heavily on Ed for political advice and strategy. I called Ed and he, too, encouraged me to pursue the job. With such backing, my candidacy progressed smoothly. I went through a series of interviews, including finally with Kitty herself. Ed called me to say that Kitty was happy and it looked like a done deal. The appointment was making its way through the governor's office for final formal approval when it crossed the desk of Mark Lawton. I believe that Mark was the first deputy budget director at the time, soon to become the director. I had known Mark well from his prior job as deputy commissioner at State Parks, particularly since he had a strong personal interest in the Maritime Museum project. A few days later, Ed Kresky called to tell me that Mark had killed the appointment. Word was that Mark had described me as disloyal and not to be trusted.

I was shocked and could only conclude that Mark had found my merger proposal not just unacceptable but subversive. The state Maritime Museum had apparently been his pet vision, and he presumably found my suggestion for a new direction traitorous. I had kept Orin Lehman apprised of what I was doing, but that did not seem to count for Mark. This was the only time in my entire professional career that I felt stabbed in the back—and it was devastating. Ed counseled that with that kind of indictment, the situation could not be salvaged and I should accept it. I obviously had no choice. But, as things eventually turned out, Mark had unwittingly done me a great favor.

Licking my wounds, I realized that I had to get out of my present position. I did not have the support I needed, and the future of the project was cloudy at best. I could not conceive of another public-sector job that would work for me. I had had the best jobs I could imagine at both the city and state levels. It was time to move on and look to the private sector.

In August 1979, as the final punctuation to my public-sector career, I received the NYU Graduate School of Public Administration Distinguished Alumnus Award "for dedication to the public service and outstanding contributions to the community." Ed Kresky received the same award some years later and deserved it far more. The dean, Dick Netzer, with whom I had always had a prickly relationship, presented the award to me but, with the justification of expediting a crowded program, forbade me from saying anything. That took some of the air out of what should have felt like a valedictory celebration.

TEN

REAL ESTATE YEARS

I had enjoyed my time working for the city at the mayor's Office of Lower Manhattan Development, focusing on urban planning and design issues and discovering the stimulating world of architects and their craft. Equally satisfying and engaging had been my work at the Urban Development Corporation and then with Jan Pokorny on Schermerhorn Row. Real estate, I thought, might be a good next step, and it had the obvious attraction of paying well. I decided to consult my old boss.

I had kept in touch with Al Marshall, who had moved on to become president of Rockefeller Center. In that role, he moved among the top echelons of the real estate world in New York. Al would occasionally invite Mary Kresky and me to join him and his wife, Sarah Marshall, for lunches in his private dining room, called simply The Apartment. It had been built by the Rockefellers in the early 1930s for theater impresario Samuel "Roxy" Rothafel,* who had gained fame popularizing silent movies in opulent movie houses enlivened by live musical accompaniment. Most famous was his Roxy Theatre in Times Square, where he introduced rigorously choreographed dancers, whom he called the Roxyetttes. When he took over Rockefeller Center's palatial new Radio City Music Hall, the troupe was renamed the Rockettes—the new name smoothly combining the two

* His name, originally Rothapfel in German, means "red apple." It would be nice to think it was the origin of New York City's nickname, the Big Apple, but this is not the case.

sponsors. Rothafel hosted entertainers and show business executives in the art deco elegance of The Apartment. Now it was the private preserve of the Center's chief executive, and our lunches were long and enlivened by old political war stories that echoed against the domed ceiling of the dining room. I phoned Al and asked to meet with him.

Over lunch, I told Al about my idea to try commercial real estate. I knew he dealt with some of the city's leading players. Could he point me in the right direction? After listening carefully, he said, "Why don't you come to work here?"

I was surprised by his question. I had not realized that Al had turned the previously staid business of managing Rockefeller Center into a wide-ranging and powerful national real estate company. Rockefeller Center, Inc. (RCI) had acquired Tishman Construction as its construction arm. It had bought Cushman & Wakefield and its sprawling brokerage operation. Al had transformed the management company from a local to a national enterprise. Finally, he had created the Rockefeller Center Development Corporation (RCDC), a developer of major office buildings around the country, and had brought in John Burnett, my old boss at UDC, to run it. All this was news to me. "Go see John," Al said, "and see what he can do for you."

I went to see John Burnett, and in October 1979, he hired me as a project manager. Once again, I was being hired to manage something about which I did not know very much. But now I was operating from a position of authority, coordinating the efforts of superb professionals. This was my comfort zone. Whether John was told to offer me the job or not, I never knew, but I had landed safely—and what a landing! RCDC was a first-class operation engaged in major high-profile projects nationwide, and it was aggressively looking for more. It enjoyed access to the capital and prestige bestowed by the Rockefeller name. My colleagues were an accomplished and impressive crew. The camaraderie and professionalism of that staff and the unique experience of working for John Burnett led to deep and lasting bonds. Forty years later, several of us including Bill Maloney, Peter

Herman, Les Smith, Alex Cooper, Bob Jackson, Wendy Rowden, and others still get together periodically to compare notes about our current lives and to revisit that special time.

Bill Maloney is the unofficial shepherd of the RCDC alumni. Bill is another classic New York product. Growing up in a rough section of Washington Heights in Manhattan in the 1950s, he attended a Catholic high school and Manhattan College before being drafted. He landed at the finance section of RCI in 1973 despite lacking a CPA or an MBA at the time. He transferred to RCDC a couple of years before I arrived, and he quickly impressed John Burnett, Peter Herman, and others. Eventually he would succeed John as president of RCDC, having gained the full confidence of senior RCI management and David Rockefeller. He later served as project manager for both the MoMA expansion of 2004 and the new downtown Whitney Museum, completed in 2015. Bill grew from a numbers guy to a fully rounded real estate executive who maintained a high professional—but low public—profile. He is a master of New York Yankees trivia, and even more so of World War II history. Bill also possesses a devastatingly quick wit, which makes for lively evenings whenever we get together.

My first assignment was to work on a proposal for a new one-million-square-foot operations center for Irving Trust on a parcel adjacent to the World Trade Center in Lower Manhattan between Barclay and Murray Streets. We were competing to become the owner-developer and then net lease the entire space back to the bank. Because it involved no leasing risk, this was an almost perfect deal structure for a developer.

The site was located in the Greenwich Street Special Zoning District, which OLMD, my old office, had created. Along with certain zoning constraints, the main purpose of the special district was to create an upper-level pedestrian walkway at the same elevation (thirty-two feet above sea level) as the plaza of the World Trade Center. Because it separated pedestrian activity from the street level, this may have been the worst idea to come out of OLMD and was subsequently abandoned. But the requirement was operative at the time, and we had to come up with a design to accommodate it and the rest of the provisions of the district. The entire deal depended on successfully navigating the city approval process—the dreaded Uniform Land Use Review Procedure (ULURP)—which could be as long and treacherous as its off-putting acronym. Since I was intimately familiar with the Special Zoning District and ULURP, I was comfortable with this assignment.

John Burnett had brought in Skidmore, Owings & Merrill, the prestigious architecture firm of major office buildings, well suited to institutional-type projects. At Irving Trust's insistence, Turner Construction would handle the construction. We worked almost around the clock for about ten days to produce a glossy proposal document showcasing Skidmore's design; Turner's cost numbers; and the development fee, lease, and financing terms put together by our people. We won the competition and I spent much of my time at RCDC working on this substantial undertaking.

Skidmore had done such a good job of incorporating the second-level walkway through the building and meeting the other requirements that we sailed through ULURP in the minimum six-month time frame. To manage the day-to-day design and construction issues leading up to the groundbreaking, we held weekly meetings of the "Gang of Four" project managers, as we called ourselves: Tony Guasco of Irving Trust, Carolina Woo from Skidmore, Roger Lang from Turner, and me. Carolina and Roger were seasoned practitioners and graciously accepted me into their world. We all got along well and, despite the intense budget and time pressure, became good friends. We worked under the supervision of Andy Rendino, the project executive at Irving, who was demanding but fair. The monthly meetings with Andy and John Burnett were often tense and difficult, but we managed to handle the operational issues and the resulting cost overruns that relentlessly arose. The building, 101 Barkley Street, now the Bank of New York Corporate Trust Operations Center, was later damaged during the 9/11 disaster but survived.

At some point during 1979 before I arrived, an individual New Jersey developer, Les Smith, approached RCDC through a Cushman & Wakefield broker, Ty Maroon, looking for backing for an unusual venture in the wilds of northern New Jersey. Les had acquired rights to more than six-hundred acres of land in Mount Olive township fronting on Interstate 80. Les proposed that the centerpiece of the proposed development should be something called a "foreign trade zone" (FTZ), which no one at RCDC had ever heard of. Les had persuaded the State of New Jersey, where he was politically well connected, to designate the site as the official New Jersey foreign trade zone. Then, in 1980, Congress amended the existing legislation authorizing FTZs to allow goods that had been brought into the zone to be further assembled or manufactured into higher-value items with duties charged only on the raw materials. This made FTZs far more attractive to international companies and interest in them was burgeoning.

Still, to say that John Burnett, Al Marshall, and the rest of the conservative Rockefeller Center financial hierarchy were skeptical of a New Jersey FTZ would be to put it very mildly. RCDC's expertise was downtown office buildings. Its partners were normally major financial or corporate behemoths like Continental Insurance, Wells Fargo, and Ford. But Les and Alan Goldstein, his local attorney, persisted. To every question they had reasonable answers. They were exceptionally astute, exuded decency and integrity, and were willing to give RCDC controlling interest in exchange for its financial underwriting. After months of due diligence, Burnett received approval to go ahead. RCDC was all in.

Shortly after my arrival in 1979, I was also assigned to be the point person for our side of this unusual project. I spent the next several years working closely with Les, Alan, and Joe O'Connor, their expert on foreign trade zone operations, and a host of consultants on the planning, permitting, and marketing of the zone. Alex Cooper—the highly regarded architect, urban designer, and former city employee, who had recently launched his own firm in our offices—handled the site planning.

A highlight of this project for me was our marketing trip to Japan. In the early 1980s, Japan was viewed as an economic miracle. With innovative business practices and strong government support, many Japanese companies, from auto manufacturers to watchmakers, from electronics to banking, seemed to be leaving their American competitors in the dust. The Japanese were able to achieve both quality control and market dominance, a combination that was the envy of western economies. Japanese companies seemed to be a natural to anchor our FTZ. Using David Rockefeller's international business contacts, access was assured at the boardroom level to some of the largest enterprises in Tokyo and Osaka.

John, Les, and I boarded a Pan Am 747 bound for Tokyo in the fall of 1981. We flew first class, of course, and found ourselves alone in the upper level of that glorious aircraft with three lovely stewardesses (they were still called that). We had what amounted to a private party for the duration of the twelve-hour flight. The next morning, in the lobby of the Okura Hotel (still the nicest hotel I have ever stayed in), we met our liaison from the public relations outfit that had made all the local arrangements.

Presenting the foreign trade zone in Japan, 1981 (from the far right: Les Smith, John Burnett speaking into the microphone, our translator, and me).

We made the rounds of the executive suites, toting the heavy projector and screen that were needed in those days for our slideshow outlining the benefits of our FTZ for their companies. John, as was his infuriating but endearing style, helped lug and set up the equipment. We tried to tell him that David Rockefeller's personal representative should not be doing that kind of heavy lifting; that it would diminish his stature in the eyes of the Japanese. It was no use.

We were taken to some of Tokyo's best restaurants. In offices and restaurants, we would be served by young kimono-clad women, who would bow deeply as they entered the room and would then, never standing upright, back out of the room so as to never turn their backs on us. Late at night, we would repair to the mandatory bottle clubs in the Ginza district, where etiquette demanded drinking until a very late hour. Some of the junior Japanese staffers were required to join us. The senior executives all had apartments nearby, but the others had long commutes to their distant homes and so got very little sleep. The next day, as soon as we dimmed the lights for our slideshow, they were sound asleep.

After four or five days in Tokyo, we headed to Osaka, the other major commercial center of Japan. I had noticed that 12,300-foot Mt. Fuji lay along our route. It was a weekend and I had brought basic hiking gear. While John and Les went ahead on the bullet train, our PR representative had made arrangements for me on the mountain and gave me instructions for how to get there. I took a local commuter train that stopped every few minutes. As we approached the time I was supposed to get off, I looked out for the sign for my stop. All the signs were in Japanese, so I had no idea if it was the right one. Trusting the phenomenal punctuality of the Japanese rail system, I got off at the exact time as instructed, and of course I found myself at the correct station. I then managed to identify the right bus to take me to the base of that classic mountain, which now loomed immediately in front of me. I located the trailhead and set out. Because it had been raining intermittently for a few days, almost no one else was on the mountain, which is usually crowded with hikers for whom ascending Mt. Fuji is an almost sacred pilgrimage.

It is about a 6,000-foot climb from the trailhead to the summit, requiring some seven to ten hours of hard slogging. I made my way up in muggy, damp conditions. Endless switchbacks crisscrossed the kind of scree I recalled from Kilimanjaro. The entire cone of Fuji is barren, with almost no vegetation or significant rock formations. Essentially it is just a big ash hill. At one point, I encountered a woman descending. To my surprise, she called out my name and managed to convey that I was expected higher up. The firm that had made all the business arrangements for us in Tokyo and Osaka had done the same for me on the mountain, in yet another demonstration of astonishing Japanese efficiency.

My plan was to reach the high hut, at 11,000 feet, by nightfall and then rise early to be on top for Mt. Fuji's fabled sunrise. As I climbed higher, the drizzle increased, the wind strengthened, and the temperature dropped. For rain protection I had only a flimsy plastic poncho. As darkness fell, I arrived at the hut soaked, exhausted, and shivering badly. My hosts greeted me and served me some dinner while I sat at a table and dangled my legs over a pit warmed by a small fire. Only a couple of other climbers were there, already asleep in their bunks. The man and woman in charge of the hut were arguing in front of a TV that was miraculously playing at that isolated aerie. I gradually figured out that he wanted to watch the news about the flooding caused by all the recent rains, while she wanted to watch the all-star baseball game. She prevailed.

I doubted that it would make sense for me to try for the summit in the morning. There would be no sunrise, and conditions might make the attempt even a bit dangerous. I curled up in my bunk feeling quite forlorn about this turn of events. I had agreed with my hosts that they would wake me early only if the weather improved. It did not. Rain was still falling. As I finished a small breakfast and was preparing to head down, a large group of at least a dozen climbers arrived, fully outfitted with stylish raingear. I told myself, *If they go up, I'll follow—at least I'll be sure of the route. If they go down, I'll go down.* After a few minutes of consultation and deliberation, they headed down and I followed. At the train station, I boarded the Shinkansen, the bullet train, to Osaka. Dripping and bedraggled, I must have been a curious sight to the elegantly attired businessmen in the first-class section of the train. Some hours later, I staggered into our hotel in Osaka and was greeted with great amusement and considerable kidding by Les and John.

Other moments from this mind-expanding trip stand out in my memory. Fairly early in the trip, we were having lunch in one of the fine restaurants of the Okura Hotel. Seated at a large table nearby were seven people: two older couples, one on each side facing the other; a young couple at the foot of the table; and a middle-aged woman at the head. It appeared to be some sort of ceremony. We asked our liaison what was going on. She answered that an arranged marriage was being finalized. "The woman at the head of the table is brokering the matter," she said. We were astonished.

A few minutes later, a buzz went through the room, and our guide pointed to a young man walking briskly across the far end of the large space. Our guide said he was the son of Akio Morita, the famed founder of Sony. The son had just announced that he was going to marry a film star who came from the lower classes. It was a huge scandal in Japan.

The woman who was our prime liaison and the female translator, both of whom accompanied us on our visits, were curious about the lives of working women in the United States, where the feminist movement was gaining real momentum. The two women vowed that they would not marry, because in Japan that would mean staying at home with sole responsibility for the household and no opportunity for professional fulfillment.

I remember our farewell session over drinks with the male member of the PR team. We had come to know each other quite well over the previous ten days. After exchanging gifts (cigarette lighters, I am quite sure), we felt free enough to smile and ask him, "Do the Japanese have a word for 'No?'"

He was amused. "We never use it," he explained. "It is considered impolite. Let me give you an example. If someone was about to cross the street and a truck was coming and the person asked, 'Is it okay to cross here?' we would answer, 'Yes, it is okay but you will be killed by a truck if you do.'" We all laughed with new understanding.

He then turned to us and politely asked, "May I offer you some advice about how to market your project to our country?"

"Of course," we answered eagerly.

He said, "You have talked only about how many cost savings there are in a foreign trade zone. We are not so interested in saving costs. We want to grow market share. Tell us how we can increase market share."

The three of us were aghast at how much work we had put into a presentation that had little relevance to their primary concern. We clearly had much more to learn. We also came away with the distinct feeling that Japan's dynamic new commercial society was a thin veneer atop a still very traditional culture.

As RCDC became more committed to the foreign trade zone project and excited about its prospects, the specter of serious competition emerged. The first foreign trade zone in the United States, FTZ #1, was operating somewhat sleepily at Newark Airport under the auspices of the Port Authority of New York and New Jersey. Given the enormous political and financial resources of that powerful agency, Al Marshall wanted a guarantee from Governor Brendan Byrne of New Jersey that the Port Authority would not go after the same tenants we were targeting, offering occupancy deals and public financing that we could not match. We were, after all, the official State of New Jersey FTZ and the governor could make that clear to the bistate agency. Les and I felt that we had been given adequate, albeit informal, assurances to that effect, but we suggested to Al that we meet directly with the governor, just to nail down that promise. Al asked if we were certain that the meeting would yield the result we needed. Naively, we said we were sure it would.

We all traveled to Trenton and were ushered into a large room. It was a setting that felt more like a hearing room than a cordial meeting. Al briefly presented our case and asked for the governor's commitment. Byrne turned to his aides, who said nothing, and then declared, "I can't do that. The Port Authority is a public agency and is responsible to the public to carry out its business as it sees fit."

Al gathered up his papers, stood up, and said, "Well, I guess this meeting is over." He then turned and walked out as Les, John Burnett, and I scrambled after him. The governor and his staff looked on in amazement with their mouths half open. They were not used to the kind of steely self-assurance that Al possessed after years of representing Nelson Rockefeller. On our way back to the city, Al was obviously annoyed with us but merely commented, "When you meet with people at that level, you'd better be certain of how the meeting is going to turn out before you sit down." Another life lesson!

In January 1981, Les Larsen, who was loosely attached to our staff and who handled David Rockefeller's real estate portfolio, departed along with Bill Maloney to join Cadillac Fairview, an aggressive and expanding Canadian real estate firm. At Les's suggestion, John Burnett asked me to assume the responsibility as the point person for David Rockefeller's interests, which included two major development projects. Embarcadero Center in San Francisco was a joint venture between DR (as he was often referred to) and Prudential, with the entrepreneurial architect John Portman holding a small equity position. The project consisted of four large office buildings, three of which had already been completed, plus about 150,000 square feet of retail space and the Hyatt Regency Hotel. The Hyatt was one of Portman's signature "Jesus Christ" hotels. Why the deity? Because his hotels featured soaring atria that rose hundreds of feet, and when arriving guests walked into the lobby, they could often be heard exclaiming in astonishment, "Jesus Christ!"

I came very late to this project, participating in the grand opening of the final office building. The first three buildings were almost fully leased and the overall project, after struggling for many years, was finally becoming a success. It is difficult to appreciate how pioneering this undertaking was at the time. Downtown San Francisco, like all large American central cities in the late 1970s, was struggling against the competition of its suburbs, and downtown investments were widely viewed as high-risk. Since this project had a highly competent local staff to oversee the daily construction and management issues, my role was mostly to make sure that major problems requiring ownership attention were anticipated and handled in a timely fashion. On my occasional trips to San Francisco to review pending matters, I was accompanied by Peter Herman, our attorney. Peter was a partner at Milbank in its real estate practice and would later inherit the top spot from Larry Nelson, whom I had known from my Seaport days. Peter had been with the project from its inception and knew every detail of its history and intricate structure.

Peter Herman deserves a special place in my story. A real estate lawyer of almost incomparable breadth and knowledge, he is even-tempered, unflappable, and diligent. He is also one of the nicest and most generous of people and is a deeply loyal friend. Everyone I know likes, respects, and confides in him. For me, he was both companion and consigliere. Peter was our lawyer on all of our projects, and he had been tutoring me in commercial real estate from the day I joined RCDC. Fellow bachelors at the time, Peter and I became close friends on our trips to San Francisco and later to Atlanta. Like Ed Kresky, Peter would play an ongoing and critical role in my professional career.

Peter was a wonderful mentor to others as well. He had a talent for hiring extremely competent associates to work in his practice group. I recall that at one of our many project meetings he was accompanied by his top assistant, who was called out of the room mid-meeting to take an urgent phone call. When she returned, she apologized for the interruption. "I'm afraid I have to excuse myself," she explained calmly. "I've just been appointed president of Barnard College." Her name was Ellen Futter. At age thirty-one, she became the youngest college president in the country. Ellen served as Barnard's president from 1980 until 1993 and has served as the acclaimed head of the American Museum of Natural History ever since.

DR was a partner with Stavros Niarchos in Interstate North, a large suburban office park in Atlanta. At the intersection of I-75 and I-285, today it consists of eleven buildings and almost one million square feet of space. In 1981, it was about half developed. Relationships with the on-site staff were not nearly as smooth as with the Embarcadero crew, and the financial status of the project was much shakier. I set about restructuring the staff and redoing the master plan to improve both our control and its future prospects. Peter Herman came with me on some of my frequent trips to Atlanta, but our partner's representative, Don Broad, was my regular companion. Don, a down-to-earth Brit with no formal training in real estate, looked to us for the more technical parts of our oversight, but he was extremely insightful and had enormous common sense. He more than held his own in our meetings and document reviews. Don was also an absolutely delightful person. We thoroughly enjoyed his stories about his annual trips to the Niarchos center of operations in Monaco and his periodic assignment to oversee the counting of Niarchos's bars of gold, stored in the subterranean vault of the Dominion Bank of Canada in Toronto.

In 1982, George Humphreys came to me and said somberly, "I need a big favor." Given our very close friendship and the way he prefaced the request, I knew this was serious and important.

I had no choice but to say, "Of course—what is it?"

At that time, George was the chief of staff to the assembly minority leader, James Emery, a conservative Republican from Rochester and Monroe County. "Jim is running for governor," he said, "and I need a treasurer for the campaign. I have not been able to find anyone I trust yet. Will you do it for a couple of weeks at most, until I find someone?" George knew well my liberal politics and how big an ask that was.

"Okay," I said angrily, "but it better not be long."

Each day, an envelope containing checks would be delivered to my office. I would store those campaign contributions in a cardboard box—literally—in my desk drawer and deposit them once a week. By today's standards, it was a minuscule financial operation, but it was still a gubernatorial campaign in a major state. I knew almost nothing about campaign finance rules, but I did know that if anyone went to jail, it was the treasurer. As week after anxious week went by, I grew more and more furious as George kept failing to come up with a replacement. Finally, I went to him and said I would do the job no longer, forcing him to find another option. Jim Emery lost the primary but then ran for lieutenant governor on the ticket headed by Lewis

Lehrman, who lost to Mario Cuomo. I could not help holding a grudge and did not speak to George for several years thereafter.

Otherwise, life was good at RCDC. Our projects were challenging and beneficial to their communities; my professional colleagues were smart, fun, and honest; and we were well-paid. Being part of a Rockefeller enterprise meant that everything was top-tier and a bit larger than life. A perk that we especially enjoyed—and were not above abusing—was convening for periodic lunches up in the Rockefeller Center Luncheon Club, a members-only facility in the space that at night became the elegant Rainbow Room, a legendary nightspot. At lunch we would spend a few minutes talking shop, to justify the expense account tab, and then relax and socialize. I could easily imagine spending the rest of my professional life in this comfortable cocoon.

It was not to be. An unpleasant change was coming. It must have been early in 1982 that Al Marshall left Rockefeller Center, not entirely of his own choosing. The story as we heard it was that, in return for his many years of service and for turning the staid and stagnant Rockefeller Center enterprise into a vibrant and enormously valuable business operation, Al felt deserving of some equity participation—an actual piece of ownership. Despite his extraordinary record of service both public and private, his assumption apparently crossed that invisible line that always seemed to separate family from staff, no matter how loyal. Soon Al was gone, replaced by Richard Voell, who had an operations background with Beatrice Foods and Penn Central. Voell brought an entirely new mindset and a radically revised direction at the behest of the family. An atmosphere of uncertainty seeped into our offices.

The senior Rockefellers of the "Brothers" generation—Abigail, John D. III, Nelson, and Winthrop—had died, and Laurance and David, the remaining two children of John D. Jr., were aging. The next generation or two, always referred to as the "Cousins," now numbered almost two dozen and were more interested in cash flow than in accumulating long-term assets such as the office properties that RCDC had been developing. At some point, the decision was made to largely close down RCDC, particularly any new development initiatives, in order to invest in cashflow–oriented businesses. That meant real estate project managers would no longer be needed.

On a Friday in the fall of 1982, with little warning, several of us were told that John Burnett and a human resources person wanted to meet individually with us. I was the first in. In short order, I was informed that I was being let go. I would be given a couple of months' severance plus outplacement services. That was that. I emerged from John's office and saw several pairs of eyes looking questioningly at me. I said nothing but pulled my tie around into a hangman's noose position. Everyone understood.

My days at RCDC were over. I was shattered. This had never happened to me before and I found myself almost literally shaking with anxiety at what lay ahead. I had given up smoking several weeks earlier and was still in the throes of withdrawal. I headed for the elevator, intending to go down to the lobby and buy a pack of cigarettes. I got as far as the counter of the newsstand and stopped. No, I would not let this disaster justify another debacle. I turned around and never had another cigarette, except in many nightmares for years to come.

The next months were very painful. We were given office space from which to pursue our job searches, but I felt embarrassed and awkward. The few RCDC employees who were retained were cordial and supportive, but they could not help looking at us as if we were dying or already dead. We imagined that we smelled bad. We wrote our résumés and practiced interview skills. I watched the video replay of a mock interview that I thought I had handled very well. I looked like a sniveling sad sack whom I would never hire. I had a long way to go.

That spring, Marilyn decided that it would be a good time for me to escape New York for a while and see where she came from. She had not been back to West Texas in a long time. It was a good time for a sentimental journey. We flew to Midland, where her father, always called O. B., was living with his new wife, Myrtle. He was pleasant but taciturn; she had a thick Texas twang. After a night or two—in separate bedrooms, of course—we headed north to spend the night with O. B.'s brother, Uncle Ed, and Aunt Dess, his wife. They lived near Lubbock, in the aptly named city of Levelland. On our flight to Midland, I had grumbled to Marilyn that it would be very awkward for me to answer the inevitable question from her family—"What do you do?"—since I was unemployed with no immediate prospects. "Don't worry," Marilyn said, "they won't ask. It's too personal a question." And no one ever did. I began to understand where she came from.

The next morning, after an alcohol-free dinner and Jell-O for dessert, Marilyn told me that Ed had asked her if I had grown up on a farm. It was the highest compliment he could have paid. We then drove about one hundred miles north to the small city where she was born: Hereford, in Deaf Smith County. We drove around until we found the house where she had spent the first few years of her life—a tiny forlorn-looking bungalow on a side street. Another hour-and-a-half drive northwest past Amarillo brought us to the town, actually named Panhandle, where she had spent her youth. It was a dreary place of fewer than 2,500 people without a traffic light, at 3,500 feet of elevation in the dustbowl of the northwest Texas panhandle.

We had tea with the town librarian, who had befriended and encouraged Marilyn during her childhood in Panhandle. There was a copy of *The New Yorker* on her coffee table. The next morning, as the wind kicked up—as it did almost every day—we went to the cemetery to visit Marilyn's mother's grave. I stayed in the car as Marilyn and her father trudged up a small hill to the site. In my mind, the image of the two of them in that bleak setting, with a single wind-bent tree as a backdrop, captured the austerity of Marilyn's beginnings.

Back in New York, after several frustratingly empty months, I finally landed an interview for a job advertised in the *New York Times*. A Midwestern manufacturing company was looking for someone to lead a project it owned on the Staten Island waterfront, near the ferry terminal, called Bay Street Landing. The company was renovating abandoned warehouse buildings into upscale residential loft units for sale as co-ops. One of its executives came to New York for my interview and I was then invited to the company's home base outside Detroit to meet with the CEO. Both meetings left me concerned that the project was in pretty deep trouble. One large warehouse was largely finished and partially occupied but involved in litigation against the contractor for allegedly faulty work. I would be working with Chris, the young lawyer who had been heading the development. He was supposedly great at deal-making and finance but needed help with management and implementation. The CEO said he hoped that we would make a great team. I later was told that the young lawyer was sleeping with the CEO's daughter, never a welcome complication.

I made a list of the pros and cons of the job. The number of items under "cons" was long and persuasive. Under "pro," there was one entry: it was a job. I had been unemployed and scared for more than eight months. I recalled one of Al Marshall's favorite aphorisms: "There are times when one must rise above principle." The sole "pro" won out and I took the job. It was late June of 1983.

I had good reason to be worried. The young lawyer proved impossible to work with. The company CEO's management style (which he assured me had worked for him in his rise through the firm) was to deliberately leave lines of authority and responsibility unclear and see who rose to the challenge. While Chris and I managed to maintain a respectful working relationship, I took the lack of clarity to be the CEO's tacit encouragement to me to gradually assume more and more authority. I did, and Chris finally left the project entirely. What remained was a nightmare.

Whenever it rained hard and the wind blew from a particular direction, the main building leaked. Furniture was ruined, tenants had to be relocated, tempers flared. The most valuable apartments on the top floor and the unfinished penthouses above them suffered the worst damage. We continually patched the roof but could not stop the leaks in the worst weather. The building was an old concrete structure, which would allow the rainwater to course undetected along its beams. Where the water came out gave us no clue about where it was getting in. We spent months working on the roof and thought we had the problems solved. Then, in September 1983, tropical storm Dean hit New York and flooded the top floors again—worse than ever.

Meanwhile, a marina had been planned for the waterfront and was minimally operational, but it lacked an adequate breakwater to quiet the waves and wakes of New York harbor. This was a prerequisite if we were to attract the larger yachts that would make the marina financially viable. Chris had tried cabling old tires together and throwing them into the water. That was laughable. I convinced the CEO to let me hire some professional marine engineers to try to solve the problem. But then the tropical storm tore up what little infrastructure we already had in the water.

At the same time, we were trying to complete the second set of buildings—low-rise brick structures that also housed our dingy office. I managed to get permission to hire an experienced assistant to oversee building operations and an administrative officer to handle finances and security, but the parent company was not happy. It was a cost-conscious manufacturing outfit in which the heads of the various components held equity positions in the whole enterprise. Chris had engineered a leveraged buyout that was enriching the senior officers, so they had tolerated his management shortcomings. Now, however, he was gone, and the leadership of the other divisions, which were highly profitable, looked upon our Staten Island project as an endless hemorrhage that could slice chunks out of their net worth. Corporate money for my staff or for adequately addressing our issues was very difficult to come by. It was seen as "throwing good money after bad." Still, by the middle of 1984, we had finished basic renovations of the apartments in the brick buildings and sold nearly all of them. But on the adjacent open land stood the eyesore skeletons of two more large warehouse structures, and there was little appetite to tackle their redevelopment in the foreseeable future.

It had been a miserable experience for me, and I had been sending out feelers for some months. I had had one interview, again from a *New York Times* ad. I met with Sheldon Solow, a major New York real estate owner, in his 9 West 57th Street building, to discuss becoming his personal assistant. I knew of his reputation as perhaps the most litigious developer in the city. Our interview consisted mostly of his assuring me that he really was a good guy. He insisted that his dog and his long-time secretary liked him and that he got along really well with Gordon Bunshaft, Skidmore's famed architect, who had designed the building we were sitting in. I consulted some of my friends, who were unanimous in advising me against accepting the position. One said that a second lieutenant on Omaha Beach on D-Day had a longer life expectancy. Reluctantly, I listened to their advice and did not follow up.

The unpleasantness of the Staten Island job lasted a long time. After I left, some of our tenants, led by a relentlessly aggressive lawyer, filed suit against our company. It was a civil RICO suit, the kind of litigation that is normally used to prosecute mobsters. We were accused of conspiring to defraud the tenants and I was a named defendant. The litigation was fundamentally frivolous—not the residents' complaints, but the charge that we had engaged in a malicious conspiracy. Nevertheless, it dragged on for several years, thanks to the bitterness and intransigence on both sides. I did have a letter of indemnification from the company, but the litigation still posed the remote risk of generating catastrophic financial consequences for me. That led to many sleepless nights before the case was finally settled out of court some five years later.

During the past two rollercoaster years of my professional life, my personal life was also undergoing major upheavals. Marilyn and I had started living together in 1980. I had been resisting making a full commitment, unable to shake my admittedly self-absorbed but nevertheless nagging notion that perhaps, just perhaps, there might be someone else, some absolutely perfect person, out there somewhere. On my birthday in January 1982, Marilyn announced that we were going to have dinner with our friends, Harvey and Celia, at their considerably less than elegant apartment, aptly nicknamed "The Pit." I was mildly annoyed, since I had thought we might go out to a nice restaurant. I was further perturbed when Marilyn added that we were bringing the dinner.

When we arrived and they opened the door, I looked down to see an adorable kitten sporting a blue ribbon around its neck. The cat was a birthday present for me! Harvey and Celia knew from our previous visits to their house in the Hamptons that I loved cats. With Marilyn's permission, they presented me with the pick of a recent local litter—quickly adding that, of course, I could give it back. I instantly grasped the gravity of the situation. I knew I would be hooked. This was clearly the first step down the inexorable path toward what I thought I dreaded most: *commitment*. I was quietly furious but began to contemplate accepting the inevitable. The tabby kitten's shelter name had been Sahib because it had a prominent orange spot on the center of its forehead. On closer inspection, Sahib turned out to be a female, and Memsahib did not have the right ring to it. We renamed her Kathmandu, or Kitty for short. She proved to be a great cat—playful, loving, and fearless.

Then came the RCDC debacle and the months of pain and embarrassment of unemployment and job-hunting. Marilyn stayed with me and her support never wavered. I gradually came to appreciate her love and loyalty. On the deck of the little house I had bought in 1981 near Phoenicia in the Catskills, I proposed and she accepted. I was forty-three; she was forty-four.

We agreed to marry quickly before either of us could change our minds. Marilyn made that seem like a mutual possibility, but it was her wise way of ensuring that I did not back out. We picked a date only a few weeks away: Saturday, July 16, 1983. Courtesy of Marilyn, we had tickets to a Yankees game the day after my proposal. I called my brother from the Stadium and asked him to be my best man. When he agreed, we fixed the date. We knew that my father and stepmother could not come because they were at their house on the Attersee in Austria. They were disappointed at being unable to attend but were delighted at my finally having come to my senses. They had met Marilyn many times and were very fond of her.

We found a cute little church in Mt. Tremper, the Shandaken Reformed Church, that was near our house in the Catskills and was available on the date we wanted. The minister would be happy to marry us. We invited only our closest friends. Including my brother and his wife, the group totaled twelve. Marilyn's father came from Texas to give her away, which made her very happy. The ceremony was simple but felt just right, and then we adjourned to our deck for an informal outdoor reception. It was a step I never regretted.

With wedding plans behind us, I agreed to sign on for the Staten Island job, under one condition: that I could take a substantial honeymoon in September. I wanted to show the Himalayas to Marilyn and share that experience with her. On the day after the tropical storm that caused so much damage to our project, Marilyn and I were due to leave for our trip. At the airport, I heard how much devastation there had been. We hesitated over whether we should leave, but not much purpose would have been served by canceling the trip at that point. With enormous relief, we boarded our flight to India. We spent several days sightseeing in Delhi and then, like countless newlyweds before us, headed to Agra to visit the most famous human tribute to love, the Taj Mahal. No matter how many photos one has seen of it, the real thing is even more beautiful.

Celebrating with Marilyn at the end of our honeymoon trek in Nepal, 1983.

The moderate two-week trek required no serious climbing. Still, we would camp for two weeks and traverse a 15,000-foot pass; it was far from a luxury honeymoon. Marilyn suffered the fleas and leeches of a late monsoon without complaint, as was her nature. After a week of damp weather at relatively lower altitudes, we finally emerged from the forested hillsides on a glorious sun-brightened day. We were in western Nepal, and in the distance, we could see the magnificent snowcapped Annapurna massif sparkling in the rarefied air. Exhilarated, I pointed to the majestic peaks, exclaiming that *this* was what a Himalayan trip was all about. Marilyn smiled pleasantly but did not seem overwhelmed by the magic of gazing on that fabled range. It dawned on me that perhaps she was not as thrilled by this adventure as I had hoped she would be. But as was her wont, she never uttered a word of complaint.

Marilyn was stoic. After all, she had grown up in that bleak part of Texas where hardly anyone, especially women, expressed emotion. Her father was a soils engineer, an ironic occupation in the barren terrain of that part of the country. But he had a job during the Great Depression and a pension afterward. Her mother had died of breast cancer in her fifties. Marilyn had visited Mexico on a class trip in her senior year of college. A mariachi band had serenaded her at her hotel on her birthday, and the trip had changed her life. She discovered a world of color, romance, and excitement beyond West Texas, and she was determined to experience it. Her parents, to their credit, understood and gave her luggage at Christmas. She had four older brothers, but she was the first to go to a four-year college. She took a year off from North Texas State (now the University of North Texas) to care for her dying mother and then graduated in 1961, the same year I did.

As Marilyn was fond of saying, she caught the first plane out of Texas and it carried her to New York City. She had an uncle in New Jersey, but no other anchor or support in the area. She had only some modest savings from having worked in an atomic bomb plant near Amarillo. When she arrived in Manhattan, she found a room at the Evangeline Home for Women, a Salvation Army refuge on West 13th Street. Donning a pair of white gloves, she started looking for a job as a secretary; it was her only option at the time, but she could type and spell really well. After a number of dispiriting rejections, she happened to tell a woman on a bus of her disappointing experiences. The woman said that a friend had told her of a place that might be looking for someone. On a slip of paper, she wrote: *Room 5600, 30 Rockefeller Plaza.* "You might go there and see if they have something," she said.

The next day, Marilyn went to that address. She walked out of the elevator and through glass doors that gave no indication of what kind of place it was. She asked if they were looking for a secretary and was told that yes, in fact, they were.

She took the typing test, did very well, and proceeded to an interview. When the woman interviewing her asked her where she had come from, Marilyn mentioned that she had stopped in Puerto Rico to visit a brother before coming to New York.

The interviewer said, "Oh, perhaps you stayed at our Dorado Beach Hotel while you were there?"

"No," Marilyn answered quietly. Then, wondering who might own that luxury resort, she asked, "Where am I?"

The interviewer, a bit surprised, replied, "The Rockefeller family offices."

Marilyn was hired and worked for Laurance Rockefeller's section, mostly for Henry Diamond, for about eight years.

By 1970, with the feminist movement gaining traction, Marilyn was eager to move on and spread her wings. Charles Goodell, who had been appointed by Nelson Rockefeller to fill Robert Kennedy's Senate seat, was running for reelection. Marilyn was hired to manage his New York City office for the campaign. Goodell secured the Liberal and Republican lines on the ballot but was challenged by Conservative James Buckley (Bill's brother) and by Democrat Richard Ottinger. Buckley won the three-way race, so Marilyn was looking again.

Nancy Hanks, who had been close to Nelson Rockefeller and had become the first head of the National Council on the Arts, frequented 5600, as the office was simply called, and Marilyn became friendly with her. Nancy was anxious to help an eager and ambitious young woman. Nancy introduced her to people at NBC, which was also headquartered at 30

Rockefeller Plaza, and Marilyn went to work there as a sales and marketing rep in its affiliate relations division. She visited radio and television stations to manage existing clients and recruit new ones. She started in the upper Midwest, which meant traveling to exotic locations like Bismarck, North Dakota.

She later moved on to similar work at Home Box Office, which proved much more exciting. HBO was taking off like a rocket ship, exponentially expanding its staff and reach. Cable TV was a new phenomenon; it was the future, and HBO intended to dominate it. By the time Marilyn and I started living together, HBO had grown almost tenfold in staff, and she had risen to an executive level and was making more money than I was. She had come under criticism for not using her expense account enough, so we obliged by having her take me out to dinner at our favorite high-end restaurants using HBO's account with a black-car service (something brand-new in the early 1980s). We were having a very good time.

Marilyn had become an avid skier when she was single, having learned by sharing Vermont ski houses and taking vacations in the Austrian Alps. She had bought a ski condo in Steamboat Springs, Colorado, where her youngest brother lived. I had tried skiing a few times when in Albany but had not taken to it. We agreed early on that she would go hiking if I would learn to ski. I took lessons in Steamboat Springs and became a moderately decent skier, but no more. Over the years, we spent a lot more time on hiking trails than on ski slopes.

During the oil crisis of the 1970s, travel plunged, and with it, the value of vacation rental properties dropped. Her Steamboat Springs condo became a yoke instead of a cash cow and we had been trying to sell it. It was under contract when a renter in a neighboring unit dumped the ashes from his fireplace on the porch woodpile. The result was an historic conflagration that burned some sixty units and led the evening news in Denver. Marilyn's insurance company required rebuilding, which we were loath to do, so we gave the bank the keys. It then took several years for Marilyn to regain good standing on her credit reports.

When we returned from our Himalayan honeymoon, I made an appointment with my doctor. We had had to have physical exams before being cleared for the trip, and mine had revealed a small lump on my throat. The doctor said it probably was nothing, most likely benign, but I should have it removed when we got back. As I was being wheeled into the operating room at St. Vincent's Hospital in Greenwich Village, the surgeon put his hand on my throat. His eyes widened a bit and he said, "That's a lot bigger than it was"—not exactly comforting words at that moment.

As I emerged from anesthesia, I had the vague sense that I had been under a long time. The first words I heard were from Marilyn, whispering urgently, "You're going to be all right; you're going to be all right."

I thought to myself, *Oh shit—I'm not all right.*

I had indeed been under for almost seven hours. My condition was diagnosed as a papillary carcinoma that had spread to several lymph nodes. The surgeon had performed a modified radical thyroidectomy. Fortunately, he was able to stop just short of leaving me with a major concave disfigurement; all I ended up with were some very impressive zipper scars on my throat and neck. I spent about a week in the hospital and returned to work about ten days later.

Then came the hard part. Several weeks later, I had to return to the hospital to undergo radioactive treatment to destroy the right thyroid, which the surgeon had not removed in order to preserve the parathyroid on that side because it serves some useful function that I did not understand. I had to swallow an enormous pill that oblated my remaining thyroid, destroying it but leaving the parathyroid undamaged. I was then locked in a sealed room. Food was slipped through a slot in the door. I could not be near anyone and had to destroy the books and clothes that I had brought to the hospital because they had become highly radioactive. I then had to go off my thyroid medication for several weeks in order to rid myself of any residual thyroid function so that I could have a full-body scan to determine if the cancer had spread. I felt absolutely horrible, lacking sufficient energy or initiative to undertake the simplest physical or mental task. I could only think of

Superman laid low by proximity to a big hunk of kryptonite. Fortunately, the scan came up clean and at last I could begin full recuperation.

That started with several weeks of physical rehabilitation at a Staten Island hospital to work on the pain and the limited movement of my neck and left arm, and on slowly rebuilding some of the muscle tone that had atrophied. It was a slog, but I eventually returned to normal. I have had a checkup annually for thirty-five years with no sign of a recurrence.

A few weeks after I returned to work, Marilyn was scheduled to head to the Dominican Republic for an HBO Super Bowl party, held annually in a warm getaway for senior staff and major clients and renowned as one of the best corporate junkets anywhere. Spouses were invited. Four or five days gratis at Casa de Campo, the most luxurious resort on the island, sounded like the perfect antidote after my recent ordeal. My boss in Michigan was not at all pleased to hear that I was "taking more time off" (as if major surgery had been simply time off), but I went nonetheless. Everything was complimentary and first class. We played tennis and there were ball boys. If we wanted to "hit a few" with Australian tennis legend Roy Emerson, we just had to sign up. (We opted not to take advantage of this opportunity but still named our next car, whose color was Australian Blue, "Roy.") Football greats Nick Buoniconti and Len Dawson were there to personally comment on the game as it was shown on a huge screen near the pool. I was the only male corporate spouse and received a bouquet when we arrived home, in gratitude for my "sacrifice" in attending. (It was supposed to be a complimentary facial until the corporate planners realized that a facial might not be ideal for me.) Life as part of the HBO family helped offset the tribulations of my job on Staten Island.

While I was in the early stages of my recovery from the thyroid surgery, Marilyn and I flew out to visit my father, who had recently had a heart attack. He and his wife, Ilse, were now living in Charlottesville. They had been driving around the South looking for a suitably warm place to spend their winters. In Lynchburg, my father had felt chest pains and went to an emergency room. The ER doctor referred him to the University of Virginia medical center in Charlottesville. It turned out that he needed a quadruple bypass operation. This was happening while I was going through my cancer crisis. My brother, in Washington, DC, was relaying messages back and forth, shielding each of us from each other's bad news. Then, with both of us mending properly, we decided to get together and share our medical stories.

Dad and Ilse appreciated the excellent care he had received and liked the university-town ambience of Charlottesville. They settled there and would ultimately spend the rest of their lives there as their home base. We would visit at Christmas and for other celebrations, and Charlottesville became our family anchor. The meals of *Wiener schnitzel* and venison, the familiar Christmas cookies, and chocolate *Mozartkugeln*, along with the handmade tree ornaments, all made their apartment feel very much like the home I had grown up in.

Dad had met Ilse on a tour of the Greek islands the year after my mother died. He had gone on the trip to grieve and to indulge his long-held interest in the classical world. He and Ilse spent time together among the German-speaking sections of the tour. In Ilse he had found a kindred soul who could finish his quotations of Schiller and knew almost as much Homer as he did. They were immediately drawn to each other, and after a brief letter-writing romance, they decided to marry. Ilse arrived in November 1967, and I accompanied my father to meet her when her ship pulled into New York Harbor. I was the best man and sole guest at their little wedding in Westchester County.

Ilse Kunert was born into a German-speaking family in the contested Sudetenland of today's Czech Republic. I will give only a brief summary of the varied and colorful history that she would relate to us hour after hour over meals. She had the habit of talking endlessly, in uninterruptible detail, but somehow never repeating herself. Ilse had a forceful mind and a curious intellect that enjoyed roaming over any subject that captured her interest. She was completely attuned to the natural world around her, knowing the flora and fauna, and she used local materials to make gifts, decorations, and useful household items. She did her best to pass these skills along to the rest of us, with mixed results. Ilse was an environmentalist long before it became the norm, recycling everything and relying less on the power grid than anyone around her. She was struck with macular degeneration at about age seventy. With minimal eyesight and legally blind, her lifestyle barely changed. She continued to maintain the household, host family visits, and take care of my father until he died in 2003.

As a naive graduate of the Hitler Youth, Ilse had worked for the Nazi Wehrmacht, serving as an admiral's assistant. She had helped a linguistics scholar develop a dictionary for an obscure eastern European language, probably of a region that Hitler hoped to conquer. She and her family had suffered retribution after the German defeat when the Czechs regained sovereignty over their historic territory. Ilse and her first husband, a former low-level SS officer home from the Eastern Front, fled to Salzburg, where she lived for much of the next two decades. At some point, he had an affair with her best friend, which ended the marriage.

Finally, she lived in Munich and worked in a United States Army hospital in the psychiatric ward. In Munich, she befriended a very difficult neighbor, and characteristically showed the woman kindness when others shunned her. Years later, when the woman died, she left her prized vacation home on the Attersee to Ilse with just a small mortgage left to pay. The Attersee is one of the spectacular bodies of water in the Salzkammergut, an area of transparent blue-green lakes and snowcapped mountains near Salzburg. Dad and Ilse would spend their summers in that idyllic setting for more than twenty years.

They would host friends and family and treat us all to the bucolic life of fresh food and gorgeous surroundings synonymous with that region. They welcomed Pierre's son, Eric, who spent several summers with his grandparents, learning crafts, nature skills, and passable German. Ilse made the last thirty-five years of my father's life peaceful and happy. It was an odd pairing: a Jew, albeit a reluctant one, marrying an Aryan archetype and former adolescent participant in the Third Reich. But he loved Ilse, and she was without prejudice, possessing unbridled energy and generosity, so it proved a good match.

During the summer of 1980, Marilyn and I visited them at the Attersee. My father had written to me that he wanted to take us to his favorite mountain spot from his youth in the nearby Dachstein mountains. I arranged for permits to stay in the region's mountain refuges. My father was in his early seventies and Ilse was thirteen years younger. We donned packs and began hiking not far from Schladming. I had not realized how well outfitted the huts were, and Ilse was amused by our overstuffed backpacks. After several hard hours of climbing, we arrived at the refuge. We signed the register and my father asked the innkeeper if he had registers from years past.

The man beamed and said, "Of course, all the way back to the 1950s."

My father's face fell a bit. "Oh, that's too bad," he said. "I was last here in 1932."

The next day, we hiked up a bit farther to some small glacial lakes set in a bowl surrounded by fantastic alpine shapes. It was a magical spot called the Klafferkessel. I saw tears well up in my father's eyes. Clearly, he was reconnecting with the joys of his distant past and was filled with emotion to be able to share this with his son. Watching him, Marilyn prodded me, "Go give your father a hug." That kind of emotional display was virtually unknown in our family and the thought would not have crossed my mind. I gave him the best hug that our awkwardness allowed. He returned it warmly. I remember that moment now with gratitude.

ELEVEN

TO PHILADELPHIA AND BACK

Toward the end of 1984, I received a response from one of the job listings to which I had sent my résumé in the hope of finally escaping from the Staten Island project. The Binswanger Company, one of the leading real estate brokerage firms in Philadelphia, was looking for a senior vice president to head up its newly established development activities. I took a train south for the interview and met with John Binswanger, who headed the company's commercial office operations. He and his brother, Frank Jr., who ran the industrial brokerage side, had taken over the management of the company from their father, Frank, who had founded it in 1931. John's son, David, and Frank's son, Frank III (known as Jeff), were coming up as heirs apparent. It was very much a family company, and they were justifiably proud of its longevity. Clive Mendelow, an experienced, down-to-earth man from South Africa, headed the management division; he was the only non-family member of the senior management team.

The firm was thriving and had decided, like many brokerage firms at that time, to try its hand at development. The Economic Recovery Tax Act of 1981 provided irresistible incentives for investment in real estate development projects and led to an explosion of syndicated financing. Binswanger created the position of senior vice president to head up this emerging function for them. Two office-building projects had been initiated in North Carolina, where the company had a strong presence. Someone was needed to see those projects through and to take the lead in finding and exploring other possibilities. It struck me as a job with real responsibility and potential, with a prestigious and respected name in the community. I had a good interview with John Binswanger, who was favorably impressed by my previous Rockefeller connection. I was offered the job at close to a six-figure salary, equivalent to something like $200,000 today. My office would be just one door down from John Binswanger, with only Clive Mendelow in between. It was a dark, comfortable office equipped with an impressively large desk. After Bay Street Landing, it looked positively luxurious.

Taking the job meant, of course, moving to Philadelphia. Marilyn had recently gone through a rupture of her own at HBO. Its business model was changing, and she had a conflict with her new boss. After almost a decade of excitement and success at HBO, she was let go. It was a bitter parting. With both of us having just gone through our own grim New York career purgatories, we were ready for a change. Maybe there was a good life to be had in Philadelphia. Maybe we could put down roots in new, more forgiving soil and enjoy a calmer, easier lifestyle. We decided to make the leap.

We put Marilyn's apartment on the market. It was a very good time to sell a large Upper East Side one-bedroom co-op on East 94th Street between Lexington and Third Avenues. Marilyn had been one of the fortunate buyers when her rental building converted to co-op in the first wave of such conversions. She paid about $18,000 for her unit, which we now listed at $320,000. It was a spacious unit with a small but recently renovated kitchen. Marilyn had found a talented young architect-contractor, Frank De Martini, to redo that tiny space. He did a wonderful job, and we became good friends. I hired him at Bay Street Landing to do one of our model apartments, which also turned out very well. Frank went on to work at the Port Authority and ended up heading their interior design and construction division. Years later, he came to see me for some career advice. He confessed that he was feeling worn down at his Port Authority job and wanted to move on. We had a good chat, but at the time I had no useful leads to suggest. A few weeks later, Frank died in the 9/11 attack, heroically trying to lead people out of the buildings that he knew so well. I wish I had been able to give him wise and actionable advice that might have led to a different fate.

One of Marilyn's colleagues at HBO, whom she had hired and mentored, snapped up our apartment. Meanwhile, John Binswanger did his best to ease our transition. He put us up in a nice rental apartment right on fashionable Rittenhouse Square while we looked for our own place. The Binswanger offices were also on the Square, so I had a two-minute commute to work and could even walk home for lunch. After a month or two, we found an appealing townhouse in Society Hill, the old section of Philadelphia not far from Independence Hall. Our new home was in a newer courtyard development among the old restored brick buildings that made the neighborhood so charming and attractive. We moved from a one-bedroom apartment to a three-bedroom townhouse with a dining room, a small garden, and a garage—all for less than the selling price of our New York home. We were ecstatic. There *was* a good life to be had outside of New York!

I happily immersed myself in my new responsibilities. Binswanger had purchased a site in a suburban office park near the Greensboro, North Carolina, airport. A small office building of around 60,000 square feet was underway, and I made monthly trips to work with our local architect, monitor the construction, and coordinate the leasing with our office in Charlotte. Design was also underway for a new headquarters building that we were developing for a local bank on the pedestrian mall in downtown Raleigh. The building was being designed by Ballinger, a prominent Philadelphia firm. Its lead architect, Frank Butler, and I met often and traveled together to Raleigh to work with the tenant. I also worked with John Binswanger on negotiating the lease and development agreements. I picked out the travertine for the lobby from a stone contractor in New Orleans, and for the façade, I tested the Dryvit (a synthetic stucco applied over lightweight Styrofoam panels), which budget constraints forced us to substitute for concrete. While not on the scale of RCDC's projects, these were solid real estate ventures and I had far more responsibility. I found the work satisfying, and Marilyn and I worked hard at fitting into the local community.

I joined a community leadership program. With my prior cultural credentials, I was asked to moderate a debate between the two major mayoral candidates in an upcoming primary election. I took the stage between Wilson Goode and Frank Rizzo. Goode would become mayor but would then be overwhelmed by the MOVE disaster during his tenure, when the police tried to evict a Black radical group occupying a West Philadelphia townhouse and an incendiary device set the house ablaze, destroying an entire neighborhood and killing eleven people.

At the debate that I moderated, neither candidate had much to say about the arts or anything cultural; they did little more than utter platitudes and yell at each other. Frank Rizzo was a former police chief and mayor, and a crude demagogue. His statue would finally be removed from the steps of a municipal services building during the protests of 2020.

Marilyn had a tough time finding a job. Whenever she went for an interview, the first question she invariably encountered was: "What does your husband do?" When she responded that I worked for Binswanger, she would then be asked why she needed to work. One woman to whom she turned for advice had suggested that Marilyn should just volunteer at the Children's Hospital. "That's what women like us do," she said. Clearly, the feminist movement had not yet gained much traction in the City of Brotherly Love.

Marilyn finally landed a job as a contract administrator for Comcast, the local cable company owned by the Roberts family. I sensed a little competition between them and the Binswanger family in the Jewish social hierarchy of the city. Marilyn spent part of her time mentoring the young Brian Roberts, who was just coming up in the company. Today, Brian chairs Comcast, which has become the largest provider of cable internet access in the United States. Marilyn used the opportunity of a less demanding job to take a master's-level certificate course at Wharton to burnish her business credentials.

It did not take us long to discover that Philadelphia was a very conservative town despite its large Jewish population and its many vibrant arts institutions. In my community leadership program, I was told by one of the speakers: "We need outsiders like you to save us from ourselves. Since the Revolution in 1776, we have always chosen to be too traditional. We have the inner city and the Main Line, and not much in between." When, in social gatherings, we would try to talk politics or discuss controversial books about race or other issues, we were likely to encounter polite smiles and topic-changing responses such as how to avoid traffic on the way to the King of Prussia Mall. Through her coursework at Wharton, Marilyn made some friends at the University of Pennsylvania, where we detected signs of intelligent life. Otherwise, we felt isolated. Possibly we were just too hardcore New York to be accepted into proper Philadelphia society without undergoing some extended initiation ritual that we did not understand.

One indicator of change while we were there concerned an issue that would affect one of the projects in which I became involved: a new Center City headquarters for Philadelphia Blue Cross. Several buildings were being proposed for downtown that would, for the first time, exceed the traditional (albeit unwritten) height limit. They would be taller than Billy Penn's hat—that is, they would rise above the statue of William Penn atop City Hall. Paul Goldberger, the suave architecture critic for the *New York Times,* whom I would get to know later, came to Philadelphia to deliver a lecture on the subject. In his wise and insightful style, he told the audience that, in his opinion, there were far bigger issues facing Center City—such as streetscapes and how new buildings would integrate into the urban fabric—that would have a much greater impact on the viability of the city's core than the simple question of the relationship to Billy Penn's hat.

Blue Cross retained Binswanger to be its real estate advisors for its new headquarters building. I took the lead for our firm, working with Bob Fascia, the project manager. Blue Cross intended to occupy the entire building but did not want the risk of ownership. Just as Irving Trust had done with RCDC—after realizing that as the net-lease tenant they would be bearing the full risk anyway, since all the costs were translated into financeable rent payments—Blue Cross eventually decided to opt for ownership. They hired Linpro, later called LCOR, to develop the building, which indeed was one of the first towers to exceed the historic height limit. Helping to ensure that the building was designed to their exact operational specifications was familiar territory for me after Irving Trust.

Finally, the American College of Physicians (ACP), which was housed in an historic mansion on Pine Street in West Philadelphia, decided that it needed—and could afford—to build a new headquarters. ACP retained Binswanger to be the development manager, appointed a committee of a dozen doctors to oversee the project, and looked to us to find a site and manage the entire process. To see a prestigious project like this through, literally from the ground up, was an exhilarating prospect.

Wanting a traditional look for its new home, ACP brought in Shepley Bulfinch, the successor architectural firm to H. H. Richardson, the legendary architect perhaps best known for Boston's Trinity Church. That firm had been making its mark on the American architectural landscape (including Harvard Yard) since the 1890s. I thoroughly enjoyed working with its current principal, Hugh Shepley, who was as distinguished and patrician as his surname suggested. After considering several other possible sites, particularly one in Baltimore whose proximity to the National Institutes of Health was appealing, ACP settled on a parcel on Independence Mall in Philadelphia. We then set about the detailed planning and design of the exteriors and interiors to meet its very specific needs.

Despite my portfolio of meaty assignments, I did not feel that Philadelphia was becoming a permanent home for us, and Marilyn felt very much the same way. We struggled to feel that we really fit in. We did make a few friends, in particular spending time with a couple whom Marilyn had met. Ann Duffield worked at the University of Pennsylvania. Tim, her husband, was a British landscape architect who supplemented their income by producing splendid architectural renderings. I was able to get Tim the assignment to do the rendering for the ACP building. Etched in a glass paperweight given out at the groundbreaking, a miniature version of it sits on my desk today. One evening, we were at their house for dinner when I recognized someone in a photo on the mantelpiece. "Hey!" I exclaimed. "That's Tommy Rosch. He was my classmate at Harvard." Equally surprised, Ann said it was her brother.

Our next-door neighbor in Addison Court, our courtyard complex, was a very tall man named Garrett Brown. One evening, he and his girlfriend invited us over for dinner. We had gotten to know them because Kathmandu, our cat, would climb over the rooftops and into their window. Garrett offered to let me hold the Oscar that he had received for inventing the Steadicam. It was surprisingly heavy. Still, it was apparently not enough to anchor a friendship, because ours did not go much further.

While I deeply appreciated the opportunity and support that John Binswanger had given me throughout, his management style proved at times more critical than instructive. "I guess if I want it done right," I recall him saying on more than one occasion, "I'll have to do it myself." I was struck by the demotivating effect of these words. More fodder for my management folder. It made some of our day-to-day interactions less pleasant than they otherwise might have been.

More importantly, the market for new office development was softening, and brokerage firms were discovering that they had less stomach for development risk than they had thought. They also tended to be capitalized insufficiently to ride out down markets. I sensed that Binswanger might not stick with the development business much longer. But mostly, after almost three years, Marilyn and I just wanted to get back home to New York City. On the few times when business trips took me back, I was electrified by the energy on the streets compared to Philadelphia, and casual conversations overheard in restaurants were more invigorating to us than anything we heard in Society Hill. We had honestly tried, but it just was not working. We never could develop a taste for cheesesteaks or the Eagles. New York was too deeply embedded in our psyches. I started to send out some feelers.

Mirabile dictu, the phone rang again in the spring of 1987. The caller was Alice Early, an executive recruiter from the highly regarded firm of Russell Reynolds. She told me that Cushman Realty Corporation (CRC), a Los

Angeles-based real estate company, was looking to open a New York City office. CRC had secured a major contract with Colgate-Palmolive to lead the redevelopment of its manufacturing site on the Jersey City waterfront and was looking for someone to take on the assignment. She asked if I would possibly be interested. As calmly as I could, I said that I was very comfortable where I was, but just might consider it.

Initially, I met with Erik Hansen, who had worked for KPMG's advisory arm and now headed CRC's consulting division. I liked Erik immediately, and we had a good exchange. A week or two later, I took a train to New York and had a dinner meeting with Erik, CFO Charlie Peck, and John Clydesdale Cushman III, the legendary founder and CEO of the company. John was from the family that founded Cushman & Wakefield (C&W), the international commercial brokerage company that had been acquired by Rockefeller Center. He had worked his way up in the company and headed its West Coast office, which, under his direction, became hugely successful and dominated the Los Angeles real estate market.

John had pioneered the equity lease, whereby anchor tenants would agree to occupy major portions of a new office building in exchange for significant equity participation in the overall development. Flush with this success—so the industry story went—John tried to lay claim to inheriting the top job at C&W. That was just when RCI had acquired C&W, and it was being run by the Peters brothers, Jimmy and Leon. It was Al Marshall who delivered the news to John that this was not in the cards. Without missing a beat, John took his LA office and with his twin brother, Lou (who ran C&W's Houston office), formed his own company. C&W had not protected the name and John was able to call his company Cushman Realty Corporation.

We met at a very upscale Midtown restaurant. We all ordered huge steaks and had some exceptional wine (John also owned Zaca Mesa, a well-regarded vineyard). The conversation was lively and wide-ranging. I particularly hit it off with Charlie Peck, who was a serious mountain climber. (Charlie would later climb very high on Everest, turning around not far below the summit because his partner could go no farther and had to go down. Charlie thought he could have made it to the summit, but he had just remarried and could not justify the risk of a solo ascent.) After dinner, as we parted, Erik whispered that he thought the evening had gone very well.

Some days later, Erik called to say that they wanted to proceed and that we should discuss terms. He told me that he was heading to Hawaii for an Urban Land Institute (ULI) conference and asked if there was any chance of meeting there. I had been a member of ULI, the professional association of the real estate development industry, since my RCDC days. With about a thousand attendees, the twice-annual ULI meetings were large and expensive and attracted the major players, making them a first-class venue for information and contacts. I had wanted to go to the spring 1987 meeting but had hesitated to ask John Binswanger for such an indulgence. I screwed up my courage and guiltily asked him if I could go. He agreed and I headed for Honolulu.

Erik and I spent some time together in Hawaii and Erik then went to bat with John Cushman, supporting my request for a starting salary of $150,000, a solid step up from my annual rate at Binswanger. Erik would prove to be an enormously supportive and loyal boss throughout my time at Cushman. I giddily reported John's approval to Marilyn when I returned. A good salary turned out to be something of a two-edged sword. Nearly everyone at CRC, except Erik's group, was a broker who worked exclusively on commission. John liked to say that he got up every morning naked and had to earn the clothes he put on each day. He had trouble understanding how anyone could expect to receive the same paycheck every two weeks without regard to whether he or she had closed a deal and earned a commission. He became especially prickly at year-end when annual bonus time came around. There were no ground rules for salaried employees, which led to unrealistic hopes and dashed expectations. But these were matters for the future. Marilyn and I could head back to New York with the ecstatic feeling that we were in excellent financial shape.

I broke the news to John Binswanger shortly after returning to Philadelphia from Hawaii. He was obviously annoyed, but he let slip that he would have preferred my leaving in a few months when the American College of Physicians building would be done. It seemed clear to me that he was already thinking seriously of closing down the development operation at that point and would probably have let me go as well, so the timing of my departure proved felicitous. John arranged for the very competent construction assistant I had hired in North Carolina to move up to Philadelphia for a few months to see the ACP project through.

We sold our Philadelphia townhouse to ACP's staff director, with whom I had been working. In New York we lived at first in a furnished sublet, then bought a two-bedroom apartment in an art deco co-op on the corner of West End Avenue and 87th Street. From there, I could see the brownstone where I had lived fifteen years earlier. This was the kind of building—565 West End Avenue—in the kind of location that I had long dreamt about. We were back!

In the summer of 1987, I started my new job working out of the Park Avenue offices of our client, Colgate-Palmolive, while I looked for office space. John Cushman had made it clear that he wanted a high-prestige location to signal to the industry that CRC intended to be a real player in New York. I found a suite on the fifteenth floor of 630 Fifth Avenue, part of Rockefeller Center, overlooking the skating rink. Now I really was back home. I hired an extremely capable and personable administrative assistant, Karen Kleinstauber, to anchor our office.

Colgate-Palmolive owned fifteen city blocks on thirty-four acres just south of Exchange Place in Jersey City. The site had been its principal manufacturing facility for more than a century and had even been its headquarters location in the early1900s. In the mid-1980s, Colgate decided that it needed more modern manufacturing facilities and, for distribution reasons, wanted to locate them in the middle of the country, in places like Jeffersonville, Indiana. The waterfront site was now excess real estate, and Colgate had retained John Cushman and his firm to advise the company on what to do with it and how to do it. Few things are as exciting to a real estate professional as the prospect of planning and executing a project from scratch on such a large scale and in such a prime location. From an urban planning and design perspective, this was a breathtaking and irresistible opportunity.

Model of the preliminary master plan for the Colgate Project, 1988 (the fully built-out project is remarkably consistent with the plan; Exchange Place Center is to the far right; behind it and to the left is a model of the design for the new Merrill Lynch Building at 101 Hudson Street).

Colgate's land was located along what was coming to be known as New Jersey's Gold Coast, even though it was still a mostly derelict industrial area. One new office building—the inelegant green-glass 700,000-square-foot Exchange Place Center—had been completed, adjacent to the PATH station connecting the area with Lower Manhattan, a mere three-minute subway ride away. The mass transit link was the key to the viability of the area as a cheaper alternative to the Financial District and Midtown area of Manhattan for companies seeking modern, efficient office space. Just to the north, the vast Newport complex was underway, a joint venture of shopping center developer Mel Simon and housing builder Sam LeFrak. "The scale of the undertaking is hard to imagine," the *New York Times* exclaimed. Several other significant projects were being planned south of Newport for many more millions of square feet. Many developers envisioned a great future there, as of course did the public officials of Jersey City and the State of New Jersey.

The Colgate executive who had prime responsibility for overseeing its venture was Gerald Z. Gibian. Gerry was a quintessential product of New York City: Stuyvesant High School followed by NYU for both undergraduate and law school. He was the company's lead tax lawyer and was assigned the corporate real estate portfolio as well. He is one of the most positive and even-tempered people I have ever met. No problem exists for him that cannot be resolved by reasonable people sitting down together and working out a practical solution. Gerry is still a close and valued friend.

Working for Gerry was Jack Huston, who was full-time on the Colgate Project. Jack, about fifteen years younger than me, was a Yale graduate and had worked in city planning and in the New Jersey governor's office under Brendan Byrne. We had a great deal in common and we would spend years working very closely together. Above Gerry and Jack was Bill Cooling, the chief technology officer, an aptly named Canadian with an icy temperament. At the top was Colgate's long-time chairman and CEO, Reuben Mark. Universally known by his first name, Reuben was a Jersey City native who took a personal and detailed interest in our work.

Meetings with Reuben were rare but eventful. He would grill us intensely on progress and problems and was never satisfied with our answers. On one occasion, Gerry, Jack, and I were trapped in his limo with him on a ride back to Manhattan from Jersey City after a meeting with Mayor Anthony Cucci. Reuben was particularly aggressive in his examination of our progress report. When we finally emerged back at the Park Avenue headquarters, Gerry offered, "Let's get something to eat." In unison, Jack and I exclaimed, "Who can eat?"

A signature feature of the Colgate site was an enormous octagonal clock with a fifty-foot diameter bearing the corporate logo. Facing Manhattan, it sat atop one of the old buildings due for demolition. Reuben was concerned that Wall Street analysts, who played a major role in determining Colgate's stock price, could see the clock from their windows, and he insisted that if the clock disappeared or told the wrong time, the analysts would interpret that as a sign of trouble at Colgate or with the project. He ruled that the clock had to remain visible and accurate at all times. It was moved two or three times during the demolition and construction, each time at a cost of more than $100,000. Today it is still visible and still on time at the southern end of the now-completed development.

The project team already consisted of Brennan Beer Gorman—our master plan architects—and numerous engineering, environmental, and legal consultants. While the team was engaged in creating a long-term physical master plan for the entire development, the first order of business was to clear the site. This meant getting permits to demolish the numerous manufacturing buildings and remove compromised soils and debris. While only soap and toothpaste had been produced there, the land was urban fill, making for the significant possibility of serious contamination. We were in a coastal management zone, subjecting the area to state and federal regulatory permits as well. It would take a lot of time and money to navigate this minefield.

Another problem was that in 1985, when Colgate closed the Jersey City plant, the company laid off hundreds of workers without doing all that it could have done to alleviate the resulting hardships. As a result, intense community hostility complicated the political approval process. Moreover, the site was directly adjacent to the low-rise brick buildings of the historic Paulus Hook neighborhood. The new project, even at its massive scale, would be a much more humane neighbor than the derelict fenced-off industrial complex it would replace, and Colgate had committed to funding a new waterfront park (where the clock now stands). Nevertheless, area residents thrived on making life as difficult as possible for Colgate.

There were many endless, angry evenings at public hearings before the city council at Jersey City's City Hall on Grove Street, and many long meetings with state and city officials to shepherd through the necessary site clearance permits. Jack Huston and I also spent many hours—much more enjoyable hours—poring over the options for the master plan with the architects and other consultants. The public officials wanted our project to succeed, and Colgate was willing to spend the time and money to ensure that all the due diligence and permitting were done thoroughly and correctly. Eventually, demolition work began and the project plan started to take shape.

Early on, an important decision had to be made regarding what role Colgate would play in the new development scenario. Publicly owned companies were notoriously poorly positioned to take the lead in real estate development projects, particularly large-scale ones. The degree of uncertainty and risk, the often cumbersome decision-making structure, shareholder oversight, and the impact of large, long-term debt on corporate balance sheets all militated against Colgate taking the lead developer role. But we felt that there was substantial long-term upside value to the property—if developed wisely—that would not be realized if Colgate were simply to sell the land outright to one or more real estate companies. The solution that CRC recommended was for Colgate to be the master land developer, selling parcels incrementally to individual developers over time, hopefully retaining small equity positions, to capture the increases in value that we could foresee. To preserve and enhance long-term value and returns, Colgate would require the developers of individual sites to build according to our master plan and, more specifically, according to our design guidelines.

The subject of the efficacy of design guidelines in achieving architectural and urban design objectives, particularly for multi-site phased developments, had intrigued me (and still does). The experience at Battery Park City yielded mixed reviews: while the esplanade and public spaces there were widely acclaimed, the individual buildings have been quite pedestrian. The success of design guidelines at Riverside South—which the civic community forced on developer Donald Trump in the 1990s—was even more questionable. The early buildings of that project aimed at being contextual with Manhattan's Upper West Side but proved to be ordinary at best.

My conclusion is that design guidelines cannot dictate or guarantee architectural excellence in individual buildings. They are too blunt and rigid.

They can prevent the terrible but cannot guarantee the sublime. The most likely outcome of stringent guidelines is mediocrity. Therefore, rather than focus on building details, we aimed at ensuring quality and consistency in the streetscape. Rockefeller Center is a good model. Its individual buildings are of no special distinction; its magic lies in the consistency of the street furniture and the way the buildings meet the street and function together around public spaces. The best way for a land developer or public sponsor to maximize the possibility of excellence in building design is to hire first-rate developers and, when possible, utilize design competitions. The more competitive the real estate market, the better the chance that individual buildings can afford the incremental cost of great architecture.

The most difficult urban planning issue we wrestled with was retail. The project's fifteen blocks would be a mix of primarily office space, some residential buildings, and a hotel and conference center that would total eight million square feet of space—the equivalent of downtown Kansas City. We aspired to create a vibrant urban center, but we knew it would be incomplete and sterile without active street-level storefront retail. How could we ensure that the bases of the individual buildings, constructed over time by different developers, would contain the variety of shops that would make for a real neighborhood? An additional challenge was that office and residential developers were neither expert in nor comfortable with including a significant amount of shopping space on their ground floors.

Again, the experience across the river at Battery Park City told us that overcoming this challenge would be extremely difficult. The retail concourses there were often barren. Only upscale chains chose to locate there initially, which hardly served to enliven the neighborhood ambience. We looked to experienced retail experts for advice. Those who pretended to that kind of expertise were generally suburban shopping mall aficionados. They wanted to close the streets and surround the project with parking. We wanted a genuine urban experience. How could we mandate—or at least effectively encourage—what we wanted: organic, street-level stores offering both convenience and discretionary goods like any successful, mature city?

To try to find out, we toured several cities whose waterfronts were known for their appeal to residents and tourists alike: Baltimore's Inner Harbor, Seattle's Pike Place Market, Boston's Faneuil Hall, Vancouver, and Toronto. Mostly we learned that what we wanted to do was hard work and took a long time. We did our best to require what we wanted in the guidelines for each building, but we knew it would be difficult to achieve—let alone maintain—our objectives in the crunch of final deal negotiations.

Late in the winter of 1988, John Cushman decided to host a strategy session at his ranch in Idaho, which had a splendid view of the west face of the Grand Tetons. Gerry Gibian, Jack Huston, John, Erik Hansen, and I flew out on John's private Gulfstream II, landing at the airstrip near Driggs. One or two others from the LA office joined us. We spent two intense days and three well-lubricated evenings reviewing the financing, development, and marketing strategies that we were to pursue. One outcome was a marketing trip to Japan that John Cushman, Gerry, and Erik took some weeks later. Despite my previous experience, I did not join them.

Another result of our Driggs session was finalizing the financial plan. Dale Schlather, John Cushman's young numbers guru (now an executive vice-chairman at Cushman & Wakefield), created an enormous and complex spreadsheet showing development expenses and projected land sales for all fifteen blocks over a fifteen-year period. It was a tour de force of assumptions and projections. Jack Huston told me not long ago that despite decades of changes in market conditions and uses, the model had proven remarkably on target.

After a few months, John Cushman hired Brian Dugan, an experienced corporate real estate executive, to assist with the marketing of the project. John also insisted that I get my broker's license, even though he knew this was not my strength or primary interest. Over a quiet Christmas period, Brian and I laboriously compiled a list of all tenants occupying over 250,000 square feet of space in Manhattan, thinking that these companies would constitute the prime targets to anchor new buildings in the Colgate Project. One advantage we could offer was that several of our sites were 80,000 square feet—almost two acres—and could accommodate the large floor sizes that financial institutions needed for their data centers and trading floors. New York was reasserting itself as the center of global commerce, and companies like Chase, Merrill Lynch, Bear Stearns, Lehman Brothers, and others were seeking competitive advantages via more efficient trading operations. Huge operations facilities with energy-intensive mainframe computer centers and flexible floor plates to accommodate ever-changing technology needs were essential for their success. The exercise that Brian and I undertook, requiring weeks of scouring printed source materials and laboriously checking lobby directories, could be done today in hours, if not minutes, with today's online databases.

As site preparation and detailed planning progressed, Colgate decided that it needed to revisit its real estate legal representation for the lease, land sale, and development negotiations to come. Colgate was not happy with the firm that it had retained after a rigorous interview process. It turned out that my friend Peter Herman had been part of that original competition, finishing a close second. I was able to put in a good word for Peter and his unparalleled development expertise. Colgate decided to turn to him with no further vetting. Peter undoubtedly merited the assignment on his own, but I was delighted to play a minor supporting role and to repay a fraction of the debt I owed him. I was also thrilled that we would be working together again.

At some point early in 1989, I received a phone call from Bernie May, whom I had met during my city government days. He was now a corporate real estate executive at Merrill Lynch. Bernie told me that they were in the market for a sizeable amount of space to expand their operations, and he wanted to see what the Colgate Project might offer. Initial meetings and site visits followed. Merrill's interest seemed genuine, and our project—with the ability to provide large trading floors at the base of a building and efficient executive office space above, plus a short commute to Lower Manhattan—appeared to offer what they were looking for. It was time to identify a developer for a new building to meet their specific needs. Since they were looking to occupy about two-thirds of the million-square-foot building planned for our first site, Merrill was a perfect candidate for one of John Cushman's signature equity leases.

We had met with several developers in the previous months, mostly those with a track record of undertaking large-scale projects, including Olympia & York, the Canadian company that had built the office complex at Battery Park City. None of them liked our scenario. They did not want to take the risk of developing an initial building in a relatively unproven location and, if successful, not having a guaranteed right to future sites at previously established prices. They wanted to be master developers of all or most of the Colgate Project. But it was basic to our game plan and projections that Colgate at least share in the future upside of success as well.

I knew that LCOR, which had developed the Blue Cross building in Philadelphia, had recently established a presence in New York and was aggressively seeking new opportunities. I had worked well with Kurt Eichler, the son of CEO Eric Eichler, and phoned him. They were interested. Eric and Kurt came to New York for a meeting with our project team. They were willing to play by our rules with a handshake promise that they would be given an equal and full shot at the next deal. We had a sound basis for moving forward.

Many months of discussions and negotiations ensued to create the voluminous and complex set of documents—lease, construction, long-term financing, development agreement, and so forth—that were necessary for a several-hundred-million-dollar transaction. Merrill, Colgate, LCOR, and the banks all came armed with their own lawyers. Colgate, which knew how to buy and sell companies in a week, could not understand why real estate deals took so much longer to finalize. But they do. On New Year's Eve 1989, all the parties gathered at the offices of the White & Case law firm, two blocks from Times Square. Colgate, confident of concluding the deal by year's end, had already declared the approximate proceeds of the transaction (which were "material" enough to require this) in its report of estimated annual earnings, which it provided to the investment community (and to the Securities and Exchange Commission). The deal had to close that night or Colgate's stock price might be savaged for failing to hit the company's announced income projections. No one else at the table had the same sense of urgency, making for an unhealthy imbalance of negotiating strength in the final hours. An environmental attorney from Jones Day used her leverage to press for draconian cleanup and liability provisions, mostly to impress her bank client. As midnight approached, she finally relented, and the last documents were inked. The deal had closed in time.

Peter Herman's wonderful wife, Alice, had smuggled in a jelly jar full of Jack Daniel's, which she knew to be my favorite, and we celebrated briefly. Gerry Gibian calmly put a check for $22 million in his wallet and casually walked to Grand Central Station to catch his late train to Greenwich. I raced home to celebrate the New Year with Marilyn, but 1990 arrived while I was still in the subway.

I did not know that on January 2, Gerry would deliver the check to Colgate's corporate treasurer as his last official act. He left to join Estée Lauder. Jack Huston took over Gerry's worldwide real estate responsibilities and hired a new project manager, Alex Twining. Swiftly, our lives began to change. As smart and capable as Jack was, he proved much more guarded and protective than Gerry. Perhaps because he was so determined to succeed in his new role, he and Alex treated all of us at Cushman Realty as a problem rather than as a partner. The Merrill deal was literally the New York area's last major real estate transaction of the 1980s before the market softened substantially in the 1990s. We soon found that there was just no one in the market willing to make the kind of major space commitment needed to justify another new financeable deal. Nevertheless, at Bill Cooling's relentless insistence, Jack and Alex continually badgered us to produce the next miracle.

There was little doubt that the very substantial annual retainer that Colgate was paying CRC was unsustainable in this new economic environment without a reasonable prospect of more transactions. I believe that Gerry Gibian's style would have been to sit everyone down at some point and say, "This is just not working; can we figure out a way forward to keep the partnership together?" We might not have been able to do so, but everyone's cards would have been on the table, and we would have been able to maintain the mutual respect and goodwill that we had shared to this point. Instead, the pressure on us continued to increase, and criticism—spoken and silent—intensified. As 1990 wound down, and throughout 1991, the atmosphere steadily deteriorated.

The completed Colgate Project as seen from Hudson River Park, 2020 (Exchange Place Center is to the far right with 101 Hudson Street behind it; the relocated Colgate Clock is at the far left, still visible from Manhattan and still keeping perfect time).

By early 1992, as our relationship with Colgate was coming to an end, John Cushman was looking to the New York office to become a more traditional commercial brokerage operation focusing on tenant representation, which was CRC's trademark. Brian Dugan was comfortable with this; I was not. Brian and I had become great friends while working together on the Colgate Project, learning from and appreciating each other. We talked often about the unpleasant direction of things. By the spring, it was clear that I needed to have a heart-to-heart with John Cushman. I understood that I either had to move into a broker's role or move on. I regretfully told

John that at the age of fifty-two, I just was not cut out to reinvent myself as a commissioned broker. He generously accepted that and pledged to be helpful as I looked for a new job while bringing my time at CRC to an end.

Working for John Cushman had been a marvelous experience. He operated in the stratosphere of the real estate business. Unlike many of his competitors who fought in the trenches, John marketed himself and our services at the corporate boardroom level. I recall that soon after I joined Cushman Realty, we were in the offices of Drexel Burnham. John knew a senior executive and we were to meet with him about marketing and financing for the Colgate Project. It was Monday, October 22, 1987, which came to be known as the infamous "Black Monday." Computer-driven trading programs triggered a massive sell-off in an already frothy market that saw shares fall twenty percent in a single day. We walked unnoticed past desks manned by young traders who were staring helplessly in shock at their computer terminals. The squawk box was blaring a message to contact Drexel's clients and try to assure them that everything was going to be okay. It was surreal. John was unfazed.

John Cushman was unique among commercial real estate brokers in his comfort in prowling the offices of corporate giants. He understood the mindset and concerns of Fortune 500 CEOs, and he knew how to talk to and socialize with them. He created opportunities rather than responding to them. He recruited smart, talented people and treated them extremely well (except, that is, when it came to sharing major commissions, when the office environment resembled hyenas and lions around a carcass, with John definitely in the role of the alpha lion).

But John's work style could be infuriating. During difficult meetings or negotiations, he would open his briefcase and start going through his back-logged pile of memos and mail, seeming to lose interest in what was going on. Then he would suddenly jump back into the discussion, showing that he had not missed a thing. Or he would purposely toss a virtual hand grenade into the conversation, raising some entirely new issue or question to throw the others off stride. John's mind was so quick and his focus so sharp that he loved injecting chaos when others were seeking order. He felt, I believe, that he operated better than others in turbulent air and it gave him an edge. His style clearly worked for him but was hard on others. He was a legendarily tough—although never petty—negotiator, and I was very glad to be on his side of the table. I learned an enormous amount from being around him and am deeply grateful to have had the opportunity to work for him.

I worked hard during the years I spent at Cushman Realty, but still found time to sustain my addiction to adventurous travel, now with Marilyn. In the early days of our marriage, we talked about perhaps having a child. Given Marilyn's age, we had very little time. Then my cancer intervened and the issue became moot. Neither of us was consumed by the need to have children, so we did not seriously regret this turn of events. Over the next twenty years, we would spend the better part of the cost of a college education on travel and still put aside a decent amount for retirement.

I had discovered the catalogs first of Mountain Travel and then of Wilderness Travel, and together they would become my new "Book of Marvels." I did my best to go on as many of those adventures as I could. I had taken their trips to Dhaulagiri and then to Kilimanjaro and Island Peak. In 1986, while I was still at Bay Street Landing, Marilyn and I trekked for a week on the Inca Trail to Machu Picchu, which was a magical experience. Each night on that trip, we read aloud from the book describing the discovery of the site by Hiram Bingham, father of the man who had saved my family in Marseille. We read the last chapter at our camp overlooking the ethereal ruins. At that time, Marilyn was still hanging on at HBO and had to return home after the first week. I continued on for a trek in the Cordillera Blanca.

In 1987, we joined a group on a very strenuous trip to the Pyrenees. Our guide was Martin Zabaleta, who had recently become the first Spaniard to climb Mount Everest. He was from the Basque region of Spain and created a major stir when he planted the separatist flag on the summit. Nevertheless, he was a national hero and was given a celebratory welcome wherever we went. He had prodigious strength and stamina and became a bit impatient with us amateurs. To save a few hours, he took us on a "shortcut" down a sheer rock wall, which dropped endlessly away. Some metal spikes stuck out of the face, providing some handholds, but the descent was breathtakingly frightening. Our inexperienced group spent many more hours navigating this so-called shortcut than the original route would have required.

Marilyn wrote a vivid description of this trial for a creative writing course that she took the following year:

Shivering, we pulled on parkas, gloves, and hats against the pre-dawn chill. Martin distributed harnesses, ropes, carabiners, and other technical climbing paraphernalia among those with room in their rucksacks. By sunrise we were trudging up a loose gravel switchback toward the notch. Soon we could see the Brecha, a snaggle-toothed crest smiling in the morning sun, inviting passage through its gap to unknown wonders and mysteries. Once there, it seemed all of Spain spread out before us. Valleys, mountains, green, gray, and brown. We rested, then headed down—a long scramble over intermittent boulders, cliffs, and meadows to a grassy plateau 2,000 feet below. Finally, lunch near a cool stream, resting and watching young men scale rock pinnacles in the distance.

The spell broke when Martin led us to a spot out on a promontory from which the earth fell away. Massive 2,000-foot rock columns like Manhattan office towers dominated the space. He and Raphael (our Kamikaze bus driver/ mountain guide/Spanish good ole boy) laid out the ropes and other climbing gear and began to outfit the most visibly terrified of the group, Elsa.

A doctor's wife from Little Rock, Arkansas, Elsa had come alone on this trek in her personal odyssey to recapture physical strength and emotional grit after thirty years of nurturing a family. They strapped her into a harness that encircled each thigh individually, connecting to a thick waistband, a kind of chastity belt. Then they uncoiled the ropes attaching one end to her harness. With each action, Elsa's face became more contorted. Her lips quivered, her eyes darted wildly—the perfect countenance of imminent, painful death. We called out words of consolation and encouragement as Raphael led her like a lamb to slaughter toward the abyss.

She disappeared around the corner. Silence. We talked softly among ourselves, waiting. Some retreated to protected corners to struggle with private fears. It seemed an eternity before we heard a shout from below: "Elsa says it's a piece of cake!" Cheers.

Klancy, a veteran of Outward Bound, having faced her extreme fear of exposed edges, asked to go next. I, a virgin of such endeavors, was eager to take on the adventure, so the two of us stepped up to be harnessed. Raphael led Klancy around the corner, instructing me to keep the safety rope linking the two of us always taught. I stepped around the corner, grinning and waving to the group, excited about what lay ahead. That's when reality set in. I stood on an eight-inch-wide ledge next to a waist-high boulder whose bulk intruded onto that small area, inducing a need to bend in the middle in order to maintain contact with the ground. Behind me was nothing but space. Somewhere ahead, probably twelve feet distant, were the spikes. I knew Klancy was on them because I could hear Raphael directing (in Spanish) where to step and where to hold as she moaned and whimpered. I could not look. Doing so would have meant acknowledgement of that overwhelming void.

The rope became taut, signaling my obligation to step forward into space. Narrow iron protrusions, eight to twelve inches long, grew out of the rock at eye and foot level. Running horizontally at chest level and secured periodically to the surface was a cable, which served as an additional safety device. Martin followed close behind, directing hand and foot placements as I worked my way across.

Slowly, slowly, hugging the rock and stepping spike to spike, I made my way, heart pounding, palms sweating. As I moved across, the umbilical cord connecting me to Klancy dramatically changed its angle. Instead of continuing to traverse, she was going downward, something I had not expected. I glanced down and saw her clinging to the spikes, sobbing. My hands became wetter, my concentration faltered. I hesitated. Panic. It was time to give up the security of the fixed cable and follow her.

Raphael parked Klancy, clinging to the wall, and rushed over to direct my feet. Martin lowered me down by the harness until I made contact. Down, down. Then a level path again about eight inches wide with nothing to hold on to except the rock wall.

"Wait here," Martin commanded, then disappeared. I stood with my face pressed against the wall, certain the slightest movement would send me out *into the chasm. When finally instructed to move, I clambered down a narrow twenty-foot rock chimney fitted with intermittent spikes to a luxurious two-foot-wide landing. Klancy stood there, eyes moist, grinning. We squeezed each other's hand tightly, hugged, paused, and then shouted our lie to the awaiting victims. "Marilyn and Klancy are down. Piece of cake!"*

I was next, and I knew enough not to believe them.

The summer of 1988 saw us camping on the beaches and in the forests of Hawaii. We started the trip by celebrating our fifth wedding anniversary at a luxury resort on Kauai and then joined our group for rustic lodge accommodations on the Garden Isle before moving on to Maui, Molokai, and the Big Island. We skipped the final beach luau and moved for the last two nights into the Mauna Kea hotel, a Rock Resort, where the quality of detail and artwork on the walls attested to Laurance Rockefeller's personal attention. The architecture, landscaping, furnishings, and entire ambience exuded quiet, understated luxury

In 1989, we went back to Europe for a magnificent trek in the Alps, beginning in Chamonix, France. The Mont Blanc circuit is one of the world's classic hikes. It takes about two weeks to walk around the tallest peak in the Alps, from France into Italy, on to Switzerland and then back into France. Classic scenery and extraordinary cuisine make this one hundred-mile hike one of the special experiences for mountain lovers. We had two leaders for the trip: Roland and Béatrice, both of whom were members of the renowned Chamonix guides. We learned from Béatrice (whose name sounds very lyrical when pronounced the French way), who was very attractive, that her husband had been severely injured in a mountaineering accident. She and Roland made little effort to hide that they were having an affair, a very French thing to do. During our lunch stops, she would strip to the waist to sun herself, another very European thing to do. We prudish Americans were quite agog.

When not traveling, Marilyn and I spent our weekends at the small country house that I had bought in 1981 outside the village of Phoenicia in the Catskills. Until then, the idea of owning a vacation house had not really entered my head. At first, Marilyn said she wanted to rent a vacation house as she had done in her single years (a beach house in the Hamptons in summer and a ski house in Vermont in winter). Since I loved hiking in the Catskills, she proposed renting a house there for the summer, or even buying one. We had briefly considered buying a vacation house in Westhampton but had been defeated by the interest rates at the time, which were close to twenty percent. Paul Volcker, the legendary chief of the Federal Reserve, was waging war against runaway inflation, and loans for second homes had become almost unobtainable.

I agreed to give the idea of buying a house in the Catskills exactly one day. We contacted a broker and told her that we were looking for a cabin by a lake. Not much fit that description, but the second place we saw was a charming little house on a dirt road with a community pond nearby. It was priced at $50,000. We took about fifteen minutes to decide that we wanted it. We found a local savings bank that was willing to give us a mortgage at a credit-card-like rate of 17.5 percent, which after a year or two, we were able to refinance on more conventional terms. We closed shortly after the Fourth of July weekend in 1981 and enjoyed our country house together for more than a dozen years. That was the beginning of my deep love affair with the Catskills, which continues to this day.

TWELVE

RPA AND BEYOND

It was now 1992, and I had been compelled to start thinking about what I might possibly do after Cushman Realty. The real estate market was in the doldrums; development projects were going belly-up all around the country. Workouts—restructuring and repackaging existing distressed properties such as shopping centers and apartment complexes—was about the only sector hiring anyone, and I had no experience or interest in that kind of job. One day, while standing on the platform of the Seventh Avenue subway line—my usual commuting route—I ran into Richard Anderson, president of Regional Plan Association (RPA). I had been an admirer of RPA since studying its Second Regional Plan (released in the 1960s) while working on my NYU master's degree, and my friend and colleague Peter Herman had a long history with RPA. As a young associate at Milbank in the 1970s, he had done pro bono work for the association and had remained actively involved. He was now one of the mainstays on its board of directors and served as de facto counsel. I had attended various RPA events and was keenly interested in its work.

Richard Anderson (known as Dick) surprised me by asking if I knew of any opportunities in the real estate world. "Why are you asking?" I replied. "You have the best job in New York." He told me that he was leaving RPA. The hairs on the back of my neck stood up. *That would be my dream job,* I thought.

As soon as I got home, I called Peter Herman. He laughed and said, "I was about to call you. I couldn't do so before Dick's departure became official, but by all means, get me your résumé."

I soon found myself meeting with RPA's search committee, which consisted of several directors including Peter and Richard Ravitch, who had chaired the Urban Development Corporation in the 1970s and led the rescue of New York City's subway system from its imminent collapse in the 1980s as head of the MTA. I had met him on several occasions.

I soon learned that my main competition was Robert Yaro, the chief planner at RPA. Bob was a recognized scholar and authority in regional planning who had been brought in to lead RPA's effort to create a Third Regional Plan. Work on the plan was behind schedule and the organization's finances were precarious. The board wanted the new president to right the ship and make sure the plan got finished. For all of Bob's intellectual brilliance, there were questions about whether this kind of management was his strength and might divert him from getting the plan done.

I had a follow-up interview with Gary Wendt, RPA's board chairman. He was the CEO of GE Capital, the incredibly successful financial arm of General Electric. Gary's brusque style told me that he was a product of Jack Welch's "take no prisoners" school of management. A couple of days later, Gary called me and said, "Okay, the job is yours until you blow it." I asked him what my relationship with Bob Yaro should be. He said that it would be like a baseball team; I would be the new manager, but Bob was the star center fielder, and it was my job to keep him happy and motivated. It was a challenging assignment, but I was thrilled beyond words. And I didn't even miss a paycheck.

RPA has a national reputation for serious, objective, and impeccably researched policy recommendations to improve the economic and social well-being of the Tri-State Metropolitan Region. Founded in the 1920s, the organization is a major player in the civic life of the region. Here is how RPA describes itself on its website today:

RPA is America's most distinguished urban research and advocacy organization. RPA works to improve the prosperity, infrastructure, sustainability and quality of life of the New York-New Jersey-Connecticut metropolitan region. Some of the region's most significant public works, economic development and open space projects have their roots in RPA ideas and initiatives, from the location of the George Washington Bridge to the revitalization of downtown Brooklyn, Stamford and Newark to the preservation of open space and development of parks in the Palisades, Governors Island and Gateway National Recreation Area. RPA has pursued these goals by conducting independent research, planning, advocacy and vigorous public-engagement efforts.

RPA was founded by business and civic leaders to create a blueprint for the rational growth of the region in the wake of the rapid but helter-skelter economic expansion of the 1920s. Issued in 1929, the First Regional Plan became part of the sacred scripture of metropolitan planning in the United States. The Second Regional Plan was undertaken in the 1960s in response to the explosion of growth after World War II, which mostly took the form of ugly suburban sprawl. This was the "plan" that I had studied at NYU. Why the quotes? Because it was actually a series of highly regarded research volumes rather than a plan *per se*; despite the rich trove of studies and findings contained in these reports, no final plan document was ever completed. It was a time of reverence in some quarters for participatory democracy and bottom-up planning. There seems to have been a feeling that RPA should not tell people what to do but rather offer a forum for discussion. Televised town meetings about the "plan" were the highlight of its so-called completion.

This mindset bothered me. I was determined to prod RPA out of what I saw as its passive role, and to guide its evolution as a true advocacy organization committed to seeing its recommendations implemented. Approximately once per generation, RPA issued a comprehensive vision of the steps needed to ensure the region's continued economic and social success;

I wanted to see RPA spend the next twenty-five years actually engaged in trying to make that vision a reality.

In the fall of 1993, a little over a year after I joined RPA, Rudolph Giuliani was elected mayor of New York. Mike Bailkin, my lawyer and friend from the mayor's Office of Lower Manhattan Development, called me and suggested I throw my résumé into the hopper for consideration by Giuliani's transition team for a major job in the new administration. Mike had established his own law firm, Stadtmauer Bailkin, and was well on his way to becoming one of the most influential and politically connected lawyers in town. Mike probably had a two-fold motive: he genuinely wanted to do me a favor; and it wouldn't hurt his kind of firm to have as many friends in high places in the new administration as possible. Mike added that, even if nothing came of it, it wouldn't hurt to have Giuliani's people get to know who I was. Given my desire to move RPA into a more politically visible and effective stance, I agreed.

I also was aware that Richard Parsons held a very senior position in the transition. I had gotten to know Dick when he was a wunderkind on Nelson Rockefeller's staff. Finishing first in his class at Albany Law School in 1971, he was recruited for a spot in the counsel's office. Dick quickly displayed his extraordinary talent for problem-solving and consensus-building, which would mark his later meteoric rise through the top echelons of corporate America. Rockefeller had brought Dick with him to Washington in 1974 to help staff the vice president's office.

Almost certainly, it was thanks to Dick's intervention that I was called in to interview with Randy Mastro, one of the mayor-elect's senior advisors, about heading the city's Economic Development Corporation (EDC). Ironically, this was the successor agency to the development offices that had been folded together during the fiscal crisis. I had a good discussion with Randy but told him that unless the job could be combined with that of deputy mayor for economic development, I was not sure I would be interested. Randy said he did not think that combining the jobs was in the cards but would pass along my concern. I was then called for a meeting with the mayor-elect, which is usually tantamount to a pro forma blessing. Giuliani told me that the deputy mayor's post was pledged to someone else, but the EDC position was available. The meeting ended without any clear commitments from either side.

The attraction of being back at the center of the political action was acute. Certainly, the idea of heading a major city agency in a new administration was tempting. But I knew that if I had to report to a deputy mayor, rather than having direct access to the mayor, I would have little leverage to truly affect public policy, nor would I have much of a political future. Leaving RPA under those terms would not be worth it. Giuliani was not a very well-known quantity yet, and he was a Republican. I had not had any problem working for Rockefeller, but it was clear that Rudy Giuliani was not cut from the same GOP cloth. Most importantly, I treasured my position at RPA, and shepherding development of the new Third Regional Plan was an unparalleled opportunity.

I decided to stay at RPA and wrote the mayor to that effect. Later I managed to make the mayor's enemies list (of which I became quite proud) and was barred from City Hall meetings. I doubt that my turning the mayor down was the primary cause for my banishment, but it certainly did not help. I asked my friend George Humphreys, who had a back channel to Peter Powers, the first deputy mayor, if my blacklisting was personal. The word came back that it probably was not. Powers reported that the mayor just did not like regionalism. For him, the term was just a synonym for stealing jobs from New York City.

At this point, work had been underway for several years on the Third Regional Plan. But it still needed a lot of work to pull it together into a completed product worthy of being called a "regional plan" and living up to RPA's previous products. Bob Yaro possessed an unusually fertile mind and a restless intellect. He could synthesize new planning concepts and solutions and find ways to express them that captured people's imaginations. He was not as good at making firm decisions and pushing people to get things done. That was my job. We developed mutual respect and a good working relationship, but we did not become close. We were just too different for that. I also sensed how much Bob wanted—and felt he deserved—my job, which kept a certain unspoken tension lingering in the air.

RPA's staff of about a dozen professionals was, on the whole, superb. They were experts in their fields, self-motivated and dedicated to the high intellectual and academic standards that RPA was noted for. They needed support, recognition, and structure but not close supervision or micro-management. An immediate problem, and one that would continue to plague us, was our office space. We did not have the financial resources to pay Midtown Manhattan rents. Yet Manhattan was the transportation center and beating heartbeat of the region, and it was home to most of our corporate board members. We needed to be there but could not really afford it, so we had to take any opportunity that presented itself.

At that time, we were in space donated by one of our board members, but it was on an interim basis and we would have to move soon. Gary Wendt came to our rescue. He gave us space at 570 Lexington Avenue, GE's wonderful art deco former corporate headquarters. Near Grand Central, it was an ideal location for us. But GE was planning to divest itself of the building, so we would have it only for a couple of years.

Facing a second move, I was finally able to arrange for us to be housed with Con Edison, one of our most loyal supporters. We occupied half a floor in its landmark building on 14th Street. In order to satisfy the Public Service Commission's requirement that it be an "arm's-length" transaction, Con Ed had to charge us something close to a market rent. We were barely able to meet that requirement, but RPA stayed in that space for more than twenty years.

Our finances were a constant bedevilment. Bob Yaro, a student of RPA's history, would refer to the situation as RPA's "seventy-fifth annual budget crisis"—not much of an exaggeration. RPA had about a $2 million annual budget at the time, about half of it coming from our corporate board members in the form of unrestricted gifts. The other half came from foundations for restricted program grants that Bob was constantly pursuing. Those familiar with nonprofit fundraising and budgeting know that the key to non-profit financial health is attracting unrestricted support that can be used to pay for basic staff and operations and to do what the organization wants to do. Restricted program grants require that the funds be used for the donor foundation's objectives, which may be consistent with the nonprofit's goals but may not match its most critical needs. In addition, the administrative overhead that comes with program grants (and government contracts in particular) almost never covers the true cost to the organization. In short, restricted program grants are welcome and often indispensable to keep nonprofits afloat, but they come at a cost.

Our unrestricted giving had been shrinking slowly but inexorably for some time. We were caught up in a broader trend: corporate philanthropy was undergoing a seismic change. In the years following World War II, local business leaders—the heads of the banks, utilities, insurance companies, newspapers, etc.—tended to have a direct stake in the health and well-being of their communities. In those days it was part of a CEO's basic job to serve on the boards of nonprofit organizations such as RPA. Now most of those companies were becoming global enterprises, and global competition was relentless. It was partly for that reason that boards of directors increasingly looked to CEOs to focus exclusively on stock price, which meant concentrating on next-quarter earnings projections rather than on long-term commitments to stakeholders including workers and their communities. Now CEOs' windows looked out upon the world, and their interest in the communities that actually housed them was secondary. We encountered more and more difficulty convincing companies that they should support an organization like RPA that was working to improve the region where they were physically located. Maintaining the interest of CEOs was key to maintaining their financial involvement with us, but they were increasingly moving in a direction that I could not figure out how to reverse.

One existing staff member, with the colorful name of Aram Khachadurian, intrigued me. Aram had an inchoate array of responsibilities. A microbiology major in college and a former banker, he had a restless energy and intelligence that struck me as capable of being far better employed. And I just was drawn to him. Aram was gay and HIV positive. In those days, that was close to a death sentence, but Aram attacked his illness with the ingenuity and fierce determination that I would find were his hallmark. I feared that I would have to attend his funeral in the near future, but I was determined to invest in him. I made him our sorely needed director of development. Aram could not overcome our basic financial problems, but he brought order and direction to that difficult operation. Relating the rest of Aram's career would require a book of its own to capture his imagination and spirit of adventure, and to catalog the many hair-raising places where he has chosen to spend time. Suffice it to say that he is healthy, and we remain close friends to this day. He stays in touch from his home base in Tunis.

Gary Wendt was feeling frustrated and impatient about our financial condition. We would meet with him for periodic reviews at his office in Stamford, Connecticut. Necessarily, we divided our budget reports into the restricted and unrestricted categories, each of which had different accounting rules, especially governing how we booked the revenues. That made it difficult to discern exactly how bad our situation was at any given moment. Gary ran one of the most sophisticated financial enterprises in the country, but he wanted to see a single bottom-line number. "Just tell me," he would bark, "if I had to sell RPA tomorrow, are we in the toilet or not?" We could never give him a simple answer.

One of the main things we looked to our chairman for was to recruit someone to chair and lead the fundraising for the Regional Assembly, our annual conference. We gathered the civic-minded constituency for our work in a hotel ballroom and in breakout areas each year to hear presentations about—and provide feedback on—the key issues we were working on. The chair of the Assembly did not even have to show up; he just had to commit to lend his name, come up with a sizeable lead contribution, and let us use his mailing list to pursue other contributors. One year, Gary called me to say that I should meet him the next day in the lobby of the AIG building at 77 Pine Street in Lower Manhattan. Gary said he had asked AIG's titanic

CEO, Maurice "Hank" Greenberg, to headline the Assembly.

When I met Gary in the lobby, I asked, "Why does he want to meet with us? Chairing the Assembly can't be that big a deal for him."

Gary smiled sardonically and replied:, "I don't know, but we're going to find out."

We took the elevator and a private circular stair to the peak of that historic building and were led to Greenberg's private dining room. As we sat down, Greenberg turned to Gary with a steely look and said, "Okay, you've got your twenty-five grand, now let's talk about the Far East."

AIG was founded in Shanghai and had long been a major factor in high finance in that part of the world. GE Capital had been making inroads in underwriting major investments there as well. The rest of the tense conversation had nothing to do with RPA; it was all about whether they could avoid beating each other's brains out in competition in that part of the world. I sat and watched. They did not seem able to find any common ground. The conversation might have proven fascinating to an antitrust lawyer, but for me it provided a rare glimpse into a very different arena.

My time at RPA was not limited to just worrying about administrative and budgetary matters. Almost as soon as I arrived, I started attending regular meetings of the Riverside South Planning Corporation (RSPC) which had been formed in the early 1990s by six civic organizations, including RPA, in response to Donald Trump's scheme to build a mammoth project on the former Penn Central railyards between 59th and 72nd Streets on the far west side of Manhattan. To be called Television City, it would boast "the tallest building in the world" at 150 stories, as well as several 75-story towers. It was truly gargantuan; Donald's outsized ego was already on display. Both the initial plan for Television City and several subsequent modifications stirred up a firestorm of community opposition led by a group called Westpride. Despite the woeful state of the real estate market and the city's hunger for new development at the time, it was very doubtful that Trump could have won the necessary approvals to proceed. Among other things, he and then-mayor Ed Koch were waging a bitter war of words in the press.

The six civic groups got together and presented Trump with an alternate plan, still large but restricted to housing, some of it affordable. If Trump would agree to their plan and agreed to build a park over a torn down West Side Highway, the civic groups would support the project. Donald agreed, and Riverside South Planning Corporation was formed to advocate for the project and to monitor compliance with the plan. Donald also agreed to fund a small staff headed by the remarkable Richard Kahan, a member of Ed Logue's team at UDC, who later turned Battery Park City into a success story. RSPC consisted of RPA, the Municipal Art Society, the Natural Resources Defense Council, the Parks Council (later called New Yorkers for Parks), the Riverside Park Fund, and Westpride. It was close to an all-star team of public advocacy groups. Even the normally skeptical Paul Goldberger wrote in the *New York Times* that the outcome "now stands a real chance of being a cause for celebration rather than embarrassment." The civic groups met monthly among ourselves, and roughly quarterly with Donald, with Kahan handling most of the communication with Trump and his development team. The meetings were divided between political advocacy and architectural reviews to ensure that the buildings would comply with the detailed design guidelines that had been developed. The political advocacy involved securing the necessary city approvals, including ULURP, and trying to get federal funding to tear down the highway. Responding to the civics' demand for first-rate architecture, Donald had retained Philip Johnson to design the first couple of buildings. At a review meeting, one of the civics complained to Philip that his design was a fairly bland attempt at contextualizing with the Upper West Side's traditional brick residential architecture. He haughtily responded, "Don't blame me; you designed the buildings, I'm just filling them in." I thought the moment precisely captured the imperfect outcome of design guidelines.

The real estate market of the time still did not support large-scale construction in such a pioneering location. With the market delays and persistent litigation from community opposition, the consortium of banks led by Chase lost patience with Trump's outstanding and delinquent pre-construction loan of over $200 million. He professed not to care, famously proclaiming, "When you owe the banks $2 million you have a problem; if you owe them $200 million, *they* have a problem." Nevertheless, he sold his controlling interest to a Hong Kong development group but continued to be the public face of the project. It was clear to us that the real power was wielded by the Hong Kong investors' representative, who began to attend our meetings.

Our experience dealing with Donald Trump was decidedly mixed. He was undeniably obnoxious and arrogant, but he essentially lived up to all of the commitments he made to us and to the project. We never succeeded in getting the federal money to tear down the highway, but he seemed to use his political connections toward that end as much as he could. He did build and pay for the scaled-down park that now exists along the Hudson River from 59th to 72nd Streets. A biography of Donald written not long after this episode quoted me as saying, in response to a question of why he had acted relatively responsibly, that I guessed he did so "not to do the right thing, but to be admired for doing the right thing." At that early stage of his descent into demagoguery, he still craved the approval and respect of the civic community. He invited us all to his fiftieth birthday party in the lobby of Trump Tower. While we all found him personally despicable, I doubt that any of us saw in him the capacity for the catastrophic political hubris, human insensitivity, and constitutional assault that he would demonstrate as president.

As work on the Third Regional Plan progressed, we had to prepare for its release, publication, and promotion. I was convinced that unless we could get it on television, it would not have the impact we all wanted. I was introduced to Steve Anderson, a public-spirited documentary filmmaker. He got excited about the idea of producing an hour-long film about the plan and getting it on public television. He came up with a minimum budget of $400,000 to produce it. I crafted as persuasive a memo as I could to Gary Wendt justifying the importance of the effort and asking his help in raising the money. My memo came back promptly with one word scrawled in the upper right-hand corner: "Ugh!" At first, I had no idea whether he thought it a ridiculous idea or was commenting on the difficulty of finding the money. Fortunately, it turned out to be the latter. He called me a week later to say, "Okay, I got you the first $200,000 and I'm working on the rest. Get to work."

Shortly after the plan was released, the film was shown during prime time on Channel 13 and other regional PBS outlets, hosted by local NBC anchor Chuck Scarborough. Steve Anderson had succeeded in distilling the plan's complicated public policy recommendations into visually interesting story lines. He also proved to be fearless and effective in rounding up political and community leaders to participate. All three regional governors—as well as Mayor Giuliani, Felix Rohatyn, Calvin Butts, and other opinion leaders—made cameo appearances. Today the videotape sits on my bookshelf and is one of my prized RPA mementos.

We did not have the money to produce a glossy print version of the plan. We needed a publisher. Bob Yaro had contacts at Island Press, a public policy-minded publisher that specialized in environmental issues. They were interested, but beyond the very limited market of urban planning schools and libraries, they could not see much sales potential. Bob Yaro was somewhat recognized in the field, so Island Press insisted that his name be on the cover along with that of Tony Hiss, whom Bob had recruited to help with writing the final document. Tony was a well-known and respected writer for *The New Yorker*. The plan was the work of the entire staff, and it grated to have our organizational product personalized in this manner, but we had no choice. When I reviewed the first draft of the early pages, I was troubled by the breezy, Talk-of-the-Town style. It was highly readable, of course, but it did not convey the gravitas that I thought the document should contain. I edited out the contractions and some of the informal wording. Tony and Bob reluctantly but graciously accepted my corrections. Numbered copy #2 of the plan now also has a special place on my bookshelf. I doubt that Gary Wendt still has his copy #1.

We had long discussions about what title to give to the final document. The plan cataloged the many problems facing the region, which was still rebounding from the crash of 1987. It was, in our view, a fragile recovery.

The growing economic inequity, underinvestment in infrastructure, and lack of concern for environmental degradation all seemed to pose serious threats to sustained growth. We represented these challenges in a Venn diagram of three overlapping circles: economy, environment, and equity. We labeled the common area at the center "quality of life," which was the common theme that our business leaders had identified as essential to attracting and retaining businesses and employees. Trying to strike the right balance between threat and opportunity, we called the plan *A Region at Risk*. Most reactions were supportive, but we did get some passionate pushback that the title sent an unduly negative message.

The ultimate litmus test of newsworthiness is coverage on the front page of the *New York Times*. Aspiring to this, we promised an exclusive to the *Times*, which we told the other media we would not do—not an uncommon ruse. Marian Heiskell, who had been so helpful to me at State Parks and was on RPA's board, contacted her nephew, Arthur Sulzberger Jr., publisher of the *Times*. She could not directly affect the paper's coverage; the editorial staff adamantly maintained its independence. She did, however, arrange for a "publisher's lunch," the most prestigious ritual that the fabled newspaper could offer.

A few days before the formal release of *A Region at Risk*, having provided the *Times* an advance copy, Bob Yaro and I arrived at the executive floor of the 43rd Street offices. We were given souvenirs of the occasion—coasters showing historic front pages of the *Times*—and were asked to sign a register of those who attended these lunches. I was awestruck to see that two of the names above mine were Bill Clinton and Yitzhak Rabin.

Arthur Sulzberger Jr. greeted us and led us to a huge round table at which were seated the revered leadership of the *Times*. The editors of each major section of the paper were there, along with a couple of *Times* reporters assigned to cover the story. I began by thanking them profusely for taking the time to meet with us and for giving us the privilege of discussing the plan with them. I am fairly certain that it was Abe Rosenthal, the former executive editor and at that time a columnist, who spoke up and said, "No, the privilege is ours. It is so nice to finally have someone here who has something to say."

That moment is seared in my memory as the highlight of my time at RPA, if not of my entire professional career. His comment was not, of course, about me. It was a tribute to RPA and its long history of professionalism and objectivity. But I felt a special and profound gratitude and pride to be able to represent that tradition. The next day, the article about the release of *A Region at Ri*sk was indeed on the front page, above the fold, a space traditionally reserved for the most important stories of the day.

One of the three major pillars of the plan was the environment. RPA's focus, which is now about climate change and resilience, was then on preservation of open space. Bob had harked back to Frederick Law Olmsted's Greensward concept to highlight our proposals for creating more parkland within the region's ever-enlarging development footprint. While the focus was on a greenbelt on the periphery of the urbanized core, I spent my energies more on proposed park spaces around the city. I joined the steering committee advocating the creation of Hudson River Park, launching a long friendship with Al Butzel, the pioneering environmental lawyer. Al had led the opposition to Westway and was now working to shepherd legislation creating the Hudson River Park Trust through the state legislature.

Bob Yaro had secured funding from the Kaplan Foundation to begin planning for a park on Governors Island in New York Harbor. It had long been a military post but was declared surplus by the United States Coast Guard in 1995. I led this initiative and may have spent more time on it than on any other project while at RPA. Our staff, led by Rob Pirani, worked with architect Jane Thompson to develop a concept plan for public open space plus sufficient suitable private development to minimize the carrying costs of the project. In order to accept President Clinton's offer to sell the 172-acre island to the city and state for one dollar, it was essential to secure support from Mayor Giuliani and Governor Pataki. Both were leery of the costs of building and permanently maintaining public open space on the island. We fended off proposals for casinos, luxury housing, and golf courses while researching ideas for educational uses and conference centers.

We opposed housing of any kind, fearing that the island would become the private preserve of a small number of residents who would fiercely oppose public access. In 2000, the mayor and governor finally agreed to create a joint city-state entity to develop and maintain the island. I testified on behalf of the plan before then-Representative Charles Schumer's congressional committee, along with State Parks Commissioner Bernadette Castro and newly elected Senator Hillary Clinton. As one of his last official acts in January 2001, President Clinton designated the most historic twenty-two-acre section of the island as a national monument, to be owned and managed by the National Park Service. It took until 2003 for ownership of the rest of the island to be formally transferred to the city-state partnership, protected by covenants prohibiting housing and casinos. We enjoyed a great victory for civic advocacy.

Early in my tenure, RPA was asked to undertake a new plan for downtown Brooklyn, building on work that RPA had done in 1983. Revitalizing the core areas of the region's centers beyond Manhattan had been an RPA mantra since the Second Regional Plan. I led this effort, and in 1999, I was invited to join the board of the Brooklyn Bridge Park Coalition. Consisting of more than a dozen community groups, the coalition had defeated plans by the Port Authority to erect high-rise luxury housing on the obsolete shipping piers that stretched south from the Brooklyn Bridge for one mile to Atlantic Avenue.

Now the coalition was advocating for a magnificent park to be built along this iconic waterfront. Tensie Whelan, the coalition's brilliant and shrewd executive director, decided to recruit for the board several of the more visible civic figures. She approached Al Butzel, Kent Barwick of the Municipal Art Society, and me. Her goal was to give the coalition greater credibility and city-wide influence to pursue its ambitious agenda. It was an irresistible offer, and I enthusiastically joined in. Our vision for Brooklyn Bridge Park, a world-class, democratic urban oasis, has now been largely fulfilled. It has become one of New York's crown jewels and one of its most heavily used parks. My active and ongoing involvement in this project has been among my most satisfying civic commitments.

Soon after the Third Plan was released, Gary Wendt resigned as chairman of RPA. He was going through a bitter and highly public divorce and wanted to withdraw as much as possible from the public eye. In addition to leading the Regional Assembly effort, the other major job of RPA's chair was to identify and recruit a successor. We pressed Gary on this, but he kept saying that he could not find anyone. Among our concerns was that Gary had little use for most of the other members of the board, who he felt did not pull their weight or help with tough decisions. Consequently, he convened the fewest possible board meetings and alienated most of the directors with his abrasive style. It seemed unlikely that we would find an adequate replacement within the existing board. We desperately needed someone with the clout to raise serious money and influence elected officials.

Brooklyn Bridge Park, 2020.
(Courtesy of Etienne Frossard.)

With only a few days left before his departure, Gary called me to say he might have the answer. Felix Rohatyn had agreed to meet with us. I immediately called Felix's office (he was universally known by his first name) and was able to set up a meeting on short notice. Feeling excited and nervous, Bob Yaro and I went to his Lazard office in Rockefeller Center. Was this too good to be true? Felix unquestionably had the stature to recruit corporate leaders for our board and to raise money at levels we had only dreamt about. His proposals for a public infrastructure bank aligned with RPA's priorities. Having played a key role in rescuing New York City from its fiscal crisis, he had an unsurpassed reputation for civic leadership. Our discussion went well. Felix was cordial, gracious, and insightful. As our meeting ended, he said that this was the kind of thing he was looking to do, but he wanted to sleep on it.

Peter Herman and me at an RPA event, 2006.
(Photo by Matthew Borowick, courtesy of Regional Plan Association.)

Bob and I were ecstatic. It was the middle of the day, but we adjourned to a nearby bar for a celebratory drink. Suddenly, RPA's future appeared secure and our lives were about to get much easier. The next day, the news broke that Bill Clinton intended to appoint Felix Rohatyn to be the next United States ambassador to France. So that was why Felix had wanted to sleep on it! Our superlative high came crashing down.

I thought about our predicament overnight. We needed a chairperson immediately and had no viable candidates. I consulted with some board members, particularly Jill Considine, head of the New York Clearing House. Jill was extremely smart and pragmatic, and she had been a great source of advice and support. We concluded that I had only one viable option. We went to see Peter Herman and asked him if he would serve as chairman on an interim basis, which would not be an unusual role for a counsel. We knew that we could rely on Peter to be fair and judicious. We also knew (and he readily acknowledged) that as a service provider rather than a client, he could not help much with fundraising. But he was liked and respected by everyone on the board, and no one understood better or revered more what RPA was all about. Peter likes to tell the story, which is essentially true, that I made three promises to him: 1) that RPA was not in financial trouble; 2) that he would have to serve for no more than a year until we found someone else; and 3) that under no circumstances would I leave RPA before he did. Of course, it turned out that I lied about all three. RPA was *always* in financial trouble; he served as chairman for thirteen years; and I definitely did leave before he stepped down.

The policy and physical centerpiece of the Third Plan was the Regional Rail Express (Rx) concept. We proposed thirty-five miles of new transit connections, to be built in four phases over twenty-five years, to create new capacity and to better knit together the entire regional public transportation network. A new and expanded version of the Second Avenue Subway would be the central element of a network that would provide "airport access by connecting the Long Island Railroad to Grand Central Terminal, Lower Manhattan, Kennedy Airport, and LaGuardia Airport; direct access from New Jersey and Long Island to the East Side and Lower Manhattan; direct service from the Hudson Valley and Connecticut to the West Side and Lower Manhattan; through service from New Jersey to Connecticut and Long Island; and service between the boroughs in a new circumferential subway line."*

We did not put a specific price tag on Rx, lumping it in with the rest of our recommendations, which totaled $75 billion. That was a staggering number but did not represent that much of an increase over historical infrastructure spending and, we argued, was well within the region's capacity to afford. We were not surprised when most critics contended that it was a laughable overreach. Particularly subject to ridicule was our call to resurrect the decades-long stalled Second Avenue subway as a key spine for the integrated improvements that we proposed.

* A Region at Risk: A summary of the Third Regional Plan for the New York-New Jersey-Connecticut Metropolitan Area, (Regional Plan Association, 1996), 11.

Our advocacy efforts included a program of ads in the subways and buses humorously highlighting the poor performance and crowded congestion of the transit system. Working with Elliot (Lee) Sander (former New York City commissioner of transportation under Mayor Giuliani), Bob Yaro had put together an impressive coalition of transportation interest groups and secured funding for the campaign. The MTA refused to post our ads and we sued in federal court on First Amendment grounds. Litigation was highly unusual for RPA, but we felt we had an ironclad case. The lawsuit generated more publicity than we could ever have hoped to produce on our own, making us giddy with gratitude for the MTA's intransigence.

Peter and I attended an initial hearing on the litigation along with representatives of the MTA before a United States District Court judge. The judge quickly made it as clear as propriety would allow that he considered the MTA position to be untenable; he almost pleaded with the authority to allow the ads to appear before being ordered to do so. Several days later, the MTA relented and our ads went up. The publicity, coupled with the undeniable merit of our proposals, began to give us some real political traction. As a result, we were able to arrange a meeting with the state's top transportation and economic policy officials under the auspices of MTA Chairman Virgil Conway. Also attending were Charles Gargano, head of the state's economic development agency, and his deputy, Kevin Corbett, a good friend of RPA's. Finally, and perhaps most importantly, Brad Race, Governor Pataki's chief of staff, was there and basically ran the meeting.

Bob and Jeff Zupan, our transportation guru, took the group through our slideshow and were at their persuasive best. The transit access to airports, the integration of disparate elements of the system, and the improved travel times to Manhattan for many outlying areas all made basic sense.

At the end of the presentation, Brad turned to the MTA chairman and said, "Virge, I know we don't have the money. But, tell me, is this a good idea?"

Conway hesitated a moment and then sputtered, "Yeah, I guess so." We felt we had taken a major step in the right direction.

Although the following story may be somewhat apocryphal, we heard that the real and fateful decision was made over a pasta-and-Chianti dinner in Albany several weeks later. Senator Alfonse D'Amato, from Long Island, proved keenly interested in Rx. He was mostly drawn to our identifying the dormant Long Island Railroad connection to Grand Central Terminal as a key and early component of our plan. D'Amato was known as "Senator Pothole" for his notorious focus on local issues. The LIRR/GCT link would save 40,000 of his prime constituents about forty-five minutes a day on their commutes. That was a big pothole indeed.

D'Amato was instrumental in George Pataki's political rise, and Charles Gargano had been a Long Island contractor before joining the Pataki administration. Reportedly, the three met for dinner in Albany to discuss our plan. D'Amato said he could secure federal funding for the LIRR project and got Pataki's support for that. What may not have been discussed were the ripple effects of that decision. Bringing that many new commuters into the East Side of Manhattan meant that an estimated 18,000 more passengers a day would jam the Lexington Avenue subway stop at Grand Central during rush hour. That station was already dangerously overcrowded. At least some portion of the Second Avenue subway would have to be built to relieve this unacceptable increase in congestion.

Our version of the new subway was much more ambitious. It would have gone from the Bronx to Lower Manhattan and even on to Atlantic Terminal in Brooklyn via a new tunnel. Today's very modest Phase One is in operation from 96th Street connecting to existing lines at 63rd Street, and plans are underway to extend it north to 125th Street. Whenever I ride the new Q line to visit my climbing friend, Jim Berger, I smile as I think about this story and hope that successors will have new stories with even more impressive outcomes. The LIRR link has been a much more troubled project, running years behind schedule and astronomically over budget. A few years ago, I visited the construction site deep below Grand Central. I was overwhelmed by what a gigantic undertaking it was and how spectacular and important it will be when finished, still two or three years away.

My view of the future was not always so clear-eyed. At some point in 1999, Jeff Zupan came to me advocating an interesting proposal to repurpose the dilapidated elevated CSX freight line into a park. I scolded Jeff, arguing that no one in their right mind would want to preserve a structure that was such an obvious blight on its neighborhood. I also predicted that the city would never fund such a zany idea. I was a bit right about the funding, but I was completely off base about the vision. There have been few more successful adaptive reuse stories in the United States than the High Line. An elevated oasis, it offers a unique perspective of the urban streetscape. I now live near its southern terminus and often enjoy having been so wrong.

While at RPA, I was able to continue to indulge my love of hiking and travel. Marilyn and I still tried to spend almost every weekend at our house in the Catskills. We had built a new deck, upgraded our landscaping, and created a small vegetable garden, which we fenced in to protect it from the ubiquitous deer. We were "aspirants" for membership in the Catskill 3500 Club. To become a full member, one had to climb all thirty-five peaks in the Catskills with summits above 3,500 feet. Half the peaks do not have maintained trails, which means using a compass to work one's way up the mountain in search of a small canister mounted on a tree at the very top. Not being above the tree line, the summits are forested and indistinct, making finding the canister (and signing the register within) quite challenging. We became member numbers 713 and 714. As of 2021, the list now totals over 3,200 while some 5,300 climbers have summited Mt. Everest. I would never claim that there is any real comparison, but I found some of the Catskills climbs almost as demanding as anything I would do in the Himalayas.

We had occasional guests to help enjoy the outdoor grilling and hiking in all seasons. Our most frequent guest was John Bing, my dear college friend. In the early years, John was between marriages and would bring a parade of girlfriends for our review and testing on the trails. In 1992, he brought Cass Mercer, a sharp, practical, gentle woman. This was obviously different and serious. He proposed to her on our deck when we were away, and they were married in 1993. I was the best man and we have shared much of our lives ever since.

The most memorable of our Catskill 3500 experiences involved Southwest Hunter. It is a subsidiary peak to the well-known Hunter Mountain, one of only two summits barely above 4,000 feet in the Catskills. Southwest Hunter, a trailless peak, is only a little above 3,500 feet but is notorious for its indistinct top, erratic compass readings, and dense balsam trees. John, Marilyn, and I set out one summer day to add it to our list. We hiked up the Devil's Path from the end of Spruceton Road for about 2.2 miles to the Devil's Acre lean-to. This looked like a good takeoff point for a compass heading to the top, which was only about a half mile farther. After more than an hour of wandering around in the deep forest, unsuccessfully searching for the canister, we came upon a small clearing. Marilyn sat down and announced that she had had enough. We could go on looking, but she would stay there. In a monumental error of judgment, we told her to wait there for a bit while we stubbornly kept searching. John and I stumbled around for perhaps another forty-five minutes or so, getting more and more disoriented before giving up and heading back to the clearing. Or so we thought. We could not find it. Increasingly frantic, we yelled and yelled, but got no reply. John and I had all our gear, including the water and compasses; Marilyn had nothing but the clothes on her back.

I looked at the map and saw that if she went down the wrong side of the mountain to find a stream leading out—a traditional emergency backwoods survival strategy—it was unlikely that she could find her way. I was hyperventilating with panic. We made it back to the lean-to, reset our compass heading, and charged back up, yelling the whole way. Furiously following the compass, we actually found the canister marking the top but did not find Marilyn. We headed back, fruitlessly calling and yelling, and once again emerged at the lean-to. This time, we found it occupied by a camper.

"Did you see a lone woman come out this way?" we asked anxiously.

"Oh, yeah," he calmly replied. "She said she was going down to get the ranger."

We were engulfed with relief. As we approached the trailhead, up the trail came Marilyn with a ranger in tow. With considerable embarrassment and profuse apologies for our stupidity, we thanked the ranger and limped, exhausted, the few steps back to our car.

Marilyn calmly explained that she had noted the sun's position on the way in, and when she concluded that we might be lost, she simply headed back in the opposite direction and found the lean-to without any problem. She had then knocked on the door of a house near the trailhead and phoned the rangers from there. It was a good thing that Marilyn was a born problem-solver because we had committed a cardinal sin of hiking: never get separated! It was a life lesson, learned with some difficulty but with no negative consequences except a story that we would retell often.

The move from Cushman Realty to RPA gave me a feeling of sufficient comfort and security to launch a project that Marilyn and I had been talking about for some time: building a special new country home for ourselves. In 1993, spurred on by Tracy Kidder's book, *House,* published in 1985, and Witold Rybczynski's *The Most Beautiful House in the World* (1989), we began looking for the right piece of land for our Catskills dream house. The search proved a bit harder than we anticipated. We wanted to be away from Woodstock and its built-up areas and to be near the hiking trails. But, thinking that we might someday retire to the Catskills, we did not want to be too far from Kingston and its shopping, medical facilities, and other amenities. We wanted mountain views, but above all, we wanted quiet. That combination was problematic. Accessible sites perched on steep slopes with good views almost invariably overlooked highways from which traffic sounds beamed up directly, disturbing the serenity we were most seeking. We finally discovered a fifteen-acre site in Mount Tremper, in the Riverby subdivision that had been put together by Jerry Wapner, a prominent local attorney. He had reserved this centerpiece lot for his children, but when they decided that they could not afford to build on it, they put it on the market. The land was covered in mountain laurel, which put on a spectacular show every other spring. Set well back from approach roads and partway up Mt. Tobias, the site was supremely quiet.

We bought the parcel for a little under $100,000. We found a local architect named Carey Cook who had designed some wonderful houses in the area. I was confident that, with my real estate development experience, I could oversee and control a seamless and successful project. Despite the lessons described in Kidder's and Rybczynski's books, I failed to appreciate how different building a home in a rural area is from developing a downtown office building. But we got off to a good start. Carey had the inspired idea of flying over the property in a small plane to orient ourselves to its topography and relationship to the views that we would need to cut through the surrounding trees. At an airstrip in Kingston, we rented a pilot and a plane for forty-five dollars an hour. We flew for a bit more than an hour, but the pilot gave us a break and charged us only the minimum fee. That was the last time we stayed within budget.

We spent almost a year refining the design. Carey insisted, correctly, on square rooms as the most livable. To accommodate all of the elements that kept popping into our heads, he kept expanding the house by four-foot modules, claiming that it would hardly cost any more. He had also argued that it made no sense to hire a contractor at a fixed price since none of them had the financial resources to make good on any overruns. Why pay for risk that they could not handle, he reasoned. That sounded persuasive, but it was a decision we would regret. We hired Carey Cook as both architect and construction manager for a very reasonable combined fee. Marilyn and I would be the general contractors.

At a meeting of Riverside South during this period, I told Philip Johnson about my house plans and said that my instruction to the architect was that I wanted a combination of Philip's Glass House and Frank Lloyd Wright's Taliesin. Philip looked at me ruefully and merely sighed, "Oh, the poor man." I realized too late that I had said something hopelessly glib and sophomoric to the august Philip Johnson.

We broke ground in April 1994. By then, our initial budget of $250,000 had swollen to an estimate of $349,000, based on the final drawings. We would have a huge and splendid home on two levels totaling about 4,600 square feet plus a two-car garage. Carey warned us that he was not proficient at budgets and that we should maintain and monitor the project spreadsheet. Marilyn was good at this. She had always handled our finances and taxes and happily took to this new task.

Site work began with cutting a 1,000-foot driveway up to the location where Carey insisted that the house belonged, overruling my preference for a slightly lower site with a more level approach. The slab was poured and the frame started to go up. Carey's son was the framing contractor and soon proved not up to the job. A second framer also failed to perform. Nevertheless, Carey assured us that the house would be enclosed before the winter so that interior work could proceed without interruption. That did not happen and we were, in construction terms, frozen out for the season.

Work began again the following spring and crept along. Every Friday evening, Marilyn and I, along with Kathmandu, would arrive hoping to see real progress. Not once were we pleasantly surprised. One drawback of being our own general contractor—that was not mentioned by Carey—was that no one cleaned up after the workmen. We spent almost every weekend sweeping and lugging trash so that the work could resume on Monday. It was dirty and discouraging work.

The budget kept climbing. At one tense session, Carey admitted forgetting about one line item: "finish carpentry." That included all the interior trim and carried an estimated price tag of $70,000. Our budget climbed into the stratosphere. The final cost of the house was $565,000. In a bow to the more than doubling of the original budget and construction time, we dubbed the house "Overrun."

Not surprisingly, our relationship with Carey Cook soured. We had become friends and had socialized at the outset. Now we were barely on speaking terms. We obtained the final certificate of occupancy around New Year's Day 1996. We proudly hung our framed 3500 Club certificates in the entry foyer. The bitterness of the building process slowly waned, and we did get to enjoy our "dream house." It was a beautiful place with glorious views of Cornell and Wittenberg, two of the taller 3,500-foot peaks. John and

Cass visited often, sharing countless evenings on the deck and innumerable hikes in the mountains.

I doubt that the stress of building Overrun had much to do with it, but at about this time, I was diagnosed with a duodenal ulcer. I felt no pain, but the loss of blood left me weak and disoriented for several weeks. I was put on a heavy regimen of antibiotics and had to give up alcohol for an entire year. I started drinking again on the day my one-year sentence expired, and I went back to Dr. Hillel Tobias for a final checkup a few days later. All my tests were perfect.

Dr. Tobias looked at me sternly and asked, "Have you started drinking again?'

"Yes," I answered honestly.

"Well," he went on grumpily, "whatever you're not doing, keep not doing it!"

I used that line often in many different contexts, and when I saw him again some twenty years later, we shared a good laugh over it.

In 1997, Marilyn and I did a tough Mountain Travel hiking trip in the Dolomites and went on for a few days to Venice. We then did a trip on our own to Switzerland, spending glorious days hiking around Saas Fee, and then Wengen and Mürren in the Bernese Oberland. Arizona was our next destination in the late winter of 1998, hiking the Madera Canyon on our own.

That summer, we signed up for a Wilderness Travel trip to the Highlands of Scotland. Prior to our departure, we received the trip roster, which contained only six names. In addition to the two of us, we saw the names of two single American women and a couple named Buck and Deborah Griffin from Atlanta. *Buck?* We groaned, assuming that we were about to be stuck with some culturally alien Southern conservatives. On the morning when our little group was to gather, we went to breakfast in our small hotel in Inverness. I was hunched over my eggs and haggis, trying to look as unfriendly as possible, when a sandy-haired man with a broad grin approached the table and stuck out his hand. "Hi, my name is Buck," he announced in a deep Southern drawl. "I think we're on this trip with you." I cringed, convinced that my worst nightmare had just come true. I shook Buck's hand and mumbled a chilly Northern greeting. He beat a fairly hasty retreat.

Little was said during our van ride to our first destination, a lovely old inn near the coast. Wine over dinner and several single malt whiskys afterward helped facilitate conversation and the sharing of histories. It turned out that Buck had gone to Harvard a few years before me, and we were soon belting out Crimson fight songs to everyone else's mildly amused annoyance. His and Deb's politics were even more liberal than ours, and they were as interesting and delightful a couple as anyone we had met in a long time. We bonded instantly, shared future vacations, and developed a long and deep friendship. Buck was profoundly generous and kind. He had a gentle and wide-ranging intelligence and boundless curiosity. Every person whose life he touched was drawn to him as a mentor, friend, confidant, advisor, and companion. Sadly, Buck died recently at age eighty-five, much too soon for all of us, especially Deb, who is every bit as special a person in her own right—practical, resourceful, wise, and loving. She remains a treasured friend.

Marilyn and I flew to Costa Rica the following winter, visiting the tropical east coast, the central rain forests, and the arid western part of that spectacular country. As a birthday present several years earlier, Marilyn had taken me on a birding weekend to the Mohonk Mountain House in the Shawangunk Mountains just south of the Catskills. I took to it more than I ever expected, becoming and remaining an enthusiastic amateur birder. Costa Rica opened an entirely new world for that hobby.

With Deb's fiftieth birthday approaching—May 15, 1998—the four of us decided that we had to be somewhere special on that day. Wilderness Travel offered a moderate walking trip at just that time in Tuscany, where none of us had been. It looked perfect, and it was. We were guided by Lise Apatoff, an American expat who had married an Italian and now lived in Florence. She was knowledgeable, efficient, and delightful, showing us corners of that magical region we would otherwise never have found. Her passion for

Tuscany was infectious and we caught that delightful disease. We would stay in touch and draw upon her expertise for years. In 2001, Marilyn and I went with Buck and Deb, with their friends Larry and Marsha Large, on a wonderful trip to Sicily. It was essentially a clone of a Wilderness Travel trip but privately led by Lise's husband, Mario.

As the millennium approached, I was just beginning to feel the first twitches of restlessness. I had been at RPA for more than eight years. I was no longer sure that I was as fully engaged as I had been initially and as I knew I should still be. I began to feel that I might well have already done everything that I knew how to do for the organization. Perhaps it was time for someone else. And I again felt the tug of the Himalayas. I had not been back since 1983 and had not attempted a serious climb since 1978. Perhaps I just resented not having gone back for one last shot?

In 1995, I had toyed with the outlandish idea of actually joining a climb of Everest itself. The era of guided climbing was beginning in earnest. *Seven Summits* had been published, telling the story of two wealthy businessmen who had set out to climb the highest peak on each of the seven continents. Aconcagua in the Andes was serious, but of course Everest was the big prize. One of the men, Dick Bass, succeeded in 1985, and the book popularized the idea that almost anyone with money, training, and guides could do it.

In an issue of *Outdoors,* the Appalachian Mountain Club's magazine, I saw a notice announcing an Everest expedition exclusively for "seniors" planned for 1996. "Over 50? Want to climb Everest? Sign up here!" The ad stated that the organizers thought maturity was more important than technical skill on Everest, and that seasoned mountaineers, even with no serious Himalayan experience, should apply. The thought sent a shock wave through me. Was it really possible? Here was the challenge of 1973 all over again, but this one was deadly serious. I understood enough about high-altitude fatalities to know that many climbers, even the most skilled, had perished in the "Death Zone" above 25,000 feet, where no amount of acclimatization or technique can protect against the mountain's horrendous and unpredictable conditions. I also knew in my core that I did not belong up there. But I had to find out more.

The brochure arrived about a week later. It was a fairly amateurish xe-roxed job in a plastic binder. This expedition would head up the imposing north side of Everest, from Tibet, rather than from Nepal and the more common approach from the south. Like the notice in the magazine, it emphasized the value of experience and mature judgment over youthful energy and strength. Fixed ropes would line almost the entire route, it promised. The word "almost" caught my attention.

I decided to put this fantasy to rest by calling the climbing leader, a well-known mountaineer named Ian Wade, who had summited Everest a few years before. I would tell him of my age and experience, and he would no doubt agree that this was not for me. He returned my call promptly. I asked him about "almost." He replied that the only place where it would not be feasible to place fixed ropes was along a narrow lateral traverse at about 27,000 feet. "We could short-rope you across that section," he said matter-of-factly. I did not know but could imagine what that might mean. "We think that is where Mallory and Irvine fell in 1924," he added almost lightly. Chilled, I offered that I had lagged far behind Martin Zabaleta in the Pyrenees. Ian laughed, "I've climbed with Martin, and I can't keep up with him either," he said. Finally, I detailed my meager climbing résumé, certain that he would chuckle and demur. Not so. "You are just the kind of person we are looking for," he said. Clearly, willingness to write a check for $50,000 was the principal qualification he was seeking. I thanked him and hung up, shivering with dread and excitement.

I mulled it over and over in my head for days. I mentioned it to Marilyn, who was clearly horrified but characteristically said little. I could not escape the stark reality that I would be jeopardizing my marriage, my job, and our finances—not to mention my life—to fulfill this wild notion. I also had the conviction, regardless of what Ian Wade had said, that I did not belong high on that mountain. I simply did not have the technical skill and was too uncomfortable in exposed mountain heights. I also did not have the brute strength that some possess to overcome these shortcomings. My friend Jim, from the 1973 Base Camp trek, had that kind of stamina, and he had flamed out on Aconcagua. Finally, I decided against it and did not go.

I later heard that the trip had been organized at the instigation of Dick Bass. When he climbed Everest as part of his Seven Summits adventure, he had been the oldest person—at about fifty-five—to have made it to the top. Since then, a Chinese man had broken his age record, and Bass was intent on reclaiming it. The seniors gimmick would have been his ticket to do so. The planned expedition never got off the ground. Coincidentally, it was 1996, the year of the *Into Thin Air* tragedy when eight clients and guides died in a sudden storm on the Nepal side of the mountain.

In 1997 or 1998, Les Smith called me, knowing all too well my affinity for the Himalayas. He told me that Beck Weathers, one of those who had survived the Everest tragedy and who had been featured in both Jon Krakauer's book and the movie, would be speaking about his ordeal at a local country club in New Jersey. Typical of Les, he had gotten us tickets. Beck Weathers showed no slides; he just talked. He described the entire episode so vividly that he virtually relived it in front of us. The audience was transfixed. Afterward, I lined up with many others to say a few words to him. When I got to the front of the line, he stuck out his arm to shake my hand. There was just a stump with the remnants of a digit or two. He had lost much of his extremities and his nose to the ravages of the Death Zone, but miraculously survived. I awkwardly shook what he offered, mumbled a few words, and walked away affirmed in the wisdom of my decision not to go.

But my restlessness slowly mounted and the particular itch of another Himalayan climb remained unscratched. In late 1999, I decided to try to get it out of my system, once and for all. I would then, I thought, be able to make a clear decision about whether to refocus my energies on RPA or look elsewhere for a final chapter. I realized that this was yet another example of my seeking my identity outside of my professional life despite having a string of jobs that were as challenging and satisfying as anyone could ask for. In 1976, I had insisted on going trekking in Nepal just after being named commissioner of cultural affairs. Was I still trying to differentiate myself from my older brother and his steady and conscientious rise through the Foreign Service? Was I emulating my father, who had always looked beyond the family business for his personal fulfillment? Some of both, I suppose. Besides, those adventures did make for magnificent experiences.

No story of mountaineering adventures seems complete without an effort to explain why high-altitude climbing can be so magnetic. "Because it is there," while iconic, falls short as a satisfying explanation. My stories lack the high drama of *Annapurna* or *Into Thin Air*, but I want to offer my contribution to this lexicon. The ineluctable lure of the mountains seems to me to contain three basic elements: beauty, simplicity, and intensity. The awesome majesty of big mountains and the staggering views both from below and above are indeed compelling and provide profound emotional nourishment. Second, life boils down to simple fundamental challenges in the rarefied air high up: staying warm, hydrating, eating, attending to bodily functions, getting to the next camp. Failing at any of these can be fatal; success is easy to measure, even if only relative to one's own personal goals. In daily life, personal or professional success is rarely without ambiguity; everything tends to be shaded in grays of incompleteness or uncertainty. Not so in the mountains. Finally, one's senses and reactions are heightened, sharpened, and focused to a degree neither common nor sustainable in the denser more mundane world closer to sea level. Every detail feels so much more immediate, important, and alive. To those of us who are susceptible, the beauty, simplicity, and intensity of climbing among big mountains are unmatched and can make for an intoxicating and even addictive brew.

With such thoughts and memories percolating inside, I signed up in the spring of 2000 to climb Mt. Mera, Nepal's highest "trekking peak" at 21,350 feet. I knew that this would be my last hurrah. As you get older, your body no longer has the adaptability or reserves to adjust to the punishment of extreme altitudes where human beings do not belong. With that harsh reality weighing on my mind, I trained hard, mostly in the exercise room in the basement of our building.

Kathmandu had changed dramatically since 1983. It was congested and polluted, much like India, and its serene if backward politics had given way to upheaval and revolution. But it still had the excitement of a climbing town. Our hotel was in the compact and colorful Thamel district in the center of the city, which had exploded in population from around 250,000 to almost a million people. The trip was run by KE Adventure Travel, a UK-based outfitter. Our group included about a dozen climbers, mostly from Europe, and I was, of course, the oldest. I quickly made friends with a British couple, Mike and Amanda Arnold, who were in their early fifties. They were prodigious hikers and could also put away a prodigious amount of red wine, so we got along well. Amanda had just recovered from breast cancer and a mastectomy and was determined to fulfill a deferred dream of reaching a 20,000-foot peak. Several years later, I would learn to my great sorrow that her cancer had recurred and that she died soon after.

As we loaded up our gear at the Kathmandu airport for the flight to Lukla, I watched our equipment being packed in the signature blue plastic barrels that I had seen major expeditions use. This looked like the real thing. After landing at Lukla, we began the approach march by turning right to go up the remote Honku valley rather than left, to the east, toward the Khumbu and Everest.

Some hard days and 15,000-foot passes brought us within sight of Mt. Mera, a frightening hunk of rock and ice rising about twenty miles away. On a cloudy and chilly afternoon, we took a slight detour and I panted my way up a barren incline to a huge rock overhang. The Sherpas directed us to a cave that had been almost sealed with rocks collected from the stark surrounding hillside. Inside was a shrine with candles, simple statues of Buddha, and a variety of offerings such as candy and fruit. The Sherpas gathered some juniper branches and lit them, creating fragrant incense.

This was a *puja*, a Buddhist ritual to ask the mountain gods to protect us and give us their blessings for success. I had read of such ceremonies at base camps of the big expeditions. I was engulfed by the elemental beauty of the chanting and intoxicating smoke—and by the realization that the Sherpas thought this was a dangerous enough piece of business that it called for a puja.

It took us several more days to make our way to the Mera La, the pass at the base of the top part of the mountain, at about 17,900 feet. On the way, we had stopped for a day of training in *jumaring*, a technique to escape from a crevasse by ascending a rope. We practiced in the relative comfort of dry ground, moderate temperatures, and ropes a few feet off the ground. It was not a realistic test. Crevasses—cold, blue, fathomless chasms in the glaciers, often invisible until too late—were the great danger on our climb. Many mountaineers have perished in their depths. This was indeed a serious undertaking.

We slogged our way up the steep snow slope, roped up and wearing crampons, to a high camp at a little over 19,000 feet. Although I had planned to have my own small tent during the trip, logistics required minimizing weight and equipment at this altitude, so I shared a tent with Martin Duggan, a delightful guy from Northern Ireland who went by Duggie, his preferred moniker. The next day, three ropes set out for the summit at something like 5:00 a.m. in the thin, frigid morning air, with all of us wearing headlamps. I was with Mike and Amanda on what we called the "A-Team," with "A" standing for "aged." Our rope was headed

Mt. Mera behind me on the approach, March 2000.

by Pete Royal, our trip leader and an experienced guide, who set an extremely slow but steady pace. We inched along at a ludicrously sluggish rate, but we kept moving.

Climbing while roped together with fellow human beings is a unique experience. The fact that one is roped up already bespeaks that one is sharing a dangerous, even life-threatening experience. One is supposed to keep the right amount of slack between oneself and the climber ahead as one holds the rope between you, by constantly adjusting one's pace to the climber ahead and by remaining acutely aware of the tension of the rope behind you so as not to jerk that line as well. Through the tension of the rope, one can sense how the others are doing. Are they going strong or tiring? Are they frustrated or buoyant? Will they make it to the top or give up? Every shade of shifting mood is messaged like a telegraph wire along the undulations of the rope. Doing one's best to understand and accommodate those messages is felt and appreciated. It is an intense and profound exercise in human cooperation, and it forms a bond unlike any other I know.

Our head Sherpa led a second rope with three more of us, moving only slightly faster. Jamie, our strapping assistant leader, took the youngest, strongest threesome and they moved far ahead. As the sun rose, the day warmed somewhat and the sky turned to a deep cobalt blue, shading to black in the increasingly rarefied atmosphere. We could see Makalu, Lhotse, and Cho Oyu, three of the world's highest peaks, etched against the cloudless sky. As we crept along, Everest loomed more than 9,000 feet higher, no more than twenty-five miles away. I knew now, more than ever, how far out of my league it was. At this pace (which was my maximum), I could never have made it to the top of Everest. I was happy knowing that and being where I was.

After several more hours, we could see the Mt. Mera summit lump not very far ahead. It had begun to cloud over as it does most afternoons in the big mountains. We had already passed our agreed-upon turnaround time of noon. I was well aware that violating a turnaround time was the most common cause of tragedies on guided climbs in the Himalayas. Most deaths occurred because climbers, excited about nearing their goal but more exhausted than they knew, kept on going and then failed to make it back down to the safety of their high camps. Having used up their oxygen supply and trying to survive a night without nourishment and the protection of tents and sleeping bags, they would die of exposure. Yet, in this case, we were in sight of the summit, the weather did not seem especially threatening, and we were at an altitude that was benign compared to the Death Zone. We passed Jamie's rope. His climbers had collapsed in the snow and refused to go any farther. We urged them to get up and give it one more go; it was not far, we pleaded. To no avail. They were burned out; no amount of encouragement would work anymore. Earlier, moving rapidly ahead, they violated one of hiking's basic rules, even more applicable at altitude: start at the pace you expect to finish at. They were headed down.

We continued for perhaps another half hour and scrambled up to the top. It was completely socked in by then and we saw nothing of what we knew to be one of the greatest mountain panoramas that mere amateurs can be privileged to enjoy. After just a few minutes around the prayer flags that adorn this modest peak, we headed down in what was approaching a whiteout, a light gray enveloping mist that makes it extremely difficult to orient yourself and find the proper line. Fortunately, the leaders and Sherpas had planted a few poles and flags to mark the route coming up and we were able to use them to find our way down.

One more major obstacle lay a day ahead of us, the Amphu Labtsa (identified as the Ambulapcha La on the Khumbu Trekking map in chapter 8), a 19,170-foot pass that separates the Honku ("Hunku" on the map) valley from the Khumbu, the area around Everest. We had to go over it to complete our circuit back to Lukla. The day after coming off Mera, we set out at 6:00 a.m. and headed for the pass. It was a long, arduous climb up through a forbidding but at least stable icefall wearing our clumsy high-altitude plastic boots. I arrived at about noon at the pass. It was clouding over as usual, but I caught the last glimpses of Everest and Lhotse and saw Island Peak directly in front of us. A sheer drop of a couple of thousand feet down the other side required us to rappel down the face while our gear was lowered by ropes. It was slow and laborious work for the guides and Sherpas. One of the blue canisters holding our extra equipment crashed into the face and spilled its contents down the slopes. It took the Sherpas about an hour to find everything. My regular hiking boots were part of the cache and one of my boots was the last item to be located. I had to wait for several chilly hours huddled against the rock trying to stay warm before it was my turn to descend. Oddly, I did not suffer from acrophobia, probably because I was too cold and tired to think.

*On the summit of Mt. Mera,
21,350 feet in a near whiteout, 2000.*

We had been scheduled to camp at the bottom of the face, but our plans had changed. Earlier in the trip, the porters had engaged in a work stoppage, protesting against the adding of a rest day. They wanted to get home to their families. The dispute had been resolved by eliminating a day further on. This was the day. We had to continue a full day's hike from the bottom of the pass to a camp hours farther down at 15,000 feet. I arrived as dark fell, feeling as exhausted as I had ever been in my life. The next few days were spent returning along the familiar but no less spectacular corridor of the Everest approach route. Sorrowfully, I knew that this would be the last time I would see the magnificent Khumbu valley.

I later found out that Mt. Mera was supposedly the peak mistakenly climbed in the fictitious expedition described by William Ernest Bowman in *The Ascent of Rum Doodle*. That parody of climbing books is, at least for devotees of the genre, an absolutely hysterical account of an attempt on the tallest summit on Earth. Every evening on our honeymoon trip in 1983, we took turns reading it aloud, laughing until we spilled our after-dinner tea.

While I was eating yak stew and dal in the Himalayas, Marilyn had gone with Buck and Deb on a cooking trip to Parma and Mantua that was led by Lise. When I got back home and went to work, I concluded that my last Himalayan hurrah had not slaked my inclination for a change in my life. Yes, I was busy with the interesting challenges and opportunities that RPA always presented, but I was not refocused and reenergized. I had to admit that I was still restless and ambivalent.

I began to feel that perhaps there was another, different chapter out there for me. If so, at age sixty-one, I had better find out sooner than later. I did not know whether the next stage would be complete retirement or something else, but I knew I needed to move on. Equally motivating was my respect for RPA. It deserved full and passionate commitment, and after a decade I knew I was not quite "all in" anymore. Moreover, Bob Yaro was waiting, and not necessarily patiently, in the wings.

In the spring of 2001, I went to Peter Herman and told him that I planned to leave (and thereby break my third promise to him). I thought I should give six months' notice in case the board wanted to do a national search. I also wanted to give Peter maximum time to inform the board and choreograph my departure so that succession would be as seamless as possible. Peter had no stomach for a wide search for a new president. He felt strongly that Bob deserved the job and set about smoothing that path. We announced my departure in midyear, to be effective at year-end. Marian Heiskell helped underwrite a lovely going-away dinner at the Harvard Club. I was able to invite family and close friends and gave a heartfelt valedictory. The tragedy of September 11, 2001, had just happened. As the incoming president, Bob Yaro helped lead a civic initiative focusing on what should come next at Ground Zero. It was the beginning of a new and more visible chapter for RPA, which Bob's decade of energetic leadership set in motion.

Today, RPA is more influential and respected than ever. It is also in much better financial shape, operating on a budget twice what it was when I was president. Under the extremely capable leadership of its current president, Tom Wright, it has restored and expanded the corporate support that eluded me. It has recently released a Fourth Regional Plan, far more substantive and expansive than *A Region at Risk*. I had interviewed Tom when he was a graduate student interested, as I had been, in RPA. Recently, Tom wrote to me about that meeting:

> You shared some observations about your time working for Governor Rockefeller and RPA's role in the region's civic community. You talked about how civic groups work with city and state government in ways that made me very excited. Honestly, I walked out of your office convinced that I would work at RPA after grad school — it was clear this was where I wanted to be. It was an important meeting in my life.

Tom Wright, president of Regional Plan Association, with another president (to be), at RPA's 2015 Regional Assembly.
(Courtesy of Regional Plan Association.)

Tom did come to work at RPA, left to head New Jersey's planning office, and then came back. I did not make public my decision to leave RPA until Tom indicated to me over a lunch at the Harvard Club that he intended to return. I knew then that I could leave, secure in the knowledge that over the long haul RPA would be in very good hands.

THIRTEEN

RETIRING BODIES AND MINDS

During the months leading up to my decision to leave RPA, I concluded that our finances were in a strong enough position to retire safely and securely. Even though she had handled our investments and financial planning for many years, Marilyn was nervous. I could not get her to look at my spreadsheets and analyses. We even took the—for me—radical step of consulting her therapist, whom she had long since stopped seeing but whom she still trusted implicitly to give objective advice. Her therapist tended to think that I was on firm ground, but Marilyn remained unconvinced and was unwilling to grapple with the details. I could not understand her feelings and was upset by her uncharacteristic lack of interest in the numbers.

To celebrate and punctuate my probable retirement, we planned a trip back to La Foce, in Tuscany, a place we had fallen in love with. We had discovered this magical spot in the Val d'Orcia in 2001, after our Sicily trip with Buck and Deb. We had looked around for the most idyllic place that we could find in Tuscany and were told about La Foce by a Foreign Service friend of my brother's who now specialized in renting Italian villas. I found La Foce's history fascinating. In the 1920s, an American heiress, Iris Cutting, had grown up as an expat, living at the Villa Medici in Fiesole, just north of Florence. She knew Bernard Berenson, a near neighbor at I Tatti, and was visited by the likes of Virginia Woolf. In 1924, Iris married Antonio Origo, an Italian nobleman, and they bought a rundown villa and estate near Montepulciano. They then spent forty years buying up surrounding properties and working with local farmers to turn what had been a virtual dustbowl into the lush countryside pictured today in the famous calendar photographs of the region. Their children turned their vast holdings into an *agriturismo* haven, selling off part of the land and converting the remaining farmhouses into simply (but beautifully) furnished villas for rent. The splendid main house overlooks a stunning formal garden designed by the British landscape architect, Cecil Pinsent.

Iris Origo's childhood home in the United States was on Long Island. The estate featured buildings designed by famed architect Stanford White and grounds that had been landscaped with the help of Frederick Law Olmsted, the legendary creator of New York City's Central Park and Prospect Park. Two hundred acres of the property were bequeathed to the State of New York while allowing the family to continue occupancy. The Long Island State Park Commission assumed control in 1952 and opened the Bayard Cutting Arboretum two years later. The lovely grounds of La Foce bear testament to Iris's early introduction to, and passion for, the design and planting of outdoor spaces. Over the years, I have stayed at La Foce five times in various accommodations and have never tired of its serene beauty.

The back story of Iris Origo's life—her writings, aiding Jewish refugee children, protecting allied soldiers and partisans during World War II, and the role that she and her husband played in helping to turn the Val d'Orcia into a world heritage site—is the stuff of books, including hers. Iris Origo was a student of biography, and her writing style was polished and sophisticated. *Images and Shadows,* the story of how she and her husband developed La Foce, is compelling reading even if one has never visited. Her diary of the World War II years, *War in Val d'Orcia,* describes her heroic work with transfixing matter-of-fact lucidity.

I wanted to really settle in and explore the area and booked us to stay for four weeks at two different places there. We shopped in the local markets and cooked in the well-outfitted kitchens of our tasteful apartments. Each day we would explore a different part of the area. The Val d'Orcia is surrounded by the picturesque hill towns of Pienza, Montalcino, Bagno Vignoni, and San Quirico d'Orcia, among others. Siena is forty-five minutes north, Orvieto is the same distance south, and Todi and Umbria are each an easy day trip east. Some striking art is located in nearby abbeys: the frescoes of Luca Signorelli and Il Sodoma depicting the life of Saint Benedict at Monte Oliveto Maggiore and the Il Sodoma's paintings in the refectory of Sant'Anna in Camprena, featured in the movie *The English Patient*. Even Perugia, Cortona, and Assisi are less than an hour and a half drive away. The area offers an amazing wealth of scenic and cultural experiences.

Lester Chan and Johanna, my dear friends from my army days, who were living near Vienna, joined us for a week. Our bond remained warm and close, and I was grateful for the chance to introduce Marilyn to those special people in my life.

The Chianti country is also nearby, and we set out early one morning. I normally did most of the driving because I very much enjoy it, particularly in quiet countrysides like Tuscany. Marilyn had been an excellent driver, but I had been noticing that lately she was not anticipating merges and turns as she used to. On this day, she took the wheel. After our last stop, she backed into a truck which had some metal pipes protruding from the back. The collision with the pipes destroyed the rear window of our rental car. It was not hard to see how Marilyn could have missed the danger, but it was disturbing. We were able to get a replacement car in Florence and our credit card company eventually covered the entire cost. But my concern that something was going on—something that I did not understand—ticked up a notch.

In the fall of 2002, we took a trip to Montana to visit Buck and Deb. They had bought some land at the base of the Beartooth Mountains in the southern part of the state, near Nye. Yellowstone sits on the other side of the Beartooth range. It is spectacular country. They had just finished constructing a small home with stunning views in every direction. They met us at the Billings airport and drove us back to their place, about an hour and a half away. Along the way, Marilyn asked if they planned to spend time there in the winter or just use it in the summer. Deb responded that they were not sure but probably would use it primarily in the summer as the winters were severe. A little while later, Marilyn asked the same question. Buck glanced at me quizzically and repeated the answer. After a few minutes, Marilyn asked the same question a third time. Something was definitely amiss.

In April 2003, we took a trip to the Dordogne region in France. The first week, we did a fairly strenuous self-guided inn-to-inn hiking tour. Marilyn did most of the walks, but she uncharacteristically opted out of a couple of days. The highlight of the week was two nights at a hotel in Les Eyzies, not far from the caves of Lascaux. Most of our accommodations had been modest but pleasant. This hotel was in a different league, but our tour organizer was able to book it at no extra cost. When we arrived in our dirty hiking clothes, we were looked upon with suspicion, but our reservations were in order. The hotel had what may have been a Michelin star restaurant where we had the best meals of our lives. The second week we rented a small *gîte*, a stone cottage, near Sarlat in the heart of the region. We shopped, cooked, and hiked and adopted the local cat, Chablis, for the week. My brief trip diary reveals no hints of concerns about Marilyn's condition. That would soon change.

The signs increased ever so slowly that Marilyn's cognitive functioning was becoming affected, at first subtly. She had recognized it and had gone to be tested in February 2003. At first the tests were inconclusive. Yes, there were indications that her executive functioning and spatial relationship skills were slightly diminished, but her verbal aptitude seemed unaffected. A report in November after more tests noted that her short-term memory was unaffected and went on to say: "There has been an overall improvement in the patient's verbal memory skills. This strongly suggests that the lower scores obtained earlier this year may have been secondary to the patient's psychological status at the time. They were not necessarily due to a dementing process." Perhaps she had had a mini-stroke and would recover her acuity over time. We did not know what to think.

The deterioration continued, and we went to a neurologist for further analysis and an EEG. Her verbal skills started to suffer as well. By January 2004, the diagnosis became inescapable. Marilyn had Alzheimer's, at age sixty-five. I had not had any previous experience with the disease and was unaware that Alzheimer's had devastated her family on her mother's side. We learned that Marilyn's condition was genetically related and early-onset, making her prognosis especially grim. She tackled the new situation with her typical silent determination. She began keeping a diary and did puzzles and other exercises to stimulate her cognitive functioning. Sadly, those initiatives evaporated after a few months as she became increasingly unaware of what the disease was doing to her. For me, the most painful and profound emotional journey of my life had just begun.

Marilyn had not been working for some time. When we returned to New York from Philadelphia, she had landed a couple of cable television jobs that did not work out. She then took up executive-search work for a firm that specialized in her industry. Marilyn would once have been a natural for this type of job. She was fearless, scrupulous, and organized. While reserved herself, she had great instincts about people. But while she did well for a few years, she never managed to become an essential part of the business that hired her on a piecemeal basis over time. Slowly, that work petered out as well.

Typical of her passion for new challenges and projects, Marilyn had begun trying to become proficient at the piano. In the 1990s, she had bought a Steinway L, a junior grand, on which she took lessons and practiced diligently. She improved but could not seem to make the kind of progress that her efforts should have produced. Still, there were benefits. One evening, we attended a small recital at Steinway Hall on 57th Street. As last-minute arrivals, we found ourselves placed directly in front of the piano. We were only inches away from the lovely vocalist who was featured that evening. When the program ended, Marilyn struck up a conversation with her. Carrie Dimaculangan was a talented soprano from Australia trying to make it in New York City. She wanted to record a demo and needed a space and a piano. Our living room proved to be just what she needed.

Carrie brought an aspiring pianist, Arielle Levioff, to accompany her and they made the demo. Over the years, we lost touch with Carrie as she traveled the world trying to make her way. But Arielle became a close friend and Marilyn's piano teacher. We would host memorable evenings of chamber music just for our friends or to try to raise a little money for Arielle's musical enterprises. Much later, I would join the board of a nascent community orchestra that Arielle's father, a conductor, was trying to launch. The idea of the Seniors Orchestral Society of New York was to use retired musicians who still loved to play and needed little or no compensation to provide free concerts to outlying, underserved New York City communities. It was a great idea that was never quite able to establish itself and foundered when Arielle's mother, the project's business manager, succumbed to kidney failure and passed away. Meanwhile, Marilyn struggled more and more to maintain her focus at the piano but could not hold the ground that she had once gained. Eventually, her frustration proved too great and she gave up trying.

As for me, late in 2002, I was contacted by Bob Sellar, who had been a staunch supporter of RPA when he was at IBM. He had chaired the Arts & Business Council of New York and secured a major grant from his employer to fund an arts component for the Third Regional Plan. Bob had retired from IBM and was now running the National Executive Service Corps (NESC), providing management consulting for nonprofits. Retired business executives contributed their expertise, which kept costs extremely low. Even though NESC's consulting services were available for a small fraction of what private firms charged, few nonprofits had the budgetary flexibility much less the inclination to undertake significant organizational introspection. As a result, NESC had remained small and insular. Bob Sellar was determined to grow it into a larger enterprise. He asked me to help with marketing, working about three days a week. It sounded like an ideal way for me to stay engaged and to earn some needed income. The dot-com bubble had burst, and my retirement projections no longer looked quite as rosy as they had two years earlier.

Bob recruited two other outsiders, Betsy Rosenfield and Jonathan Goldfarb, to help with the effort. They were delightful and capable, but nothing we did seemed to help grow the business sufficiently to justify our paychecks. The lack of talent that I had previously shown for conventional business development was apparent again. Bob's leadership also proved erratic and confrontational. After about a year and a half, I decided to resign before the new structure collapsed, which it did shortly thereafter.

In the early summer of 2003, my father, now aged ninety-five, began to fail. He had had more than thirty-five peaceful and happy years with Ilse, enjoying idyllic summers at the Attersee and mild winters in Charlottesville for most of that time. His hearing, which had been somewhat compromised since age sixty, had deteriorated badly in the last few years, frustrating and isolating him. We were reduced to writing notes to him during our few times together. Then, when his doctor told him at his last office visit that nothing further could be done to arrest his congestive heart failure, my father practically sprang down from the examining table, ready for what he knew was coming and content in the knowledge that he could spend his final weeks at home.

Ilse watched over him lovingly. They completed the sale of their house in Austria during his last days, ensuring that Ilse's retirement nest egg would be healthy. "Now you are safe," were his final words to her. He died peacefully. When I got the news, it was nighttime and I was at our country house. I sat on our secluded deck looking up at the night sky that I knew so well, listening to Beethoven's *Pastoral Symphony* that fittingly played on the local classical radio station. The achingly beautiful and joyously lyrical melodies helped soothe my deep sadness over the loss of the man who had been the lodestar of my growing up. He had lived a long, rich life and died a contented soul, but for me the sudden emptiness felt profound.

Marilyn and I returned to La Foce in the spring of 2004. John and Cass joined us for one of our two weeks and were as captivated by it as we were. By now, I was doing most of the cooking and welcomed Cass's help. I cannot recall Marilyn's exact state at this time, but photos from that trip already reveal an emptiness in her facial expression that betrayed her unabated decline.

During this time, I had continued to be very active in the effort to create Brooklyn Bridge Park. In 2001, we were able to secure commitments from Mayor Giuliani, Borough President Howard Golden, and finally, Governor George Pataki to back and fund construction of the world-class park that we had championed. In 2002, Mayor Michael Bloomberg formally joined in and signed a memorandum of understanding with Governor Pataki to create a new entity to build the park and to finance its construction. The master plan called for a limited amount of commercial and housing development on less than twenty percent of the available land, to pay for the long-term capital maintenance and operation of the park. A book co-authored by present-day executive director Nancy Webster, *A History of Brooklyn Bridge Park,* details this remarkable story.

By 2004, the Brooklyn Bridge Park Coalition had changed its name to the Brooklyn Bridge Park Conservancy to signal that we were evolving from an advocate to a partner. Early in 2005, as I recall, then executive director Marianna Koval came to me with an unexpected suggestion. Her husband had died suddenly from a heart attack, and she was exhausted from her emotional stress coupled with the demands of managing the organization. She confessed that she was running it like a political campaign and knew that the maturing conservancy needed more structure and strategic direction. Would I consider stepping off the board and sharing the executive director's job with her?

Marianna was extremely smart but prickly and tended toward confrontation rather than conciliation to get where she wanted to go. Nevertheless, she had achieved remarkable results, and no one had played a more important role in securing the unprecedented public-sector commitments we had needed to build our vision. This was an offer I could not refuse. I believed deeply in the park, and this would allow me to play a hands-on role in advancing a project of regional and even national significance. Moreover, I could use the income, and I had to admit that I was strongly attracted by the thought of getting out of the house for part of the day. The progression of Marilyn's disease was a heavy burden for both of us.

Three or four days a week I traveled to the Brooklyn office of the conservancy. We were housed in the brick building that the conservancy shares today with the corporation, the government entity created to actually build and operate the park. At that time, it was in poor condition and its maintenance and operation posed a consistent headache. Marianna and I intended to split the job. I tried to focus on organizational and administrative matters to help clarify lines of authority and responsibility. But we ended up working on most of the important policy and political matters together. We jointly navigated our way through the minefields of neighborhood opposition, dealing with elected officials and negotiating agreements with the state over programming of the Tobacco Warehouse, the historic shell of a building next to the Empire Stores.* After one of the raucous community meetings, Marianna paid me perhaps the best compliment I had ever received. She said I was Atticus Finch to her Scout. Both of us have a warm feeling about our time together.

After something like two years, this experiment had run its course. The conservancy needed a single voice. At home, Marilyn's condition was worsening, and it was getting harder and harder to leave her alone during the day. I had done what I could to help make the conservancy a more stable and secure organization, and Marianna and I were finding ourselves arguing more than consulting. I went to Tensie Whelan and said I thought it was time for me to step aside. I rejoined the board, where I still serve happily today.

My memory of the years 2005 and 2006 has become a blur of increasing personal anguish and frustration as Marilyn's condition worsened. She read

* The Empire Stores are the 330,00-square-foot historic warehouses built in 1860 that were incorporated into Brooklyn Bridge Park. As noted in chapter eight, I had first struggled with their reuse while at State Parks in 1972-74. It was only in 2019 that they opened as a restored commercial marketplace.

less and less as her ability to focus and absorb written information waned. Newspapers, which she had always devoured, were no longer of interest to her. I bought books on tape for her, and they helped for a while, but she slowly abandoned them too. She would stare blankly at the TV, increasingly unable to comprehend, much less enjoy, that distraction. She became more and more anxious if I were not with her. When I was working in Brooklyn, I had to phone her several times a day to be sure she was all right. Our weekends at Overrun provided little relief. I could not leave her alone, and as time went on, she even needed to be in the same room with me or she would become nervous and agitated. John and Cass would visit and give me moments of respite. Cass would generously stay with Marilyn, allowing John and me to head out to the trails. Hiking was out of the question for Marilyn as her gait became more and more uncertain. Taking her on long drives was one of the few ways that I could divert and calm her. We had to plan bathroom stops carefully because she often needed my help to navigate unfamiliar restrooms.

At home I had to make adjustments, simple and seemingly silly ones at first. I put yellow towels in her bathroom and orange ones in mine to help her tell the difference. I had always been a fervid advocate of mounting the toilet paper so it rolled out from the bottom; eventually, this motion baffled Marilyn, but the roll coming off the top worked for her, so I abandoned that lifetime habit.

Around Labor Day 2006 we flew to Montana to visit Buck and Deb. I arranged for a wheelchair to facilitate our way through check-in and security. When we arrived, the magnificent Big Sky was filling with smoke from a huge forest fire that was working its way toward the Stillwater Valley. For several nights after we arrived, we sat on their porch and watched the angry red glow appear over the hills on the other side of the river. What looked like atomic mushroom clouds billowed high into the sky. The destructive power of the fire was palpable and frightening. Buck's and Deb's colorful neighbor, aptly named Tom Wolf, was a volunteer firefighter. He appeared one evening covered in soot, with bloodshot eyes and bent over with exhaustion, looking as if he had just escaped from hell. We went to bed wondering if we might have to evacuate the next day. At about 1 a.m., the sheriff knocked on the door. It was not mandatory, he said, but he strongly advised us to leave. If the fire jumped the river, we would be in deep trouble. "You're backed up to the Beartooth and you'd have no place to go," he warned.

We hastily packed up. Buck and Deb pulled a few pieces of art off the wall and we cleared out. They had friends, next to the river and away from the path of the fire, who would take us in. Their friends gave the four of us a place to sleep and shared an early morning breakfast. The next day, Buck and Deb managed to talk their way through several police roadblocks, returned to their cabin, and were relieved to find the place untouched; the fire had not leapt the river. Meanwhile, Marilyn and I, on their advice, headed to nearby Cody, Wyoming, and spent a delightful day and a half touring its five museums, which surprised us with their world-class collections of western art and natural and Native American history.

We headed back north toward Billings, stopping at the Little Bighorn National Monument. The rangers told Custer's story mostly from the Native American point of view, and it was compelling and deeply moving. We learned that it was much more than the saga of a reckless army general; it was a pivotal moment in the tragedy of America's native people. As I have felt in only a few places, this struck me as truly sacred ground in the imperfect history of the country that had given me so much. Standing on the knoll where Custer, his men, and many Cheyenne and Sioux braves died, I felt the sense of history being made washing over me. I have had similar experiences at Pearl Harbor, Dealey Plaza in Dallas, and later, of course, at Ground Zero where, looking into those plunging pools at the site of the World Trade Center towers, I always make a point of finding Frank De Martini's name.

As difficult as travel with Marilyn had become, the assistance of airlines, hotels, and friends made for relatively manageable experiences. Returning to New York meant returning to the grinding reality of the Alzheimer's caregiver. I needed help. Ten years earlier, Marilyn had had the great good sense to sign us up for long-term care insurance. It now came into play and made the financial part of the challenge almost a non-issue.

I arranged through the Visiting Nurse Service (VNS) for a home health aide. After an evaluation, we decided on visits three days a week of about five hours a day. That soon became five days a week. Marilyn resisted, fearful of having strangers in the apartment. I had to pretend that they were there to help me, which was increasingly true. Often, filled with guilt, I would sneak out the door. If Marilyn knew I was leaving she would burst into tears and beg me to stay. I felt under endless pressure. I found an agency upstate to provide similar visits on weekends so that I could have a little free time in the Catskills.

In the city, I went through several aides trying to find someone who could relate well to Marilyn. I explored the possibility of hiring someone more mature and professional. I was willing to pay out of pocket any additional cost. But CNA, our insurer, would cover only employees of licensed agencies, which paid little more than the minimum wage. I never was able to work around those constraints. Finally, one of the VNS aides, a vivacious young woman named Crystal, worked out well. Temporarily, at least, things became more manageable.

Still, I could feel my reservoir of emotional strength draining by the day. Normally I was not inclined to look elsewhere for help, but this was clearly not a normal situation. Overcoming my natural resistance, I joined a support group. There were nine of us, all with spouses who had fairly advanced Alzheimer's. It was important that it was solely a spousal support group. The emotional issues are fundamentally different than those facing grown children who have parents suffering from this terrible disease. For adults caring for parents, the experience is all about reversing roles and dealing with whatever baggage is left over from the growing-up process. For spouses, it is dealing with the loss of one's life partner. The person you love and with whom you have built a life and an identity, slowly disappears. Sexual intimacy is an early casualty of Alzheimer's. Without mutuality, sex feels empty and unnatural. One realizes that a personality is the accumulation of experiences and memories built over a lifetime. When those anchors dissolve, the person we know dissolves. It is agonizing to watch, and to come to terms with what is often called "the long goodbye." That is a perfect term for the endless series of letting-go moments, without closure. Grief is experienced each day, in small doses, without the catharsis of finality.

The support group was the one place where we all felt completely understood. No matter how well intentioned, no one who has not lived through Alzheimer's can fully grasp the emotional rollercoaster that the spouse-caregiver rides. Each one of us knew exactly what the others were going through. No explanations or apologies were required. One's short-comings, grief, anger, and tears were accepted with empathy and without judgment. Here one could laugh and cry without embarrassment. I also learned how fortunate I was with Marilyn. She gave up her car keys without hesitation. Her personality never changed. She became sweeter and purer as the days went by. She did not wander. There were no fights or obscenities. She slept well and was not incontinent. She was anxious but not resentful. My family and friends gave me unquestioning love and support, which contrasted starkly with the experiences that others in my group had to contend with, including skeptical children and relatives. As hard as it was for me, Marilyn's personality made it more bearable.

On a trip to San Miguel de Allende with Buck and Deb—in 2005, I believe—I told them that taking good care of Marilyn through her Alzheimer's was probably the most important thing I would ever do in my life, and I was determined to do it well. I was trying to live up to that commitment.

In 2006, the New York Times published a striking series of self-portraits by an artist depicting his own journey as a victim of Alzheimer's. It began in 1967 with a detailed, somber image of his head and face, executed before the disease manifested itself. That was followed by paintings done from 1996 to 2000. The head and face grow angrier and more despairing but, more poignantly, vaguer and less distinct. The final sketch is frightening; just an oval of lines dripping down, with the hint of an eye and mouth. The person in the face has essentially vanished. Nothing that I had read or heard about Alzheimer's, either from the patient's or the caregiver's perspective, captured as powerfully the experience of loss. The last drawings evoked Michelangelo's depiction of himself as empty flesh after finishing the Sistine Chapel.

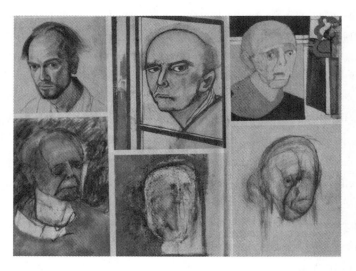

William Utermohlen's self-portraits, the New York Times, *October 24, 2006.*
(Photographs from Galerie Beckel-Odille-Boïcos, Collection C. Poilleux, Paris.)

During the winter of 2007 we made one last trip to Costa Rica to escape the cold. I could not manage a vacation with Marilyn alone anymore, so John and Cass agreed to come along. Cass helped at the airport restrooms, and the wheelchair eased the boarding process. Marilyn used the lavatory during the flight but could not unlock the door to get out; I learned how flight attendants can open lavatory doors from the outside. We rented a nice house overlooking Lake Arenal and settled in. With Cass watching Marilyn, John and I managed to get in a hike or two but otherwise we did not stray far. One evening as we were preparing dinner, Marilyn said she needed to go to the bathroom, which by then required some help. Cass offered to do the honors. John and Cass had shouldered far heavier burdens than this, but this small act of kindness broke the dam. Overcome by gratitude and fatigue, I started crying and continued to cry uncontrollably for fifteen minutes or more. This was, to say the least, a radical departure in character for me, but it was only the first of several similar emotional eruptions in the months to come. Later that year, the four of us would go to visit our friend Wayne in Colorado, but travel was coming to an end.

Harvey and Celia, who had given us Kathmandu, our cat, remained the staunchest of friends through this period. Acutely aware of the strain I was under, they established a Wednesday night supper club. Each week, Marilyn and I would go to their apartment for dinner, which Celia prepared. It gave me a welcome night off from chores and caregiving alone.

During the middle of 2007, by which time Marilyn needed almost constant attention, I began looking at nursing homes. I feared that I simply could not manage taking care of her at home much longer, even with the help I had arranged. Marilyn would look around our living room and anxiously ask where she was. She could no longer make sense of her physical surroundings. I had to admit to myself that perhaps the time had come when she would actually be better off elsewhere. As the fall approached, I learned about the 80th Street Residence on the East Side of Manhattan. The facility was exclusively for dementia care in an assisted-living setting rather than a nursing home, which gave it a slightly less institutional character. It was important that she be near enough for me to visit regularly, and this was just a crosstown bus ride or even a long walk away. Finally, the costs were manageable—considerably less than full nursing care. At last, I had found a good place. The staff came to our apartment and agreed that Marilyn was a good candidate and that the time was about right for her.

In mid-September 2007, the appointed day arrived. I did not tell Marilyn where we were going. We made the short trip in a taxi. I brought her up to what would be her private room, and she sat on the bed trying to make sense of what was going on. She was very agitated. A nurse told me it would be better if I left. I stood up, and as I turned toward the door, Marilyn said to me, "This is the end of us."

I was devastated. She might not have been able to decipher exactly what was transpiring, but her emotional intelligence was not fooled. She expressed perfectly the meaning of my walking out that door. I kept going with tears streaming down my face. It was the hardest thing I had ever done in my life.

———

I have often been asked: when did you really know that something was wrong with Marilyn? What did it feel like when you found out for sure it was Alzheimer's? Many friends have also asked: when did Marilyn know, and how did she feel? I cannot answer these questions. The process unfolded so slowly, so incrementally, that there was never a single moment when anything became clear or definitive. It just happened over time. I know that Marilyn was aware early on because she mentioned to friends that she hoped not to be a burden to me. I believe that her self-awareness then simply slipped away unnoticeably until she gradually just became a patient struggling against the cruel reality of a condition that she no longer understood.

Several months after bringing Marilyn to 80th Street, I went to see the movie *Away from Her*. Although it takes considerable dramatic license, it is the best fictional depiction of Alzheimer's I have seen. Of course, no one can look like Julie Christie, and I don't know of any real-world couple that had sex the night before one of them enters a nursing home—entering voluntarily, at that. Still, the dynamic between them and the scenes in the facility are magnificently realistic. Near the end of the movie, Julie Christie looks at her husband, played by Gordon Pinsent, and says gratefully, "You never left me; you never left me." He responds, tearfully, "Not a chance." Marilyn and I had had that exact exchange, word for word, several days before. I broke down and cried for an hour or more as I wandered around Central Park.

I visited Marilyn three times a week and she seemed to be settling in as well as could be expected. She was somewhat confused and anxious, but she did not appear agitated and did not complain about being where she was. She did not watch the endless sitcoms that played on the TV and instead wandered aimlessly around the floor, the limit of her permitted mobility. She was always pleased to see me but did not berate me for not coming more often.

After the harrowing ordeal of placing Marilyn at 80th Street, I felt an almost desperate need for a break and an indulgence. Winter was coming and, like many people my age, I was disliking the cold and dark months more and more. I had long wanted to visit New Zealand. Wilderness Travel had a seventeen-day trip to the South Island that looked perfect, and I signed up. It was a wonderful trip with a congenial group. New Zealand may well be the most scenically spectacular and varied place on Earth. We started in Christchurch and headed to the northeast coast. We swam with dolphins in the open ocean where we were the curiosity and the dolphins were the tourists. The north coast was wine country, not dissimilar from California. Coming down the northwest shoreline was just like driving along the Oregon Coast. Farther down the west coast, snow-covered Mt. Cook soars upward while its glacier flows almost into the sea, and it feels like Switzerland. Heading farther south, one enters a stark landscape akin to Scotland. Finally, there is Milford Sound, splendidly like a Norwegian *fjord*. We spent a night on a boat in the sound after having hiked for three days on the world-famous Routeburn Track. A couple of older women on the trip listened sympathetically to the story of my marriage. New Zealand gave me the pause and perspective to return and continue my vigil.

One couple on the trip had met through something called Match.com, which I had never heard of. Without allowing myself to think seriously about it, I had harbored hopes that there might be another chapter emotionally for me. But the thought of hanging out in bars at my age and trying to meet someone had been appalling. It dawned on me that, when I was ready, online dating might hold promise.

Meanwhile, in addition to returning to my routine of visiting Marilyn, I remained engaged in the civic endeavors that I deeply cared about. RPA had allowed me to remain on the board as was customary with past presidents.

The meetings always proved interesting and rewarding. I continued to serve as an active member of the board of the Brooklyn Bridge Park Conservancy and was now its vice chair. Ground had been broken for construction of the park in February 2008, but many political and policy issues remained, prompting many meetings to worry about them. The commitment that required perhaps the most attention was the Catskill Center for Conservation and Development, where I served as the president (a position now more accurately entitled "chair") of the board. I was also a founding member of the Friends of Governors Island and stayed close to the development of that spectacular place that I had spent so much of my time at RPA working to create.

The Catskill Center was like an RPA for the Catskills. Founded in 1969, it was the one regional group that took a long-term, comprehensive, nonpartisan approach to the issues that faced the area. After RPA's Third Plan was released in 1996, Geddy Sveikauskas, the publisher of the *Woodstock Times,* a remarkable local paper, ran a nice profile about me and the plan. Geddy, a remarkable individual himself and a fellow Harvard graduate, was a long-time member of the Catskill Center board and knew that I had just moved into my new house. He urged me to get involved. I had attended some of the center's meetings and was delighted to be asked. I was elected president of the board around 2001. During my tenure, the center played the central role in negotiating a settlement to a seven-year battle over the Belleayre project, a major development proposal in the heart of the forest preserve. It was a controversial agreement but was hailed in a September 2007 *New York Times* editorial with this ringing endorsement: "In the end, everyone gave up something, but the result was a victory for the environment, for the local economy and most of all for common sense."*

A victory it might have been, but we caught a lot of flak for our position and it took a toll on our donations. Tom Alworth, our terrific executive

---

* "A Watershed Agreement," *New York Times*, September 10, 2007.

director who had shepherded this difficult agreement to completion, was leaving in March 2008 and we had to find a replacement. The woman we found, who seemed great on paper and in person, turned out not to be a good fit, and within a year we would be going through another turbulent transition. All of this took a great deal of time and energy, but it was deeply satisfying work. Next to my appreciation of and attachment to New York City and all that it had meant to me and my family, the Catskills had a powerful hold on my loyalties. With John Burroughs as a pioneer of the environmental movement and the Hudson River School as the first truly American collection of painters, the Catskills occupy a special place in the nation's history. The joys that its trails, mountains, and bird life had given me were incalculable.

The other involvement that had claimed much of my time after RPA was the NYU Real Estate Institute, which was renamed the Schack Institute in 2008. Ken Patton, its dean, called me shortly after my retirement and asked me to consider joining its faculty in some unspecified capacity. I had known Ken for a long while, since his time as the city's first economic development administrator under Mayor John Lindsay. We had never really worked together, but I had long been intrigued by his eclectic persona and unusual career. As I would come to appreciate, he was a unique leader and a deeply loyal colleague.

Ken was a graduate of the Merchant Marine Academy at Kings Point in Queens. After a stint in the service, he acquired a master's degree in engineering at Northwestern. Somehow, he ended up diving with Jacques Cousteau in the 1950s, helping to resolve some underwater engineering issues for Cousteau. Eventually he found his way to corporate relocation for the Fantas Company, the most prominent firm in this esoteric practice. His understanding of why companies wanted to locate where they did attracted him to the Lindsay administration. At first, Lindsay invited Ken to join his Economic Development Council, a blue-ribbon panel of corporate leaders, which advised the administration on policies to make New York City more appealing as a place to do business. Impressed by Ken's contributions in this role, Lindsay asked him to become the city's commissioner of commerce and industry. Typically, Ken turned this lethargic cheerleading operation into an effective facilitator for businesses having problems with the municipal bureaucracy.

After Lindsay's reelection in 1969, he promoted Ken to head the Economic Development Administration, the new "superagency" charged with leading all of the city's efforts relating to support of the private sector economy. His tenure there featured, among many other things, creating the Hunts Point Market, renegotiating the Yankee Stadium lease, and helping Buzzy O'Keefe open the River Café at its iconic barge location. Later he pioneered the creation of the TKTS booth (the highly successful venue for low-cost theater tickets) and served for decades on the New York City Police Foundation board. After leaving city government, he served as the first full-time president of the Real Estate Board of New York and turned a sleepy industry group into a powerful advocacy organization. He worked for over a dozen years for Harry Helmsley, before getting fired by the impossible Leona after Harry's death. Larry Silverstein then coaxed him into taking over the NYU Real Estate Institute, which he turned into arguably the best graduate real estate program in the country.

Ken struck me as one of the most disorganized people on the planet. His desk was always piled high, seemingly with every piece of paper that had ever crossed it. He was never on time and talked incessantly, but never about inconsequential things. He would fill any vacant airtime with random speculations but loved to be interrupted if you had something to say. He walked around the city wearing earphones and listening to NPR, always hungry for more information. He would launch into a verbal torrent about some arcane subject and the listener would wonder where the hell he was going with his apparently unguided train of thought. Suddenly he would circle back to a subject you had been discussing with him and it would all make a crazy kind of sense.

Although his management style seemed equally chaotic, any organization he headed not only prospered but grew into a paradigm of what it should be. He brought in professionals whom he believed in, regardless of the organization chart. Not surprisingly, those around him returned his loyalty and friendship. He was equally comfortable with the moguls of the real estate business and with the struggling students he took the time to mentor.

I was fortunate that Ken felt I should be part of his coterie. He was not sure where I would fit into the institute, but he wanted me there and we worked together to find the right slot. We spent many evenings at Volare, his favorite restaurant on West 4th Street, drinking too much and crawling back through the great stories of the Lindsay and Rockefeller years. Our public-service bond was staunch. After a few less than successful endeavors, such as an executive seminar in public/private partnerships, he asked me to take over the Chase Competition. The bank sponsored an annual contest in which teams of real estate students from several programs around the city would identify a development project with a public purpose and then a create a proposal to make it happen. We became frustrated with the bank's ground rules, which we felt rewarded the wrong priorities. I turned the competition into a graduate seminar and it became a mainstay of our curriculum for almost ten years.

One evening, I was absorbing another of Ken's endless circumlocutions that turned into a gem of wisdom. I turned to him and said, "I think I finally get it. I think I finally understand what you are about."

He looked at me with a familiar expression of amusement and curiosity and waited.

I continued, "All you care about is the next good idea that will nudge the state of knowledge or policy another step in the right direction. You don't care how messy your desk, your life, your conversations are as long as you keep moving the ball forward."

He smiled and nodded. "That sounds about right," he said.

While Ken did not fit the popular image, he embodied what it is to be a true intellectual far more than the pompous academics who fill universities. Above all, he cared about ideas.

In 2016, at age eighty-five, Ken suffered a savage stroke while at his house near Cannes, where he and Helène, his French wife, spent part of every summer. Bedridden from then on, he died two years later, bringing to a very sad end his wonderfully rich and dynamic life.

FOURTEEN

A NEW CHAPTER

After returning from New Zealand, I continued attending my support group, but the dynamic had changed subtly. The others were still battling with the relentless challenges of taking care of their spouses at home. The stories of inadequacy, conflict, incontinence, family denial, and exhaustion were no longer as immediate for me. My concerns were now oversight, monitoring, medication, and visiting. My emotions dealt more with guilt and anticipation. I had a little more distance, and more emotional room to look ahead. The others asked me how they would know when it was time for them to take the awful step of institutionalization. All I could say—and I meant it profoundly—was, "You will know."

One could not really allow oneself to look ahead. One could not permit oneself to hope for an end. The implications of that kind of thinking were alarming and paralyzing. Still, the inchoate idea that someday it would end and that there could be another future kept me anchored and gave me strength to continue doing whatever I could for Marilyn. At the same time, I had discovered a new depth of feeling, a different kind of love for Marilyn, which was perhaps richer and more intense than anything I had known before.

Sometime in the spring of 2008, I felt the time had come that I could begin, at least, to peek into the future. I logged on to Match.com and filled out a profile and put it out into the ether. There proved to be no shortage of options. Sometimes I took the initiative, sometimes the women did.

One did need to exercise a bit of discretion. The marriage proposals from twenty-five-year-olds in Russia could be disregarded. Otherwise, I tried to read the profiles carefully for insights into character, and I studied the photos for clues of currency. Over the next few months, I met perhaps a dozen women, mostly for coffee and nothing more. I went out on a few dates with several. Nothing happened. Were there good reasons that the proverbial sparks did not fly? Was I just not ready, or was I permanently incapable of another intense involvement? In a radical step for me, I decided to consult a therapist. My friend, Richard Gordon, suggested someone he knew. Will Swift was a psychologist and a historian, which appealed to me. I went with Richard to a lecture that Swift gave at the Harvard Club, where he appeared as part of a book tour. I felt comfortable about him and signed on.

After perhaps a half dozen sessions, we concluded that I had good cause for my grief and emotional reticence. When the time was right and the right person came along, things would change. In late summer, a photo and profile popped up that intrigued me. The website announced that we were an astounding ninety-five percent match. Her picture conveyed intelligence and sensuality. I inquired, and she responded. I asked about what kind of healthcare professional she was, and she answered: a psychotherapist. "Uh oh," I quipped back, "I'll either tell you everything or nothing." She asked what "separated" in my profile meant. I described Marilyn's situation. Our email exchanges were lively, candid, and appealing. On September 11, 2008, I met Amy Edminster for a drink. She looked exactly like her picture and even better. She asked pleasantly if I would care to share a snack. I announced, "I do not snack." I explained that dinner was my religion and that I did not allow anything to interfere with its ritual, a hint of many small differences to come. I wore my blue blazer with brass buttons, only to learn later that she was not at all drawn to the preppy look. I liked her enormously. She was direct, without pretense, intelligent, and attractive.

It took me about a week to empty my Match.com dating calendar so I could follow up with a clear mind and schedule. Amy had thought that the delay meant a lack of interest, but she agreed to a second get-together over the holy sacrament of an evening meal. We had a delightful time and began to see each other regularly from then on. Amy, who lived in the West Village at the time, had been alone for several years after a long marriage and one serious relationship. I was only her second online date. The first, with a fellow therapist who looked terrific on paper, had been a dud. I was happy to be next in line. Amy's profile indicated that she had two children, who were home "some of the time." In fact, her twenty-year-old son, Zach, was living separately and her fifteen-year-old daughter, Molly, was spending part of the time with her father in Queens. How that has evolved over time is the stuff of a long-running family joke.

Amy was a rock of sympathy and understanding as Marilyn steadily declined despite her excellent care at 80th Street Residence. I was eager for Amy to meet Marilyn, both for her to get a glimpse of what kind of person Marilyn had been, but also so that Amy could better understand what I was dealing with. It cannot have been easy for Amy, but she agreed to accompany me on several of my visits. Amy would sit next to Marilyn on the couch and rub Marilyn's shoulders. Marilyn did not know who she was but seemed to welcome the comforting gesture.

Amy said she had a trip planned to join her ex-sister-in-law for a week in San Miguel de Allende in Mexico over the Christmas holiday. Having been to San Miguel with Buck and Deb and having loved it there, I said to Amy, "Why don't you extend for another week over New Year's and I'll join you?" On New Year's Eve, in San Miguel, we attended a concert that included a favorite of mine, Schumann's piano quintet. Afterward, we watched distant fireworks over the city from our rented house in the Los Balcones section of town. It was a magical evening and I sensed our relationship was deepening.

We spent weekends at Overrun in the Catskills, met each other's friends, and saw as much of each other as her profession and motherhood allowed. That summer saw us in Colorado with John and Cass to visit our friend, Wayne, in Evergreen. We no longer tackled fourteeners—the 14,000-foot peaks of the Rockies—as John, Wayne, and I had done years earlier, but we did some glorious hikes together. Amy and I went on to Ouray, Arches National Park, and the idyllic Valley of the Gods. Amy proved more than willing to join me on my now more reasonable outdoor adventures.

Shortly after we returned, 80th Street informed me that they thought that Marilyn had had a minor stroke but seemed to recover without noticeable damage. It was hard to be certain; she was retreating more and more into that impenetrable world of dementia. In September, she suffered another incident and her condition clearly deteriorated. The director of 80th Street phoned and said that, as an assisted-living facility, they could no longer provide Marilyn with the care she needed and I would have to find her a place in a full nursing facility. I had previously discovered that most of the decent ones were furiously expensive and far less personal. I visited several places around New York City before I found the Methodist Home for Nursing in Riverdale. It was modest in size and seemed to provide a caring environment. I could get there by subway, riding the Seventh Avenue line to the last stop and walking ten minutes up the hill. In mid-September, I helped move Marilyn to the Methodist Home.

My visits were agonizing. Marilyn was less and less responsive. I would wheel her to a cul-de-sac on her floor with windows overlooking a wooded area. As I watched the leaves fall, I would whisper to her that it would not be long now until she had peace. I have no idea whether she could hear me or fathom what I was saying. She just stared blankly, gagging slightly because of her failing ability to swallow. She suffered another stroke several weeks later and was hospitalized for about two weeks as the doctors tried to figure out just what had happened and how much damage had been done. Despite having medical directives to the contrary, I was persuaded to allow the use of a feeding tube so that she could be stabilized enough to run more tests. I almost certainly should not have allowed that; I discovered how difficult it is to make informed, compassionate decisions under such intense pressure. The doctors never did conclude anything useful, but Marilyn recovered enough to return to the Methodist Home, just a shell of a person.

Amy and I were in the Catskills at Overrun with John and Cass, and Amy's close friend, Malka, for Thanksgiving in 2009. A purple, blustery storm blew in during the afternoon and evening with driving rain and wind. As we sat down for dinner, the phone rang. It was the Methodist Home, reporting that Marilyn had died. Although it was not completely unexpected, I was stunned and shocked at the finality of the news. A profound sadness overtook me at the injustice of Marilyn's fate, a sadness combined with the first stirrings of relief. We quickly moved to address the logistics of the situation, spending a frantic hour on the phone making arrangements for her body to be picked up and taken for cremation. John wrote a lovely poem memorializing what we had just shared—the experience of the storm and of Marilyn's passing from us. John has allowed me to share it:

CATSKILL WINTER STORM
To remember Marilyn Russell

The pale sun seeps through burst of rain and snow
But the cold wind howls. It takes form, prowls the valleys
And the cold mountains, bending birches, oaks, pines and balsams
To its whim. Not a bird takes to the rough air, nor a stray insect flies.

The air, left to its own devices, flies into things, houses,
Slamming doors. Everything solid bends to the gale.
Holding on. The weak sun gives no comfort. Old bears make their beds.
It is the seasonal killing time. Winter does its necessary work.

Inside a house a death is announced. Winter has taken
Its sacrifice, someone willing to go so that others can live.
She had forgotten her name, so the wind swept her up in its arms
Without calling her. Her breath stopping, became part of the air.

We breathe. In the failing light, in the storm,
We knew the absence; we breathed in to let her go.*

---

* John W. Bing, *Time Signatures* (Kelsay Books, 2021), 42. Used by permission.

In early January 2010, Harvey and Celia hosted a memorial gathering for Marilyn in their apartment. About forty friends attended, each speaking about what Marilyn had meant to them. One of her HBO colleagues taped it for us. Marilyn's two remaining brothers flew in to take part. It was a deeply affecting and fulfilling experience of closure.

A couple of weeks later, my brother and his wife—along with Pierre's son, Eric, and his wife, Danielle—joined Amy and me in the Catskills. With the help of Eric's considerable youthful energy, we dug a hole under the dogwood tree and placed a container with Marilyn's ashes in the ground next to my father's. It was gray and chilly, and the yard was dusted with snow on that December day. The scene could not have been more fitting, and I felt enveloped in love and support. This part of my journey had come to an end.

In 2014, when the pain and sorrow had receded to a smaller place in a back corner of my mind, I received a letter from my army friend, Lester Chan. Johanna had been diagnosed with Alzheimer's. My heart broke for him; the knowledge of what he faced surged back into my consciousness. I immediately made plans to visit them in Horn, Austria. I wanted to see if I could provide some small bit of wisdom and support for Lester, and to see Johanna before she disappeared further. Their son, Domenic, and his wife lived nearby and were a constant presence. Johanna's sister, whom I had also met in the past, was visiting to help out. Johanna was aware of her condition and struggled to remain part of her family and surroundings. Her crystalline sweetness was unaffected. I spent three or four lovely days with them, staying in a nice gasthaus in the village. About six months later, Lester wrote to me and enclosed a medical report. It was in German; from what I could make out, he had been diagnosed with advanced liver cancer. He died not long after, and before Johanna. Even though she was in the end stage of her disease, she understood what had happened. She also knew it was the end of them. She stopped eating and died a difficult death a few weeks later. I felt a piercing sense of loss and injustice.

In January 2010, again to escape the New York winter, Amy and I went to St. John, staying in rustic accommodations at the Concordia eco-resort. I felt rejuvenated, and everything I had been hoping for seemed to be coming to pass. On one of our last evenings on the island, we went out to dinner at a restaurant nearby with the suitably evocative name of Shipwreck Landing. Amy had steadfastly seen me through this supremely difficult time. She was warm, kind, and totally without guile. I was grateful beyond words, but more importantly, I was very much in love with her. When the wine arrived, I asked her to marry me. To my surprise, it caught her completely off guard. She took it in; she did not reject the idea, but asked for some time to think it over. That caught me equally off guard, but there was little I could say or do. We talked no more about it at the time. I thought of the watchwords that Marilyn had used to describe our extended courtship: "Don't worry too much about what the other person says; just watch their feet. As long as they keep walking in the right direction, things will be okay." Amy kept heading in the right direction.

Back in New York on a late March day, we were walking in Central Park after visiting the New-York Historical Society. Amy turned to me and said, "The answer is yes." I had no idea what she was talking about and replied, "What's the question?" Laughing, she reminded me of my proposal—and I beamed happily.

A lot had to happen before we could put our lives together properly. We had two apartments. Hers was part of West Village Houses, a Jane-Jacobs-inspired series of buildings along Washington Street in Greenwich Village. It had been built as a publicly subsidized middle-income rental complex but had become a unique form of hybrid subsidized co-op ten years before. Amy was able to buy in. Now it was in the process of becoming a standard market-rate cooperative, located in what had become one of the most desirable neighborhoods in New York City. Covenants and restrictions still applied, so selling her unit at that point would mean sacrificing considerable potential value. My apartment on West End Avenue was supremely marketable. Amy's daughter, Molly, was living with us at home and was struggling with school. Minimum disruption for her was important. Amy's apartment was in need of renovation and we wanted to make it into something that reflected both of our needs and personalities. Figuring out how to handle all of these factors would take time. We decided to set a wedding date in June of the following year.

That summer, we went back to Colorado and then headed to Montana. I wanted Amy to meet Buck and Deb. Deb had also been a therapist and I knew they would take to each other. I was not wrong. We went back to St. John in the winter of 2011, renting a lovely cottage not far from Concordia, and began serious planning for our wedding. We both had many friends and lots of history, and we wanted our celebration to be something special for everyone, including ourselves.

Amy and I were married on June 5, 2011. For the festivities, we rented the event space, Ramscale, a block from our apartment, atop Westbeth, the landmark conversion of the old Bell Labs into artists' housing. About seventy-five guests attended a beautifully catered affair with delicious food and dramatic views over the Hudson River. A thunderstorm threatened but cleared in time for us to hold the ceremony outdoors on the terrace. John Bing was my best man and Amy's friend, Malka Percal, did the honors for her. My brother and his wife and both of his children were there, as were Amy's children, Zach and Molly. Arielle Levioff arranged the music. Lynn Paltrow, a dynamic civil rights lawyer friend of Amy's, who founded and runs the National Advocates for Pregnant Women, a remarkable nonprofit, got herself ordained and officiated. The phrase, "dinner is my religion," was incorporated into our vows. Lynn's partner, Sara Krulwich, the drama photographer at the *New York Times,* took photos. The ceremony and party were exactly what we had hoped for. I then sold my Upper West Side co-op in a week at my asking price. With the proceeds, we renovated Amy's three-bedroom duplex apartment, turning it into a lovely home that was indeed ours.

———

I will end my narrative at this watershed point. Marrying Amy has started a new and rich chapter. I will leave it to her and to the next generation to take up any accounting from here and to pass judgment on outcomes. The present is too immediate and the future too unpredictable for me to opine about them with any perspective or objectivity. The stories from here on will be theirs much more than mine.

Amy on our trip to Morocco, 2013.

Having put my account down on paper, I feel that I have managed a successful launch of the space vehicle that I invited the reader to share in the preface. I am relieved that the mission plan has gone generally well. For better or worse, this chronicle has found its way from memory onto the printed page about as I had intended. The major formative events in my life I can see as the stages of booster rockets, firing at different times but sequentially, launching me into the peaceful orbit of my old age. I hope the reader has enjoyed sharing the passage. My capsule is on its determined course and is not likely to change much. Time to leave the detritus behind.

My space module is comfortable but not expansive—ample for me to enjoy the remainder of my trip. My devotion to classical music is singular, but my bandwidth is ridiculously narrow and not likely to broaden. Birding is a hobby that gives me enormous pleasure, but I do not keep a life list or any real scorecard. Few things give me as much pleasure as hearing the familiar call of a scarlet tanager or rose-breasted grosbeak and following the lyrical sound until I spot one of those beautiful creatures.

My hearing is still acute enough to be able to discern those sounds better than most. I have decent eyesight, requiring only nightly drops to fend off incipient inherited glaucoma, which has been stable for many years. My hair retains most of its original color, with only a slowly increasing smattering of gray—ridiculous for my age. I am fond of opining that I wish my body would not put all its energy into keeping my hair dark while the rest of me falls apart. I get no sympathy from contemporaries for this observation. My mild COPD means that higher altitudes are a thing of the past for me and uphill hikes are more challenging, but otherwise my organ recital is mercifully short.

Now, drifting quietly in my trajectory, I can look down and reflect on what my stories have meant for me. I may never have made it to the moon, but I am more than satisfied with the orbit I have achieved. The guidance and support I received from uniquely gifted and kind mentors were indispensable to my successful flight path. Cataloguing that help on these pages has renewed my amazement and gratitude to Father Leeming, Stephen Graubard, Anne, John Capozzola, Ed and Mary Kresky, Al Marshall, Dick Bartlett, Ed Tuck, Martin Segal, Peter Herman, John Burnett, Erik Hansen, Ken Patton, and many others.

I have had the privilege of working alongside and learning from an array of supremely talented and dedicated professional colleagues, many from the public sector. I have purposefully littered these pages with their names in order to pay tribute and say thanks. I came away from my government service with a profound respect for these men and women who were, in the truest sense, public servants. I witnessed their devotion in the context of state and city governments. My brother, as a career Foreign Service officer, experienced it at the federal level. The clarion call from JFK's inaugural speech—"Ask not what your country can do for you, ask what you can do for your country"—was not just political rhetoric for our generation. It was a summons that we took seriously and responded to. My experience was that those in government worked at least as hard and were at least as honest as their counterparts in the private sector. For every corrupt public official there were thousands of others who were impeccably scrupulous. For every bureaucrat who just punched the clock at the Department of Motor Vehicles, there were thousands more dedicated public servants who put in more hours and took their jobs more seriously than most in corporate America.

Despite the inclination by some to lionize Ronald Reagan, in my personal view he did enormous harm to our democracy with his pronouncement in his first inaugural address that "government is not the solution to our problem; government is the problem." That mantra, which has taken deep root in the American psyche, is simply not true. As we have been discovering anew in a time of crisis—the coronavirus pandemic—we need good, honest, professional government more than ever. There are many things only government can do and do well. The Jeffersonian tradition of skepticism of central authority once had some theoretical basis. Too often, however, it has been used solely to justify greed, prejudice, and self-interest. I am an unabashed proponent of the Hamiltonian tradition of strong federal authority and the legal legacy of Chief Justice John Marshall, which institutionalized that concept. Our history, from the American Revolution, to the Civil War, to the New Deal, to the Great Society, to the Great Recession, and to COVID-19, among many other examples, argues persuasively, I would submit, for the validity of that heritage.

Of all the innumerable travesties that Donald Trump perpetrated upon our country—racism, xenophobia, disregard of science, cowardice and denial during a deadly pandemic, and the systematic undermining of the press and the rule of law—among the most serious was his evisceration of the professional class of the federal government. Michael Lewis's alarming book, *The Fifth Risk*, documents the initial hollowing out of career public servants particularly in the science-related agencies in the early days of the Trump Administration. That process only accelerated during Trump's time in office, underscored by the string of distinguished, competent, and dedicated diplomats who testified during the impeachment hearings, many of whom were subsequently fired. Hannah Arendt, the profound political philosopher and analyst of totalitarian governments, has pointed out that the first thing that Hitler and Stalin did on assuming power was to get rid of anyone who knew what they were doing and replace them with know-nothing loyalists. What Trump and Fox News call the "deep state" is nothing more than the professional class of public servants who form the solid basis of essential government services and who do their jobs regardless of what political party is in power. I am of the mind that Trump, most fortunately, is not nearly as smart or ambitious as Hitler or Stalin and is less interested in power as a tool for terror than in its capacity to assuage his insatiable, narcissistic need for approval. As Timothy Snyder acutely—and I believe, correctly—observed in a *New York Times Magazine* article in January 2021, "In this respect his pre-fascism fell short of fascism: His vision never went further than a mirror."*

The following quote from Arendt's *The Origins of Totalitarianism* could have been lifted from Roy Cohn's instruction manual for Donald Trump:

> In an ever-changing, incomprehensible world the masses had reached the point where they would, at the same time, believe everything and nothing, think that everything was possible and that nothing was true . . . Mass propaganda discovered that its audience was ready at all times to believe the worst, no matter how absurd, and did not particularly object to being deceived because it held every statement to be a lie anyhow. The totalitarian mass leaders based their propaganda

---

* Timothy Snyder, "The American Abyss," *New York Times Magazine*, January 9, 2021.

on the correct psychological assumption that, under such conditions, one could make people believe the most fantastic statements one day, and trust that if the next day they were given irrefutable proof of their falsehood, they would take refuge in cynicism; instead of deserting the leaders who had lied to them, they would protest that they had known all along that the statement was a lie and would admire the leaders for their superior tactical cleverness.*

Louis Menand, in his compelling new intellectual history of mid-twentieth-century-America, *The Free World,* captures Arendt's prescient analysis with concise clarity. Menand describes Arendt's identification of a new social force, which she called "the mob:" "They were people who believed that the respectable world was a conspiracy to deny them what they were owed; they were the embodiments of the politics of resentment." No present-day pundit could describe Trumpism any better.

I hope that my experience as an immigrant to this country makes me better able to appreciate the extraordinary importance—and fragility—of America's institutions devoted to equal opportunity, and our historic—though imperfect—commitment to the value of the individual. As I wrote in the preface, my story could only have happened in the United States, and for that I am profoundly grateful to this country. I also understand that being white and male were indispensable to my belated but smooth ascent up the professional and economic ladder. Extending the opportunities I was given—to the descendants of our ugly history of slavery, to Native Americans, to immigrants from around the world—must be at the core of our national purpose. It is embedded in our political scripture, even though that scripture was written mostly by slave owners. Many of our most distinguished and revered citizens have devoted their lives to making a reality of the ideals of the better angels of our nature. Trump's willingness to attack those ideals, and the widespread support he received that led

* I am indebted to my young friend, Rob Katz, for sending me this quote. It rekindled my interest in the experience that my family shared with Arendt in Marseille and stirred a new interest in philosophy—hers and others'.

directly to the assault on the Capitol, is not only a travesty of patriotism but a dire warning for the future that *yes, it* can *happen here*. At our peril, we must learn anew that the preservation of our democracy—however flawed—requires constant vigilance.

Our current turbulence may not affect me dramatically. My space capsule is fairly well insulated and should have enough fuel and oxygen for the rest of my journey. The recent political and public health crises have, however, altered considerably my view of what is happening down below. What seemed like a relatively placid picture has been upended and a dark uncertainty has been injected about what lies ahead for everyone on the planet. Millennials and recent graduates of high schools and colleges face a much bleaker and uncertain economic future than we could have imagined just a few years ago. Still, one should remember that the last pandemic, one hundred years ago, despite our having far fewer medical resources than exist today, was followed in only a few years by the Roaring Twenties. Trump's presidency has tested the limits of our institutions in ways never thought possible, revealing their weaknesses and fault lines. The insurrection of January 6, 2021, and the Republican Party's adoption of the "big lie" that Joe Biden did not win the election, are warning shots across the bow of the ship of liberty. On the more positive side, the recent protests over historic police brutality against African Americans have seen participation and support for a more equitable society from a broader cross section of the country than ever before. As I recently wrote to my friend Aram in Tunis:

As you know, I tend to be more optimistic and positive. I was reading excerpts from an interview with the late John Lewis, the titanic civil rights leader and long-serving congressman. In response to the charge that recent events have shown that nothing has changed in America, he said to tell those people to walk in his shoes. Things are bad, worse than they should be because of Trump and all that he has unleashed. But to say that things are not different than in the 1960s displays no sense of reality or of history. We have a long, long way to go; our innate tribalism and potential for violence have been on display; but the breadth and depth of the protests show we have come some distance.

I would suggest that the "American experiment" is entering a new and especially challenging phase. In a few decades, we will be a "minority-majority" nation, an oxymoron if ever there was one. Our innate tribalism is deeply embedded in human beings' DNA as a fundamental survival strategy; but so is our unique altruism. To cite almost any other country's identity—French, German, Peruvian, Ugandan, Indian, Chinese—normally conveys something about its ethnicity. Not so for being American, or at least it should not be. We are trying to become the first truly multi-ethnic nation, an unprecedented test. The self-identification of so many Blacks, Native Americans, Asians, and Hispanics as "Americans" is, I believe, our most astonishing and encouraging advantage. It gives us hope that, over time, we just might succeed.

———

For the remainder of my journey, I have excellent company. My brother, Pierre, and his wife, Hilary, supply unflagging love and support. We jointly oversee the care of our stepmother, Ilse, who at age one hundred is now in a dementia care unit in Charlottesville. Solving the problems together of attending to her needs has brought us closer and has fostered a fuller appreciation and affection for each other.

Pierre's son—my nephew, Eric—and his family bring the joy of future generations to my life. The children, Leo (twelve) and the twins, Max and Phoebe (ten), are an unexpected source of wonderful new experiences and emotions. They are the last ones carrying the family name, and I look forward to their being a major part of my final years. To them, I am known by the less than melodic nickname of GUC, Grand Uncle Claude. I came up with that moniker one day and cannot shake it, but I am just fine with it.

I am enormously fond of Eric. I was not much of an uncle to him in his early years, being preoccupied with my own life and career. I became more involved during his unsettled time at the University of Virginia. A twelve-mile hike in the Blue Ridge Mountains and a walk around Chris Greene

Lake Park helped create a strong new bond. After a bumpy but highly entrepreneurial start on the craft fair circuit, he has thrived professionally in the more mainstream world of socially responsible investing. Eric is demonstrating an ability to operate successfully in highly competitive and demanding professional environments and is contributing importantly to more responsible corporate citizenship. He has come a long, long way and it has been a pleasure to witness. But I will let him tell his stories.

His sister, Pascale, has had a more difficult time. She is African and was adopted by Pierre and his first wife, Chantal. They found her chained to a cot in a dirt-floored orphanage in Malawi, where Pierre was stationed at the time. She was rejected by her birth mother and then again by Chantal as soon as Eric was born. Despite all attempts by the rest of the family to accept and nurture her, she has resisted becoming an integral part of our family; the early damage was too severe. To her considerable credit, Pascale graduated from college and earned a master's degree in education. Recently, she spent two years in the Peace Corps in Africa, searching unsuccessfully for her roots and identity. She is now in her midfifties, teaching preschoolers in New Jersey.

Amy's children, Zach (midthirties) and Molly (late twenties), have brought fresh challenges and new meaning to this latest chapter. Zach is pursuing a nursing degree. Molly is precariously on her own in Queens. She is socially adept and has become politically passionate. Molly has shown flashes of brilliance as a writer but has not yet figured out how to mold her considerable talents into a sustainable career.

I care deeply for Zach and Molly and am frustrated that I cannot be of more help as they strive to find their places in this more complicated world. All I ever wanted was to be part of the system; they have grown up feeling alienated from and angry at it. My experiences and advice have little relevance for them. I can only hope that the stability and tolerance I have tried to provide will give them room and security to eventually lead successful lives of their own. But, again, they will be the arbiters of that.

Amy has brought me a richness and depth of emotion that was missing from my life, but we are not a ninety-five-percent match. Our mothers died of unnatural causes at the same age: fifty-nine. Our fathers were born in the same year, 1908. Both of our fathers were secular Jews, our mothers Christian. Yet we are emotionally cut from very different cloths. Our marriage has been more turbulent than my time with Marilyn, but also more intensely felt. I have had to learn that conflict and forgiving are essential ingredients in a relationship. My parents never fought in front of my brother and me, and Marilyn worked around any problems without confrontation. Previously, I equated a marital spat with a declaration of divorce. I have learned otherwise, to my benefit, though any hint of conflict still makes me inordinately uncomfortable.

Amy has met me more than halfway in our daily life and activities. She has brought a new and vibrant lode of personal relationships into my everyday life. Her professional colleagues and personal friends are now among my most meaningful connections. The family from her first marriage is now my family as well. I have indeed been given another chapter and it is better than I could have hoped for. Our bond is strong, and we live a full and happy life together, but I will let her be the one to tell this story more fully.

As my father aged, I was struck by the long arc of his life. As a six- or seven-year-old boy, he had watched Kaiser Franz Josef in his horse-drawn carriage parading down the Ringstrasse in Vienna. He had lived to see men land on the moon and to witness the Y2K computer crisis. I increasingly marvel at the long traverse of my own years, from being smuggled across a World War II border, to helicoptering over Woodstock, to living in a social media world I can barely grasp. Putting our two lives together spans considerably more than a century of unimaginable social and technological change.

Today, on my walks along Hudson River Park (which I played a small role in helping to create), adjacent to our neighborhood, I often pause at the end of a short playground pier around West 12th Street. From there, I enjoy a splendid view of New York Harbor to the south. The Colgate Project dominates the horizon to the right; in the center, I see the Statue of Liberty and the spires of the buildings on Ellis Island; Battery Park City is off to the left, where I also catch a glimpse of the Bank of New York (now BNY Mellon) Operations Center—just a few of the physical markers of my life in this remarkable city. It is a good feeling.

I am overly fond of quoting lines from my favorite movies to illustrate what I consider seminal ideas and moments. I will close by again committing this sin. I was struck by the power of the final scene of *Saving Private Ryan*. Standing with his wife and two children in front of the grave of Captain Miller (Tom Hanks), who led the team that rescued him, Private Ryan (Matt Damon) asks, "Have I led a good life?" What I heard him ask was, "Has America led a good life?"

That Private Ryan, in this final scene with his picture-perfect family, represents the United States as a country, is quite clear. The multiethnic squad that saves him, nearly all of whom perish, stands for the diverse country they were defending and the sacrifices they all made toward that end. A central point of the movie is the vivid depiction of the savage and amoral horrors of war. World War II was said to be "the good war." Still, the only way to justify the killing and inhumanity of even the "best" of wars is to live a good life afterward, to live up to the ideals we said we were fighting for. During the Trump presidency, our ability to answer Private Ryan's question affirmatively was very much in doubt. Now I am a bit more hopeful.

With far more modest implications, I am a bit tempted to ask myself the same question. I will also leave that to be answered by others, but I know this much: I have been incredibly lucky and have had a very good time.

ACKNOWLEDGMENTS

As I wrote at the outset of this memoir, mine is a quintessentially American story of personal and professional accomplishment. I was particularly fortunate, however, that my American journey was anchored for the most part in and around New York City. As imperfect as it may be, I would submit that there is no place on the planet that offers more different kinds of people more agency to lead meaningful and satisfying lives. With its ancient Dutch roots* of tolerance, representative government, and commercial opportunity, New York City is perhaps the most vital laboratory testing whether human beings on a large scale can together overcome their innate tribalism and be touched "by the better angels of our nature" to create better lives for all. I am deeply grateful to have been nurtured by this marvelous metropolis and its values, and I feel privileged to have been able to make some small contributions to its continued vibrancy.

A primary motivation in undertaking this memoir was to pay tribute to the many wonderful people—family, friends, mentors, and colleagues—who provided help, encouragement, and nourishment of all kinds along the pathways of my journey. I hope I have done them some small measure of justice.

I have called upon some of them in the writing of this book and, without exception, I received unstinting and invaluable assistance. My brother, Pierre, made sure that the family stories were as accurate and objective as we could manage. My long-time friends, John Bing, Richard Gordon, and

---

* Russell Shorto, *The Island at the Center of the World* (New York: Random House, 2005).

Aram Khachadurian, read early drafts of the work and made significant suggestions and comments. My mentor and friend, Peter Herman, provided crucial information and perspectives about the years we worked together in real estate and at Regional Plan Association. Spouses and partners, Cass Bing, Anya Taylor, and Alice Herman weighed in with added wisdom. Mary Kresky, my treasured colleague, friend, and guide through my state government years and beyond, supplied important facts and advice.

My colleagues at the NYU Schack Institute for Real Estate, Rosemary Scanlon and Warren Wechsler, reviewed the relevant section and provided valuable feedback and input. My good friend Gerry Gibian provided meaningful details about the time we collaborated on the Colgate Project.

Celia Currin, long-time board member and past president of Poets & Writers, contributed an introduction to the world of publishing, helped me navigate those waters, and added her usual powerful dose of encouragement.

One of the great joys of this endeavor has been reconnecting with my confidant from Harvard days, Tom Bethell. Despite a fifty-year hiatus in our friendship, he responded instantly and with unbounded generosity to my request for help with my story. A professional journalist and editor, he volunteered for the selfless task of an in-depth edit of the manuscript. The final version is immeasurably better in style, content, and accuracy because of his skilled hand.

The team at Mascot Books, Hobbs Allison and Jenna Scafuri, provided needed guidance and encouragement throughout the mysterious publishing process and I am especially grateful to copy editor Anna Krusinski for her impressive professional thoroughness and diligence.

Finally, of course, my wife, Amy, has been a key part of this journey. From sage advice about content and emphasis, to tolerance of my many hours at the computer, to providing the loving environment that allowed me to look back on my life with renewed gratitude and appreciation, Amy's contributions have been indispensable.

Nevertheless, despite all the help I have received, I am sure that within these pages there are errors of style, fact, and interpretation. I have probably offended some friends, omitted or gotten wrong some important details, and failed to recognize assistance provided by individuals not mentioned here. I apologize for all such errors and omissions for which I alone am responsible.

ABOUT THE AUTHOR

Henri Claude Shostal was born near Paris in 1940 and began life as a wartime refugee, escaping as an infant with his family from Nazi Europe with adventures straight out of *Casablanca* and *Sophie's Choice*. Arriving penniless and in debt, his parents managed to carve out a successful life in America, allowing Shostal to attend Harvard College, obtain a graduate degree in Public Administration from NYU, and kick-start his career by joining the staff of Governor Nelson Rockefeller in 1967. From that unique vantage point, he witnessed the drama of the urban unrest of the time, the dire political events of 1968, the Woodstock Festival, the Attica uprising, and more. He then spent almost ten years in senior positions in state and city government, culminating in being picked as New York City's first commissioner of cultural affairs in 1976. Shostal moved on to work in the private sector on transformational commercial projects during the 1980s, including the Colgate Project in Jersey City, New Jersey. He capped his career in the nonprofit world, heading the country's most prestigious metropolitan planning organization, Regional Plan Association.

Shostal has also found time to hike among many of the world's highest mountain regions, summiting Kilimanjaro and two peaks in the Himalayas over 20,000 feet. He lives in the West Village in Manhattan with his wife, Amy.

INDEX

Note: Page locators in *italic* refer to figures and page locators followed by "n" refer to footnotes.

Hightower, John, 209, 210
Hillary, Sir Edmund, 70, 174
Hill, Calvin, 150
Hill, Karl, 92
Himalayas, 171, 172, 176
Hiss, Tony, 280
Hitchcock, Alfred, 189
Hitler, Adolf, 11, 342
Hodges, Russ, 60
Hoffa, Jimmy, 128
Home Box Office (HBO), 236
Honku, 300, 303
"Horst Wessel Lied" (Nazi hymn), 16
House (Kidder), 291
Hoving, Thomas, 2, 190, 194
Hudson River Park Trust, 282
Hudson River Valley Commission, 149
Hughes, Al, 123
Hughes, Yvonne, 123
Humphrey, Hubert, 140
Humphreys, George, 156–157, 167–168, 205–206, 225
Humphreys, Grace, 157
Hunt, John, 175
Hunts Point Market, 328
Hurd, T. Norman, 158
Huston, Jack, 254, 255, 258
Hyatt Regency Hotel, 223

I

Idaho, 258
Iliad (Homer), 74
Images and Shadows (Origo), 310
Into Thin Air (Krakauer), 298, 299
Irving Trust project, 215–217, 247
Island Peak, 264
Island Press, 280
Issy-les-Moulineaux, 24, 39

J

Jack Daniel's, 176, 261
Jackson, Bob, 215

Javits, Jacob, 197
Jersey City waterfront redevelopment project, 249, 255
Jewett, T., 176, 177
JFK. *See* Kennedy, John. F.
John D. III, 195
Johnson, Lyndon, 139, 155
Johnson, Philip, 278, 292

K

Kahan, Richard, 278
Kahn, Louis, 168
Kaiser Franz Josef, 346
Kala Patthar, *173*, 177, *177*
Kaplan Foundation, 183, 282
Kaplan, Richard, 183
Kathmandu, Nepal, 172, 174, 178, 202, 299–300, 323
Katz, Rob, 343n
KE Adventure Travel, 300
Kennedy, Bobby. *See* Kennedy, Robert F.
Kennedy, John. F., 89, 93, 102, 103, 115, 116
Kennedy, Robert F., 115, 137, 139
Kennedy School, 119
Kennedy, William, 131
Keystone Press Agency, 9
Khachadurian, Aram, 275–276, 344
Khrushchev, Nikita, 93, 102
Khumbu, *173*, 177, 300, 303, 384
Kidder, Tracy, 291, 292
Kilimanjaro, 172, 199–201, 264
King, Jr., Martin Luther, 137
Kirk, Russell, 79
Kissinger, Henry, 2, 138, 139
Klafferkessel, 241
Kleindienst, Richard, 143
Koch, Ed, 198–199, 277
Kon-Tiki (Heyerdahl), 70
Koval, Marianna, 316–317
Kresky, Edward, 129–130, *130*, 161, 190, 197, 210–211, 340